CONSERVATIVES
WITHOUT
CONSCIENCE

ALSO BY JOHN W. DEAN

Worse Than Watergate: The Secret Presidency of George W. Bush

Warren G. Harding

Unmasking Deep Throat—History's Most Elusive News Source

The Rehnquist Choice: The Untold Story of the Nixon Appointment
That Redefined the Supreme Court

Lost Honor

Blind Ambition—The White House Years

CONSERVATIVES
WITHOUT
CONSCIENCE

John W. Dean

VIKING

VIKING
Published by the Penguin Group
Penguin Group (USA) Inc., 375 Hudson Street,
New York, New York 10014, U.S.A.
Penguin Group (Canada), 90 Eglinton Avenue East, Suite 700, Toronto,
Ontario, Canada M4P 2Y3 (a division of Pearson Penguin Canada Inc.)
Penguin Books Ltd, 80 Strand, London WC2R 0RL, England
Penguin Ireland, 25 St. Stephen's Green, Dublin 2, Ireland
(a division of Penguin Books Ltd)
Penguin Books Australia Ltd, 250 Camberwell Road, Camberwell,
Victoria 3124, Australia (a division of Pearson Australia Group Pty Ltd)
Penguin Books India Pvt Ltd, 11 Community Centre,
Panchsheel Park, New Delhi – 110 017, India
Penguin Group (NZ), Cnr Airborne and Rosedale Roads, Albany,
Auckland 1310, New Zealand (a division of Pearson New Zealand Ltd)
Penguin Books (South Africa) (Pty) Ltd, 24 Sturdee Avenue,
Rosebank, Johannesburg 2196, South Africa

Penguin Books Ltd, Registered Offices:
80 Strand, London WC2R 0RL, England

First published in 2006 by Viking Penguin,
a member of Penguin Group (USA) Inc.

1   3   5   7   9   10   8   6   4   2

Copyright © John W. Dean, 2006
All rights reserved

"The Modern Dilemma" chart from *The Challenge of Democracy*, Eighth Edition, by Kenneth Janda, Jeffrey M. Berry, and Jerry Goldman. Copyright © 2005 by Houghton Mifflin Company. Used with permission.

ISBN: 0-670-03774-5

Printed in the United States of America
Set in Adobe Garamond

In memory of Senator Barry M. Goldwater (1909–98),

a conservative with conscience

I only wish to observe, as an empirical matter, that no one person's ideas actually define American conservatism.

—AUSTIN W. BRAMWELL

If you think [the United States] could never elect an Adolf Hitler to power, note that David Duke would have become governor of Louisiana if it had just been up to the white voters in that state.

—PROFESSOR BOB ALTEMEYER

The administration of George W. Bush is not a dictatorship, but it does manifest the characteristics of one in embryonic form.

—JONATHAN SCHELL

CONTENTS

PREFACE

CONTEMPORARY CONSERVATIVES have become extremely contentious, confrontational, and aggressive in nearly every area of politics and governing. Today they have a tough-guy (and, in a few instances, a tough-gal) attitude, an arrogant and antagonistic style, along with a narrow outlook intolerant of those who challenge their extreme thinking. Incivility is now their norm. "During the Father Bush period, there was a presumption of civility," Norman Ornstein of the American Enterprise Institute observes, but "we lost it under Clinton," when conservatives relentlessly attacked his presidency, and "then the present President Bush deliberately chose a strategy of being a divider, rather than a uniter."[1]

Even more troubling, the right-wing presidency of George W. Bush and Richard B. Cheney has taken positions that are in open defiance of international treaties or blatant violations of domestic laws, while pushing the limits of presidential power beyond the parameters of the Constitution. It is aided and abetted in these actions by a conservative Republican Congress that refuses to check or balance the president. These patterns were apparent long before the terror attacks on September 11, 2001, but the right wing's bellicose response to the events of that day has escalated into a false claim of legitimacy. Many authors (and journalists) have described the extreme hubris now present in Washington, along with the striking abuses of power. While some of this activity has ostensibly been undertaken in the name of fighting terrorists, much of it is just good old-fashioned power corruption.

Conservatives Without Conscience, however, is not a book about Bush and Cheney. My venture here is not to expose more malfeasance, misfeasance, or nonfeasance in places high or low in Washington, nor even to try to catalog it, for the gist of what is occurring under conservative Republican rule is all too obvious. Although this is a report that cannot be given without frequent references to the administration's disquieting politics and governing, my effort, fundamentally, is to understand them, to explain why they are happening, while placing them all in a larger context, including the particular events that initially prompted my inquiry about people with whom I once thought I shared beliefs.

Frankly, when I started writing this book I had a difficult time accounting for what had become of conservatism or, for that matter, the Republican Party. I went down a number of dead-end streets looking for answers, before finally discovering a true explanation. My finding, simply stated, is the growing presence of conservative authoritarianism. Conservatism has noticeably evolved from its so-called modern phase (1950–94) into what might be called a postmodern period (1994 to the present), and in doing so it has regressed to its earliest authoritarian roots. Authoritarianism is not well understood and seldom discussed in the context of American government and politics, yet it now constitutes the prevailing thinking and behavior among conservatives. Regrettably, empirical studies reveal, however, that authoritarians are frequently enemies of freedom, antidemocratic, antiequality, highly prejudiced, mean-spirited, power hungry, Machiavellian, and amoral. They are also often conservatives without conscience who are capable of plunging this nation into disasters the likes of which we have never known.

Although I have only recently learned the correct term for describing this type of behavior, and come to understand the implications of such authoritarian thinking, I was familiar with the personality type from my years in the Nixon White House. We had plenty of au-thoritarians in the Nixon administration, from the president on down. In fact, authoritarian thinking was the principal force behind almost everything that went wrong with Nixon's presidency. I had had little contact with my former colleagues, or with their new authoritar-ian friends and associates, until the early 1990s, when they decided to attack my wife and me in an effort to rewrite history at our expense. By then I had left public life for a very comfortable and private exis-tence in the world of business, but they forced me back into the pub-lic square to defend myself and my wife from their false charges. In returning, I discovered how contemptible and dangerous their brand of "conservatism" had become, and how low they were prepared to stoop for their cause.

About 7:00 A.M. on Monday, May 6, 1991, I received a phone call that was both literally and figuratively a wake-up call, one that would dra-matically change the political world as I thought I knew it. My last politics-related activity had been in 1982, when I wrote *Lost Honor,* a book about the consequences of Watergate during the decade that fol-lowed it. Since then I had focused exclusively on my work in merger and acquisition ventures, and I no longer had any interest in partisan politics. In fact, I had done everything I could to lower my public profile and regain my privacy by refusing to give press interviews. I became a true nonpartisan, sometimes voting for Republicans and sometimes for Democrats, always determined to select the best candi-dates for the job. I paid little attention to Washington affairs other than major events. I did maintain my relationships with old friends in Washington, including some still active at the highest levels of gov-ernment and several who worked for Reagan and Bush I, but we sel-dom discussed politics too seriously. I discovered that I enjoyed life more outside of the political arena, and so I had no interest in return-ing to it.

When the phone rang that Monday morning, I assumed it was my wife, Maureen—"Mo" to family and friends—calling from Pennsylvania, where she had gone to care for my mother, who had recently suffered a stroke. I was instead greeted by Mike Wallace of *60 Minutes,* and his producer Brian Ellis. Wallace quickly got to the reason for their call. "Have you heard about this new book about Bob Woodward?" he inquired referring to the *Washington Post's* star reporter and best-selling author. "I'm talking about a book called *Silent Coup: The Removal of a President,* by Leonard Colodny and Robert Gettlin."* Wallace explained that *60 Minutes* was working on a story about *Silent Coup,* which St. Martin's Press was going to publish in two weeks, and *Time* magazine was going to run an excerpt from the book. Wallace said the book dealt not only with Woodward but also "with you, sir, John Dean."

"How so?" I asked. I knew about the book because Colodny had called me several years earlier looking for dirt on Woodward, and I had told him I had none. Later he called back to ask me some questions about my testimony before the Senate Watergate committee. But Colodny had said little about how I related to his book. I had assumed his project had died.

"Do you know a woman by the name of Heidi Rikan?" Wallace asked.

"Sure, Heidi was a friend of Mo's. She died a few years ago. What does Heidi have to do with *Silent Coup?*" Heidi and Mo had been friends before we were married and was a bridesmaid at our wedding. Wallace ignored my question.

Employing his trademark confrontational tone, Wallace began throwing hard balls. "According to *Silent Coup,* Heidi was also known as Cathy Dieter, and this Heidi/Cathy person, as they call her in the

---

*I do not record telephone calls. I do make notes, and after the conversation, if appropriate, I reconstruct the call. Most of the conversations relating to *Silent Coup* were written up within twenty-four hours of the conversation. In reporting them I have employed Bob Woodward's technique of converting them back to dialogue and the salient points.

book, had a connection to a call-girl ring back in 1971 and '72. In fact, I gather she was the madam of the operation. According to *Silent Coup,* this call-girl ring had a connection with the Democratic National Committee at the Watergate. Apparently the DNC was providing customers for the call girls. The book says that your wife was the roommate of Cathy Dieter, and she seemingly knew all about this activity. In fact, according to *Silent Coup,* this call-girl operation was the reason for the break-ins at the Watergate."

I was, understandably, stunned. I had never heard or seen anything that would even hint at Heidi's being a call girl, and I could not imagine Mo's not telling me if she knew, or had any such suspicion. And I knew for certain that neither Heidi nor Mo had anything whatsoever to do with Watergate. My thoughts raced as Wallace continued with his questioning.

"Did you know an attorney in Washington by the name of Phillip Mackin Bailley?" he asked.

When I answered that I did not, he pressed. "Do you remember an incident while you were working at the White House, as counsel to the president, when an assistant United States attorney came to your office, a fellow named John Rudy, to discuss Phillip Bailley's involvement in prostitution, and you made a copy of Mr. Bailley's address book, which had been seized by the FBI?"

"I recall a couple of assistant United States attorneys coming to my office in connection with a newspaper story claiming that a lawyer, or a secretary, from the White House was allegedly connected with a call-girl ring. As I recall, we had trouble figuring out who, if anyone, at the White House was involved. But I never made a copy of an address book." My mind was searching, trying to recall events that had taken place almost two decades earlier.

Wallace now dropped another bomb. He told me that according to *Silent Coup* Mo's name was in Phillip Bailley's little black address book. He also said that Bailley had been indicted for violating the Mann Act, which prohibits taking women across state lines for immoral purposes, specifically prostitution. *Silent Coup* claimed that my wife was listed in the address book as "Mo Biner," along with a code name of "Clout." Supposedly, Bailley's address book also contained the name of Cathy Dieter. Before I could digest this information, Wallace added more.

"According to *Silent Coup,* sir, you, John Dean, are the real mastermind of the Watergate break-ins, and you ordered these break-ins because you were apparently seeking sexual dirt on the Democrats, which you learned about from your then girlfriend, now wife, Maureen." When I failed to respond, because I was dumbfounded, Wallace asked, "Does this make sense to you?"

"No, no sense at all. It's pure bullshit. How could I have ordered the Watergate break-ins and kept it secret for the last twenty years?"

"Fair question," Wallace responded. He explained that the book claimed I arranged the break-ins through my secret relationship with former White House consultant E. Howard Hunt—Hunt, who along with Gordon Liddy, had been convicted two decades earlier of plotting the Watergate break-ins.

"I recall meeting Hunt once in Chuck Colson's office. Hunt worked for Colson. I don't think I ever said anything more than 'hello' to Howard Hunt in all my years at the White House. The only other time I have spoken to him was long after Watergate, when we gave a few college lectures together. Anyone who says I directed Hunt to do anything is crazy." Still trying to sort out the various claims of *Silent Coup,* I asked, "Did you say this book has me ordering the break-ins because of a call-girl ring?"

Wallace said the manuscript was not clear about the first break-in. Indeed, he said it was all a bit unclear, but apparently they were saying that the second break-in was related to Bailley's address book and a desk in the DNC. "Are you saying that none of this makes any sense to you?" Wallace asked again.

"Mike, I'm astounded. This sounds like a sick joke."

"The authors and the publisher claim you were interviewed," Wallace said.

"Not about this stuff. I was never asked anything about Mo, or Heidi Rikan, nor was there any mention of call girls. I assure you I would remember."

Wallace wanted me to go on camera to deny the charges. I said I was willing, but I wanted to see the book so I could understand the basis of the charges. But *60 Minutes* had signed a confidentiality agreement with the publisher, and was prohibited from providing any further information. When the conversation with Wallace ended I called Hays Gorey, a senior correspondent for *Time* magazine, who had not only covered Watergate, but, working with Mo, had co-authored *Mo: A Woman's View of Watergate.* Hays had known Heidi as well. He was aghast, and could not believe that *Time* was going to run such a flagrantly phony story without checking with the reporter who had covered Watergate for them. After a quick call to New York, he confirmed that the New York office had purchased the first serial rights to *Silent Coup,* and they were preparing both an excerpt and a news story.

Mo found the story laughable, and could not believe anyone would publish it. She had no information that Heidi had ever been involved with a call-girl ring, and did not believe it possible, because Heidi traveled constantly and was seldom in Washington. Mo had never heard of an attorney by the name of Phillip Mackin Bailley, and if her name was in his address book, it was not because she knew him.

By the time Mo returned home *60 Minutes* had backed away from the book, because neither the authors nor the publisher could provide information that confirmed the central charges. Phillip Mackin Bailley, the source of much of the information, was "not available." Notwithstanding *60 Minutes*'s rejection of the book, *Time*'s editors were still proceeding. They asked Hays to interview us for our reaction, even though he had told them the story was untrue. Hays had called a number of men he knew who had worked at the DNC at the time the call-girl operation was said to be flourishing in 1971 and 1972. They all told him it was impossible that such activity could have existed without their knowing of it. One former DNC official told Hays that had there been such an operation he would have been a top customer. Traveling from Washington to California to interview us, Hays read the material in *Silent Coup* relating to the Deans, and could not understand why *Time* was treating it as a news story. Nor could I when he loaned me his copy of the book so I could see what was being said. The material in the book relating to the Deans ran about 180 pages, and as I skimmed these pages I could not find one that was not filled with false or misleading information. All the hard evidence (the information developed by government investigators and prosecutors) that conflicted with this invented story was simply omitted. I could find no real documentation for their charges. I did not understand how the authors and St. Martin's thought they could get away with their outrageous story without facing a lawsuit from us. Hays wondered the same.

We gave Hays a statement the next morning that made clear we were preparing for legal action. Hays gave us his telephone number in Salt Lake City, where he planned to stop to visit with family en route back to Washington. Several hours later we called him, because I had had another idea, and I asked if he thought it would be worth my effort to go directly to Henry Muller, *Time*'s managing editor, to ask him to reconsider. Hays could not offer any encouragement. It was Friday evening in New York, and this issue of the magazine was heading for the printer. In addition, he confided that *Time* had paid fifty thousand dollars for the serial rights. But he gave me Muller's office number, and told me, "Only someone like Muller could pull a story at this late stage." I called Muller's office, and arranged to fax a letter. Rather than threatening legal action, I tried to appeal to Muller's journalistic good sense. They were reporting a story that *60 Minutes* had investigated and rejected, and their principal Watergate reporter, Hays Gorey, had told them the story was baseless. Surprisingly, the effort worked. Within less than an hour of sending the letter, Hays called back. "You did it, Muller pulled the story. The whole thing. We're not going to even mention *Silent Coup*. I have only seen that happen once before in my thirty years with *Time*." Hays was ebullient, clearly proud that *Time* had done the right thing.

I decided to try again to persuade Tom McCormack, chairman and CEO of St. Martin's Press, to reconsider the publication of *Silent Coup*. McCormack had refused to talk with me earlier, so I faxed him a letter to let him know he was walking into a lawsuit. A day later we received McCormack's answer, when CBS's *Good Morning America* (*GMA*) called on Saturday morning to tell us that Colodny and Get-tlin would be appearing Monday morning, May 21, 1991, to promote their newly published book and *GMA* wanted to give us a chance to respond. We faxed them the statement we had given *Time*. Clearly, a book tour was underway, but by pushing *60 Minutes* and then *Time*, we had mortally wounded the book and destroyed the carefully planned launch, which might have given the story credibility. Now it would be difficult to treat *Silent Coup* as legitimate news.

Watching the authors on *Good Morning America*, we felt encouraged. Colodny, the older of the two, who looked to be in his early fifties, was a retired liquor salesman and conspiracy buff. Gettlin, who appeared to be in his forties, was a journalist. This was their first book. Both were tense. *GMA*'s host, Charlie Gibson, an experienced journalist, was not buying the *Silent Coup* story relating to the Deans, so his questions focused on the material in the book related to Bob Woodward and Al Haig, which was as unfounded as the material relating to us. (Woodward was accused of CIA connections; Haig had allegedly plotted the "coup" of the title that had removed Nixon from office.) With St. Martin's publicity department pumping out information about their sensational new book, requests for responses and appearances became so frequent we had to put a message on the answering machine to handle the requests. Not wanting to do anything to attract additional publicity to the book, however, we declined all appearances and issued a statement explaining that the charges were false.

We watched the authors again on CNN's *Larry King Live.* Bob Beckel was the substitute host in Larry King's absence. Colodny claimed that he and Gettlin were "not making any charges against Maureen Dean." Yet I had made a note during my quick read of the book that they claimed that Mo's alleged "acquaintanceship with [Phillip Mackin] Bailley, and the true identity of her friend Heidi [Rikan] . . . [were] the keys to understanding all the events of the break-ins and cover-ups that we know under the omnibus label of Watergate." That was some "no charge." After a commercial break, well into the program, both Colodny and Gettlin simply disappeared without explanation, as if snatched from their seats by hooks. In their places were Howard Kurtz, a media reporter for the *Washington Post,* and Gordon Liddy, Watergate's most decorated felon. Beckel asked Liddy for his "theory" of why *60 Minutes* and *Time* had "pulled" their stories on *Silent Coup.* Liddy said, "Well, I don't have to go for a *theory* with respect to those two things, because they are on the record." Liddy claimed none of the people charged by the book would appear on *60 Minutes.* "They wanted to get John Dean, etcetera," Liddy claimed. "They wouldn't come on the program and face these two men. *Time* magazine just said, you know, the thing is so densely packed that it did not lend itself to being excerpted and they felt that they couldn't do it."

Liddy's remarks were untrue, for I had agreed to do *60 Minutes* (as had Woodward and Haig) and I had a copy of the *Time* excerpt, not to mention my letter, which had killed it. Mike Wallace, who had obviously been watching the show, called in to correct Liddy's false characterizations. Wallace reported that he had read *Silent Coup,* and had interviewed Colodny and Gettlin. "And we intended to go, just as *Time* magazine intended to go. We checked, Gordon. I did talk to John Dean," he said. "We objected to the fact that the authors refused or declined to let the objects of their scrutiny, these three [Woodward,

Haig, and Dean] in particular, see the book, read the book ahead of time, so that they could face the charges." As to the charge that I was the "mastermind" of Watergate, Wallace explained, "We could not, on our own, source the thing sufficiently to satisfy ourselves that it stood up as a *60 Minutes* piece. That's why we didn't do the piece." Mo applauded when one of America's best-known journalists knocked down the book's central charge.

As a hard news story *Silent Coup* was now for certain dead and would undoubtedly have been headed for the remainder table, but St. Martin's had a lot of money tied up in it, and was determined to make it a best seller. Their plan was to sell the book to Nixon apologists and right-wingers, giving them a new history of Nixon's downfall in which Bob Woodward, Al Haig, and John Dean were the villains, and randy Democrats had all but invited surveillance. Who better to peddle this tale than uber-conservative Gordon Liddy? Although we did not know it at the time, Liddy had been a behind-the-scenes collaborator with Colodny in developing, sourcing, and writing *Silent Coup*'s version of the Deans' involvement in Watergate. In fact, without Liddy's support St. Martin's might well have abandoned the project, for neither Colodny nor Gettlin had actually written it. St. Martin's had hired a freelancer, Tom Shachtman, to assemble a story based on material that Liddy and other right-wingers had helped Colodny assemble. Schactman himself was contractually immunized from any legal liability, and shortly before *Silent Coup*'s publication, St. Martin's had doubled its insurance coverage for defamation and worked out a plan for Liddy, who was already a St. Martin's author, to lead a charge to the bestseller list. To compensate Liddy for his efforts, and to give him an excuse to be out promoting, St. Martin's reissued a paperback edition of his autobiography, *Will*, with a new postscript that embraced *Silent Coup* as the definitive account on Watergate. In that material Liddy claimed, without any explanation, that I had duped him in "an exercise in sleight-of-hand worthy of The Amazing Randi himself," and that he had not truly understood Watergate until Colodny explained to him what had purportedly transpired, by telling him of Phillip Bailley's story. According to this revised accounting of history, Liddy's former partner-in-crime Howard Hunt was merely my pawn, working secretly for me unbeknownst to Liddy. (And unbeknownst to Howard Hunt as well, for he, too, denied the *Silent Coup* account.)

Liddy's involvement in this specious attack did not surprise me. He had once planned to kill both Howard Hunt and me , he had said in *Will,* but his orders to do so had never come—although he did not say who he expected would send them. "Howard Hunt had become an informer," he wrote, and when Hunt agreed to testify he became "a betrayer of his friends, and to me there is nothing lower on earth. . . . Hunt deserved to die." About me, Liddy wrote that the "difference between Hunt and Dean is the difference between a POW who breaks under torture and aids the enemy, and Judas Iscariot."[2] The subtext of Liddy's statement is that the U.S. government had become his enemy and that Richard Nixon had become something of a Christ figure for him. Attacking Howard Hunt and me was consistent with both his conservative politics and his personality. He sought to resurrect Nixon for conservatives and blame others for his destroyed presidency. His attacks on Mo, however, were inexplicable. It did not strike me as consistent with his macho perception of himself to attack a noncombatant woman, yet he traveled the country repeating the false story that Phillip Bailley had told him. Clearly, *Silent Coup* had come at a perfect time for Liddy. Since the first publication of *Will* in 1980 he had made a living by putting his dysfunctional personality on display. By the early nineties speaking engagements were becoming less frequent for him, and his business ventures, including several novels, were unsuccessful. *Silent Coup* put him back in the spotlight, where he loved to be—publicly misbehaving.

My former colleague Chuck Colson's appearance on national television to endorse *Silent Coup* truly surprised me and stunned Mo, who was deeply hurt by his gratuitous attack. Chuck and I had crossed swords at the Nixon White House only once, and even then we had not communicated directly. I had had virtually nothing to do with his office, or its nefarious activities, except for the time Chuck had wanted to firebomb and burglarize the Brookings Institution, convinced that this Washington think tank had copies of documents the president wanted. When I learned of his insane plan I flew to California (where the president and senior staff were staying at the Western White House) to plead my case to John Ehrlichman, a titular superior to both Chuck and myself. By pointing out, with some outrage, that if anyone died it would involve a capital crime that might be traced back to the White House, I was able to shut down Colson's scheme. As a result, over the next several months I was told nothing about Colson's shenanigans, such as his financing the infamous burglary by Liddy and Hunt of Daniel Ellsberg's psychiatrist's office after Ellsberg released the so-called Pentagon Papers, which was a precursor to the later Watergate break-ins.

After I eventually broke rank with the Nixon White House, Colson had set about trying to destroy me for telling the truth, though he backed off after purportedly finding God. He also became rather busy with his own problems. On March 1, 1974, Colson was indicted for his role in the Watergate cover-up, and six days later he was indicted for his involvement in the conspiracy to break into the office of Ellsberg's psychiatrist. Chuck, no doubt, sensed even more problems to come, because the Watergate Special Prosecution Force was considering charging him with both perjury and subornation of perjury.[3] He was facing a lot of jail time. However, the prosecutors allowed him to plead guilty to a single—and given what he was facing, innocuous—charge in exchange for his cooperation, although in the end he proved to be utterly useless as a government witness, since the prosecutors could not vouch for his honesty.

Chuck and I had agreed to let bygones be bygones during the Watergate cover-up trial when we found ourselves only down the hall from each other, under the federal Witness Protection Program, at the Fort Holabird safe house in Maryland, just outside Washington. Until

Colson started promoting *Silent Coup* I had taken him as a man of his word, and we had even continued to visit from time to time after Watergate was behind us. When I saw Colson promote *Silent Coup* on *Crossfire,* I was still unaware of his earlier prepublication discussions with Colodny about this invented history. (Colodny had illegally tape-recorded all of his telephone conversations.) Why, of all people, would Chuck Colson promote *Silent Coup's* conspicuously phony account of Watergate? Where was his conscience? How could he call himself a Christian? I promised myself I would find answers to these questions, because I did not understand what was compelling his behavior.

The promotion campaign to sell the book to conservatives worked, thanks to Liddy's nationwide tour, in which he appeared on countless right-wing talk-radio shows. By July 7, 1991, *Silent Coup* had peaked at number three on the *New York Times* best-seller list. On July 12, 1991, our answering machine handled a very early call. When Mo checked the message I heard her shriek, and ran to find her standing beside the answering machine sobbing and shaking. "What is it?" I asked but she could not speak, as tears poured from her eyes. As I held her I could feel every bone in her body trembling. "What is it?" I asked again.

"Liddy. He's called our house." Before Mo could explain, the phone began ringing and I answered.

"Is this John Dean?" an unfamiliar voice asked.

"Yes, it is. Who's this?"

"Wow, that's cool. This is really John Dean?"

"Yes. Who is this, please?"

"Oh, I'm nobody. I was just listening to the radio and Gordon Liddy was on, and he gave out your telephone number, so I thought I'd try it. Talk to you later. Bye."

Immediately the phone rang again, this time it was a collect call, which I refused. To prevent further nuisance calls I used a technique that makes all our phone lines busy. This diverted Mo's attention and calmed her, and she now asked me to listen to Liddy's message, so I played it.

A smug-sounding voice said, "This is G. Gordon Liddy, calling you from the *Merle Pollis Show*. John, you have . . ." "W-E-R-E Cleveland, let's get our call letters in," the host interrupted. Liddy then continued, ". . . you have promised that you will sue me and Len Colodny and Bob Gettlin. Let's get this suit started, John. We want to get you on the stand, under oath, yet again. . . . Come on, John. I'm publicly challenging you to make good on your promise to sue." The host added, "John, this is Merle Pollis, the host of the program. Would you say hello to Maureen, for me? I said she was the prettiest of the Watergate people, next to G. Gordon Liddy. I hope she's still just as pretty. I, ah, this, this new book, however, reveals some things about Maureen that irk me. I didn't want to think of her in that way, and it makes me very sad, and it also makes me feel, well, never mind. Thanks, John."

Liddy would get his lawsuit, but on our terms, not his. Rather than give him the publicity he desperately wanted, we spent the next eight months collecting evidence and preparing the case. For eight years our lawsuit made its way through the federal courts, and St. Martin's tried every possible ploy to prevent its going to trial. Had we taken the case to trial, Phillip Mackin Bailley, the key source for the story about the purported call-girl ring, might rank as the worst possible source of information in the annals of defamation law. Bailley had been in and out of mental institutions throughout his adult life. When we deposed him, Bailley's attorney arranged for a psychiatrist to testify under oath that his client's mental condition made him unable to distinguish fact from fiction. While St. Martin's and the other defendants were spending over $14 million of insurance company money trying to make us go away, it eventually became clear to them that we were prepared to go whatever distance necessary to make fools of them all, and that we had the evidence to do it.[4] By the fall of 1998 we had also accomplished our underlying goal of gathering the information necessary to show that *Silent Coup* was bogus history. Ultimately, it seems, they had hoped to win the lawsuit by simply outspending us, but when that strategy failed, they sought a settlement. Neither Colodny nor Liddy wanted to settle, however. Colodny had somehow used a rider on his homeowner's policy to get the insurance company to pay for his defense in the litigation, though ultimately his insurer forced him to settle. Liddy, on the other hand, had nothing at risk, since all of his assets were in his wife's name and St. Martin's was paying for his attorney. After we settled with St. Martin's and Colodny, U.S. District Court Judge Emmett Sullivan put an end to the litigation.[5] While the final settlement agreement prohibits me from discussing its terms, I can say the Deans were satisfied.

Despite most of the news media's fitting dismissal of *Silent Coup*'s baseless claims, the protracted litigation provided time for the book to gather a following, including an almost cultlike collection of high-profile right-wingers. Among them, for example, is Monica Crowley, a former aide to Richard Nixon after his presidency, and now a conservative personality on MSNBC, cohosting *Connected: Coast to Coast* with Ron Reagan. Other prominent media-based conservatives who have joined the glee club are James Rosen and Brit Hume of Fox News. How these seemingly intelligent people embraced this false account mystified me, and I wanted to know.

Throughout the prolonged *Silent Coup* controversy it had gradually become clear to me that St. Martin's, Colodny, and Gettlin were in it for the money. Had Phillip Bailley, or some other such source, claimed that Pat Nixon had ordered the break-in, they no doubt would have turned history upside down to try to sell that story as well. When we contested the bogus account, they all fought to save face. In addition, Colodny, who called himself a Democrat, had never been given much attention until he was embraced by the right wing, where he has found new friends. Liddy wanted revenge, even though *Silent Coup* showed him as a greater fool than history already had; promoting it did, however, provide an outlet for his aggression—not to mention that it also landed him his own talk-radio show, which has thrived. As for Colson, his reason for promoting *Silent Coup* remained a complete mystery for me, as did the motives of people like Monica Crowley, James Rosen, Brit Hume, and all the other hard-core conservatives who embraced this spurious history and made it a best seller. The only thing I could see that these people had in common was their conservatism.

As much as anything, the lawsuit made me realize that during the years I had been focused on business the Republican Party and conservatism had undergone drastic changes. The Republican Party had shifted to the extreme right, resulting in longtime hard-right conservatives like Liddy and Colson, who had once been at the fringe, finding themselves in vogue. That philosophical shift and its implications became even clearer to me when I returned to Washington for an extended period of time during the Clinton impeachment proceedings and experienced for myself the new conservative climate that has enveloped the nation's capital. Most of these conservatives had arrived after Nixon's fall, and in the late 1970s and early 1980s.

They were not good losers. So when they lost the White House in 1992 they began what would be an unrelenting and extended series of attacks on the Clinton presidency, which reached their peak when Clinton's affair with Monica Lewinsky was revealed in early 1998. At that time I began receiving an increasing number of requests for television interviews, and *Silent Coup* was all but forgotten publicly (and we were in settlement discussions). While I had no idea then whether the president was telling the truth about his relationship with Lewinsky, it was clear to me that the First Lady was correct in her contention that there was a vast right-wing conspiracy attempting to destroy the Clintons, for I still had a number of knowledgeable conservative contacts. Because each of the various scandals of the Clinton White House—the travel office firings, Whitewater, Vince Foster's suicide, the Paula Jones lawsuit, and the Lewinsky affair—was predictably declared by Republicans to be "worse than Watergate," I felt someone needed to set the record straight.[6] In reality, these scandals, even collectively, did not come close to Watergate in their seriousness. So I began to speak out. I did not speak as a partisan, but rather as someone who understood the difference between the Clinton and Nixon scandals, as well as the gravity of impeachment. (I was well versed in this topic because I had once studied the impeachment and trial of Andrew Johnson, and, of course, had firsthand knowledge of the Nixon proceedings.)

During the time the independent counsel, Kenneth Starr, was building his case against Clinton for impeachment, I agreed to work exclusively for MSNBC in Washington as an on-camera consultant, or "anchor buddy," beginning my assignment soon after Starr made a formal referral to the House Judiciary Committee on September 9, 1998, and sent the thirty-six boxes of damning evidence to the House of Representatives. Over the next several months, during Clinton's impeachment and trial, I spent more time in Washington than I had, cumulatively, in the preceding twenty-five years, and it could not have been a more eventful time to be there. One did not need to be a knowledgeable Washington veteran, though, to perceive that conservatives in Congress were hell-bent on overturning the 1996 election and removing Clinton from office.

MSNBC's studios in Washington are on Capitol Hill, not far from the Senate side of the Capitol building. A core group of on-air consultants were placed on various shows throughout the day, but during the impeachment hearings and the trial, a few of us were requested to stay on the set with the anchors as long as official proceedings continued. During the many hours I was in the studio or the green room, I probably spent more time talking with legal analyst Barbara Olson than anyone else. Barbara, who was tragically killed on the 9/11 flight that crashed into the Pentagon, was smart, savvy, engaging, and never shy, least of all in her opinion of the president and his wife. "I really hate the Clintons, and I want to run them out of town," she told me. Barbara, who frequently made calls on her cell phone during breaks, made it impossible not to overhear her conversations, and she explained to me that she was receiving talking points from her network of conservative Republicans, who were observing all of the media's coverage of the impeachment proceeding. "Do you really believe you can remove a popular president?" I asked her during the hearings. "Absolutely. It's a done deal," she said. "How about the Senate?" I asked. "We're working on it," she replied with a conspiratorial smile and a wink. I had little doubt, from the time I spent with Barbara, that votes had already been counted in the House of Representatives, and nothing was going to stop them from voting for impeachment. There were simply too many Democrats in the Senate, however, for the Republicans to muster the requisite two thirds for a guilty verdict and removal. The entire undertaking was designed to tarnish Clinton, and the Democrats.

During this period I was able to visit with members of the House and Senate, both Republicans and Democrats, who streamed through the MSNBC green room or the studios, often with key members of their staff. I had many fascinating, and informative, conversations that were invaluable to the education I received during this period. I learned, for instance, that Speaker of the House Newt Gingrich (R-GA) and majority leader Tom DeLay (R-TX) were both exerting enormous control over the GOP. Some Republicans told me that Gingrich was betting his Speaker's seat on the impeachment drive's adding additional Republican members to the House. DeLay, it was clear, had influence because the rank-and-file House Republicans feared his wrath, and he was determined to impeach Clinton. Several Republicans told me that this was payback to the Democrats for what had been done to Nixon, and when I pointed out that Republicans had been part of that undertaking, a typical response was, "Yeah, but they weren't conservative." In fact, there were conservatives involved in the effort, but I was not looking for debates about Watergate.

Notwithstanding Clinton's soaring popularity, conservatives had become myopic; they were fixated on getting rid of him. Five days after the House Judiciary Committee voted along party lines to begin an impeachment inquiry (with all Republicans, who controlled the committee, voting for it, and all Democrats voting against), a *Washington Post* public opinion poll showed that 62 percent of Republicans disapproved of impeaching the president. Knowledgeable Republicans passing through the MSNBC green room privately explained that House Republicans would pursue the impeachment anyway, on behalf of the 31 percent who wanted Clinton removed. (Seven percent of the *Post* poll of the GOP had no opinion.) The motive of the GOP leaders was simply to please the party's "base"; the wishes of the base were their command. That base was composed primarily of Christian conservatives, in particular evangelicals. Republicans with whom I spoke before the November 1998 midterm elections were convinced the party would be vindicated at the polls for its treatment of Clinton. As it turned out, however, they had misread the mood of the country, and they lost the great "impeachment election" when Americans refused to make the election a referendum on Bill Clinton's behavior. Republicans, who controlled the House and the Senate, not only gained no seats in either body, but lost five seats in the House; Speaker Newt Gingrich resigned after his plan was defeated. What was even more stunning was that the election results did not stop these hardcore conservative Republicans from continuing to push for Clinton's impeachment and, at the same time, issue increasingly stern demands for party loyalty. As someone who had previously spent over twenty years in Washington observing Congress up close, I found this new level of party discipline remarkable. I understood that DeLay scared them, but so badly that they would vote against their consciences? I was relieved that a few of the conservatives with whom I spoke believed the GOP leadership was going too far.

While not exactly naive to the ways of Washington, I was amazed, if not at times dumbfounded, by these events, and the remarkable hypocrisy displayed during them, as I watched from my ringside seat. Ostensibly, Clinton was impeached and being tried for lying about a sexual liaison. If truthfulness about extramarital affairs had been a requisite for everyone in Congress to hold their seats before they voted to oust Clinton, neither the House nor the Senate could have formed a quorum. While the people responsible for Clinton's impeachment called themselves conservatives, this was not a conservatism with which I was familiar. In past years problems of this nature had been resolved without threatening the nation's well-being. During Watergate, for example, Barry Goldwater, Hugh Scott, and John Rhodes traveled to the White House to tell Nixon it was time to resign. And in 1987, notes *Washington Post* reporter Peter Baker, "Democratic leaders agreed to forgo impeachment proceedings against Ronald Reagan for the Iran-Contra affair once former senator Howard H. Baker, Jr. took over as White House chief of staff, pledging to put things back on track."[7] In both these cases constitutional crises had been avoided. But now, so-called conservatives who controlled the House of Representatives had pushed the process for political spite and cheapened an extremely important constitutional check by using impeachment solely to attack a president of whom they did not approve. Conservative demagogues shamed themselves in ways far worse than Clinton had himself, and their behavior was certainly more threatening to the democratic process than anything the president had done.

At the height of Watergate, conservative historian Daniel J. Boorstin gave an extended interview to *Congressional Quarterly* in which he noted that radio and television enabled countless Americans to follow the proceedings. "We used to think of the conscience as being a private, intimate, still, small voice within," he said. "Now the conscience of democracy becomes the whole community sitting in their living room watching what has been done." The conscience of a democracy, Boorstin said, was "what could be called the *conscience of the marketplace*—the people's feeling of outrage at the violations of common decency, of legal and constitutional rules." This, warned Boorstin, should be distinguished from "what might be called *the judgment of the marketplace.* The judgment of the marketplace is lynch law, and that is something we must beware of."[8] If Boorstin's analysis was applied to Clinton's impeachment, the House of Representatives would be seen as having rejected the "conscience of the marketplace," and having imposed the judgment of a lynch mob.

Conservatives attracted to conspicuously false history, as occurred with *Silent Coup,* and conservatives with the mentality of a lynch mob, were foreign to me, but they certainly got my attention. In now writing about them, by myself, I am not proceeding as this project was initially conceived. It started as a joint undertaking with the late U.S. senator Barry M. Goldwater of Arizona, whom I had the good fortune of knowing almost his entire political career. His oldest son, Barry, Jr., has been my close friend since the early 1950s, when we were roommates at Staunton Military Academy in Virginia, which was also the senator's high school alma mater. Senator Goldwater was elected to the U.S. Senate in 1952, resigned in 1964 to pursue an unsuccessful bid for the presidency as the Republican Party's standard-bearer, and was reelected to the Senate in 1968, where he served until his retirement in 1985. After leaving the Senate he remained active and interested in Republican politics until his death in 1998.

I discovered Senator Goldwater's political thinking during my college years, when, like countless other college students of the early 1960s I read his book *The Conscience of a Conservative* and experienced a political awakening. The senator made conservatism respectable, unlike the witch-hunting Senator Joe McCarthy and the screwball absurdities of the John Birch Society. Senator Goldwater's conservatism was sensible and straightforward, and therefore appealing. Given the influence he had on my thinking, as well as my admiration for him, it is not surprising that I still consider myself to be a "Goldwater conservative" on many issues. Be that as it may, while my core beliefs have not changed significantly in the past forty years, the Grand Old Party to which I once belonged has moved so far to the right, that on the contemporary political spectrum I now often fall to the left of the Republican center. Like many Republicans uncomfortable with the right-wing extremists who control the party, I reregistered as an Independent.

It was not Senator Goldwater's politics, however, that prompted me to call him after the 1994 midterm elections, when the Republicans won control of Congress for the first time in forty years. I called to solicit his thoughts about the *Silent Coup* lawsuit, and to talk to him about the conservatives who were so aggressively promoting, and buying into, this false history. Following the senator's unsuccessful bid for the presidency in 1964 he had filed a defamation lawsuit against the publisher of *FACT* magazine, Ralph Ginsberg, who had claimed during the 1964 presidential campaign that the senator was crazy, a judgment he based on a ludicrous and highly partisan poll of psychiatrists. Although it took years, Senator Goldwater eventually won. His case made new law, which I told him would help my wife and me, as public figures, prevail in our suit.[9] He was aware of the attacks on Mo, and he immediately put our situation into a larger context, while counseling that we vigorously pursue the litigation.

"I heard that jackass Liddy on one of the talk-radio shows," the senator told me. "I don't think anyone believes him, John. He's a fool." "Frankly, I find it offensive that he calls himself a conservative," the senator added.

"Why's that?" I asked.

"Why? I'll tell you why. Because he thinks like a thug, not like a conservative. Conservatives seek the wisdom of the past, not the worst of it," he snapped. He continued, "I was talking with [former Arizona Republican congressman and former minority leader of the House of Representatives] Johnny Rhodes, just a few days ago. He's still got the ear of the House Republican leaders. I asked him to tell those fellows back in Washington that I don't go along with their incivility. I told them they should back off on their attacks on Hillary Clinton. They're acting like jerks too, not conservatives. If they don't, I'm going to blast them. They're driving decent people out of public service. And they're turning off voters. It's dirty politics, and it should end."

"Why do you suppose that they do this?" I asked.

Without hesitation he said, "It's these so-called social or cultural conservatives. And I don't know what in hell possesses them. I'd like to find out."*

Senator Goldwater had no tolerance for such politics, and had never attacked his own political opponents personally. He was tough as nails, yet courtly in his courtesy. During the 1964 presidential race against President Lyndon Johnson, for example, one of Johnson's top aides and close friends, Walter Jenkins, was arrested in the men's room of the YMCA near the White House for engaging in a homosexual activity. After the Johnson White House whisked Jenkins into a hospital and hushed up the story, the senator's campaign people learned of the incident and wanted to use it against LBJ. Senator Goldwater refused, despite the brutal campaign ads the Johnson people were running against him.

When I called Senator Goldwater I had only recently learned more about Chuck Colson's involvement with *Silent Coup*. I asked the senator for his thoughts on Christian conservatives like Colson, and their increasing presence in Republican politics, and he minced no words. "Goddamn it, John," he began, with a combination of anger, frustration, and sorrow, "the Republicans are selling their soul to win elections." He saw trouble coming. "Mark my word," he said, "if and when these preachers get control of the party, and they're sure trying to do so, it's going to be a terrible damn problem. Frankly, these people frighten me. Politics and governing demand compromise. The government won't work without it. But these Christians believe they

---

*Throughout I use the term "cultural conservative" interchangeably with "social conservative." While I am aware of efforts to define them separately, conservatives, the news media, and others use them interchangeably. So I have done likewise.

are acting in the name of God, so they can't and won't compromise. I know, I've tried to deal with them." He had absolutely no doubt that these people had made Washington more divisive than it had ever been, and he was concerned that their divisiveness was spreading throughout the country.[10]

My conversations with Senator Goldwater evolved into a plan to write a book together about so-called social conservatives. We would attempt to understand their strident and intolerant politics by talking with people like Chuck Colson, Pat Robertson, and Jerry Falwell. We would learn more about their thinking, and try to determine whether they appreciated what they were doing to conservatism and to Republican politics. We would title our book *Conservatives Without Conscience,* an obvious allusion to Senator Goldwater's classic. But we had not progressed very deeply into our work before I realized it could become a burden for the senator, whose physical health was rapidly failing. I slowed the project down and soon had to place it on the shelf, hoping to resume when the senator felt better. Sadly, that did not happen, but because I wanted answers, I could not abandon our task. I wanted to understand why these so-called conservatives acted in such a conspicuously unattractive manner. What caused their aggression and the hostility that was changing the nature of politics? Our litigation and my experiences during the Clinton impeachment proceedings continued to provide insights into conservative thinking, and it was not attractive. But it was my even closer look at Washington after the 2000 election, when writing about Bush and Cheney, that convinced me I had to find answers. The serious deterioration and disintegration of conservative principles under Bush and Cheney, in all branches of the federal government, with the striking shift toward a very un-American-type of authoritarianism, compelled me to complete the project I had begun with Senator Goldwater.

Unfortunately, I no longer had the senator's experience, wisdom, or insights to draw upon. But I did have notes from our conversations, as well as access to his files, which he had pointed me to before his death. His personal political papers, housed at the Arizona Historical Foundation in Phoenix, are a treasure trove of raw material relating to American conservatism, and they served as an important resource for this book. While I have quoted from the senator's papers when appropriate, I have not taken the liberty of attempting to speak for him. I have also discovered, after reading a plethora of books on the subject, that nearly every question Senator Goldwater and I had discussed about the religious right has been answered in other works—all but one.[11] That remaining question is rather basic: Why do those in the religious right act as they do? Are they motivated by religion or conservatism? Stated a little differently, is this what happens when Christians become politically active? Or do their actions simply reflect one type of person who is drawn to conservatism? In the pages that follow I have set forth the answers I found to these and many other questions about the current conservative sensibility.

Conservatives without conscience do not have horns and tails; if they did they would be easier to identify. Many of them can be quite pleasant, but at heart they are tough, cold-blooded, ruthless authoritarians. They are limited in their ability to see the world from any point of view other than their own, and they are narrow in their outlook. George W. Bush and Dick Cheney are prototypical conservative leaders without conscience. The excessive secrecy of the Bush administration, in particular, was apparent even before the 9/11 terrorist attacks, but because the mainstream media ignored this issue, I wrote about it myself in *Worse Than Watergate: The Secret Presidency of George W. Bush*. Unlike the consequences of Nixon's secrecy, those of Bush and Cheney have been lethal. Realizing that only a partisan would remain silent, I wanted to make people aware of what was happening, for I recognized that this was a dangerous presidency. In *Worse Than Watergate* I did not analyze Bush and Cheney's behavior, because I was not sure then what was driving them. However, after studying the matter, I believe that one can reasonably conclude that how they think, their policies, and their style of governing are based to an alarming extent on their own authoritarian personalities, which tolerate no dissent, use dissembling as their standard modus operandi, and have pushed their governing authority beyond the law and the Constitution.

"In his landmark book, *Privacy and Freedom,* Alan Westin . . . defines democracy and authoritarianism in terms of information policy," wrote Robert G. Vaughn, a professor at American University's Washington College of Law. Summarizing Westin's work, Professor Vaughn continued, "Authoritarian governments are identified by ready government access to information about the activities of citizens and by extensive limitations on the ability of citizens to obtain information about the government. In contrast, democratic governments are marked by significant restrictions on the ability of government to acquire information about its citizens and by ready access by citizens to information about the activities of government."[12] I did not use that quote when writing about Bush and Cheney's insistence on secrecy because I did not then really understand the true nature of authoritarianism, yet I was struck time and again by the authoritarian nature of the Bush/Cheney administration. Now I realize that Bush and Cheney have given authoritarianism a new legitimacy in Washington, and it is taking us where we should not want to go.

Conservatism is not inherently moralistic, negative, arrogant, condescending, and self-righteous. Nor is it authoritarian. Yet all of these are adjectives that best describe the political outlook of contemporary conservatism. I make these observations not as an outsider, but as a conservative who is deeply troubled by what has become of a treasured philosophy. Conservatism has been co-opted by authoritarians, a most dangerous type of political animal.

How do people—particularly those who have never put their life on the line for their country—engage in, or condone, attacks on Senator John McCain's life-defining experiences as a Vietnam POW or question Senator Max Cleland's courage in building a new life after his loss of three limbs in Vietnam? What causes them to dispute Senator John Kerry's valor during voluntary combat duty in Vietnam or to contest Representative Jack Murtha's war record in Vietnam? Do they believe that by belittling the competence of White House counsel Harriet Miers, by forcing her to withdraw as a nominee for the Supreme Court, they are engaged in legitimate political debate? Why do they remain silent, or even defend, a president who has shamed the nation forever by endorsing an unprecedented and unnecessary use of torture against our enemies? These questions have clear answers. My aim is to explain how and why these conservatives operate as they do, with the thought that others may realize that this current breed of authoritarian conservatism, the behavior of both authoritarian leaders and their credulous followers, constitute a hazardous way for politics and governing. In fact, these people cannot be trusted to exercise the powers of government responsibly.

I have not written this book with the slightest expectations of ending the vile attacks of these authoritarian conservatives or of changing their Machiavellian attitudes. They cannot be stopped because their behavior is simply a function of the way they are and how they think, their dispositions, and the way they deal with the world. However, they can be understood, exposed, and watched, and there is compelling reason to do so. While their attacks on me and my wife may be considered harmless in the scheme of things, their larger undertaking is of great concern.

Certainly, not all conservatives are the same, and not all of them are authoritarians or without conscience. In addition, many of them do not actually know very much about the belief system to which they supposedly subscribe. While some conservatives will take visceral offense at this book, for I have recast the dominant contemporary conservatism in its true light as "authoritarian conservatism," my hope is that for others—particularly this movement's "followers," a category into which most conservatives fall—it will encourage reflection. As I see it, there are three kinds of conservatives: the good, the bad, and the evil. And this book is about the bad and evil ones. Many of my friends are conservatives, and they will remain my friends after reading this book, and some may even thank me for writing it. Moderates, progressives, and liberals may appreciate that someone with inside knowledge of conservatism has finally explained what the hell has happened to these people.

For those interested in learning more about the disposition, beliefs, and actions of those who presently dominate American politics, some understanding of conservatism is required. Providing this information is easier said than done, as contemporary conservatism is a jungle of twisted thoughts and strange growths. From earlier travels I know the terrain, but I know only a few of the people now occupying it. Now that I have explained how they got my attention, it is necessary to clarify what conservatism is and what it is not, which I believe will show why it has been so easily manipulated and corrupted by authoritarians.

In Chapter 1, I explain how conservatives think, and highlight the structural weaknesses that have allowed it to be pulled from its roots by authoritarian conservatives. Chapter 2 explores authoritarians, many of whom are conservatives without conscience. This material is derived from almost half a century of scientific study, which has been inexplicably ignored outside of academia and so has not been readily available to the general reader. In Chapter 3, I illustrate how authoritarians operate in their own images, when I examine neoconservatives and Christian conservatives, who currently dominate Republican politics and policy. And in Chapter 4, I conclude with examples of the ugly politics and evil policies resulting from current authoritarian rule, the work of people who are conservatives without conscience and who are taking America in an undemocratic direction. Finally, I have placed some additional information and analysis in appendices.

CONSERVATIVES
WITHOUT
CONSCIENCE

CHAPTER ONE

HOW CONSERVATIVES THINK

To understand contemporary conservative thinking it is essential to understand authoritarian thinking and behavior in the context of traditional political conservatism, for authoritarianism has become the dominant reality of conservative thought. During its Paleolithic period, as those early days of the modern movement are now known, conservatism was easy to grasp. I recall those days well, because I signed on back then, before every schism became a new -ism, and long before authoritarians had taken control of conservatism. In the past four decades, with varying degrees of proximity, I have watched with dismay as conservatism has fallen into its present state of cluttered ideas and beliefs. It has become a potpourri of political philosophies that embrace any number of often incompatible thoughts on the right side of the political spectrum. Today's conservatism is both complex and confusing.

National Review writer Ramesh Ponnuru, who is well versed in all matters conservative, said that many people believe that there are just "two, or at most three, kinds of conservatives." Needless to say, there are many more. Accordingly, Ponnuru advises that before talking about conservatives one should know whom one is discussing.[1] It is good advice that can best be followed by addressing the key realities of modern conservatism. By examining them it becomes apparent how easily authoritarians have so effectively reshaped conservatism to their own liking.

Conservatism Cannot Be Meaningfully Defined

National polls today reveal that more people identify themselves as "conservative" than they do any other political outlook. Pollsters do not ask respondents to spell out what they mean, only whether they think of themselves as "conservative" or "liberal" or some other political position. Overwhelmingly, Republicans identify themselves as conservatives, although most cannot come up with a meaningful definition of the term. For almost a decade I have asked countless people to explain their understanding of conservatism, but my admittedly unscientific survey utterly failed to produce a good definition, which is not surprising, because there is none. Even leading conservative intellectuals acknowledge that trying to define conservatism is a futile and not particularly useful exercise.

Conservative scholar Russell Kirk wrote, "Any informed conservative is reluctant to condense profound and intricate intellectual systems to a few pretentious phrases; he prefers to leave that technique to the enthusiasm of radicals." He added, "[C]onservatism is not a fixed and immutable body of dogmata; conservatives inherit from Burke a talent for re-expressing their convictions to fit the time." Kirk offered as a working premise, however, that "the essence of social conservatism is preservation of the ancient moral traditions of humanity." He also liked to quote Abraham Lincoln's rhetorical question about conservatism: "Is it not adherence to the old and tried, against the new and untried?"[2] George Nash, another favorite scholar of conservatives, once asked, "What is conservatism?" He answered that "this is a perennial question; many are the writers who have searched for the elusive answer." Nash concluded, "I doubt that there is any single, satisfactory, all-encompassing definition of the complex phenomenon called conservatism, the content of which varies enormously with time and place. It may even be true that conservatism is inherently resistant to precise definition."[3]

William F. Buckley, Jr., founder of the *National Review* and a major force in modern American conservatism, is almost always articulate to a fault. Yet he, too, has difficulty defining conservatism. When asked to do so by Chris Matthews on NBC's *Hardball*, Buckley became tongue-tied. "The, the, it's very hard to define, define conservatism," Buckley stammered, before proceeding to offer his favorite but meaningless definition: "A famous professor, University of Chicago, was up against it when somebody said, 'How do you define it?' He didn't want to say, well, he said, he said, 'Conservatism is a paragon of essences toward which the phenomenology of the world is continuing approximation.'"* *National Review* editor Jonah Goldberg hinted that Buckley has made a career of looking for a definition of conservatism but has not really succeeded.[4]

In their recent book, *The Right Nation: Conservative Power in America*, John Micklethwait (U.S. editor of the *Economist*) and Adrian Wooldridge (Washington correspondent) sought to explain current Republican conservatism to Europeans, if not Americans altogether. They concluded that "conservatism has become one of those words that are now as imprecise as they are emotionally charged"—especially since conservatives insist "their deeply pragmatic creed cannot be ideologically pigeonholed."

In *Safire's New Political Dictionary* (1993), however, the former *New York Times* columnist and well-respected conservative William Safire defined a conservative as "a defender of the status quo who, when change becomes necessary in tested institutions or practices, prefers that it come slowly and in moderation." The *Oxford Companion to Philosophy* (1995) explained that the "conservative approach is empirical as opposed to rationalistic, cautiously skeptical rather than dogmatic, and, in certain circumstances, seeks to preserve the status

---

*E. J. Dionne, Jr., pointed out in his book on American political history, *Why Americans Hate Politics* (1991), that Buckley wrote in *Did You Ever See a Dream Walking?* that Richard Weaver's definition of conservatives was "as noble and ingenious an effort as any I have ever read." Buckley was referring to Weaver's definition when responding to Chris Matthews.

quo rather than engage in wholesale revolution or overthrow existing institutions." This source added, "It is a matter of judgment how far so-called conservative political parties are conservative in the wider, philosophical sense."

Michael Deaver, former aide to President Ronald Reagan, asked a number of high-profile and active conservatives with varying degrees of allegiance to the former president about the source of their conservatism. Deaver published brief essays from fifty-four people in *Why I Am a Reagan Conservative* (2005).[5] Paradoxically, only a few actually claimed to be "Reagan conservatives," whom Deaver rather narrowly described as those favoring "limited government, individual liberty, and the prospect of a strong America." More strikingly, none of the contributors made an effort to meaningfully define or even describe conservatism, and only a few of them could say "why" they were conservatives, although several explained "how" they became so. Perhaps a conservative—or anyone else, for that matter—is intimately incapable of the introspection necessary to understand the psychological reasons for his own beliefs and why he is a conservative. That may also explain the fact that many conservatives have easily rejected the findings of social scientists who have recently reported many of the reasons why people become, or remain, conservatives. (A subject addressed shortly in this chapter.)

Conservatives Have No Ideology, According to Their Leading Thinkers

Leading conservative scholars reject the notion that their thinking or beliefs can be described as an ideology. For conservative scholar Frank Meyer, for example, it is heterodoxy to conclude that the "American conservative movement" is anything but just that, "a movement." Meyer insisted conservatism is "inspired by no ideological construct."[6] Similarly, conservative intellectual icon Russell Kirk has adopted the mind-set of John Adams, the first "conservative" president, in refusing to classify conservatism as an ideology. Adams claimed that the "proper definition" of ideology "is the science of Idiocy. And a very profound, abstruse, and mysterious science it is . . . taught in the school of folly."[7] Michael Oakeshott, another prominent conservative political philosopher, has remarked that "conservatism is not so much an ideology as it is a disposition to enjoy the fruits of the past and to distrust novelty." Ronald Reagan, throughout his political career, sought "to downplay ideology and translate the tough theory of conservatism— its libertarian harangues and traditionalist asceticism—into accessible anecdotes and sunny sloganeering."[8] William Safire quoted Reagan as saying, "I think 'ideology' is a scare word to most Americans." Republican senator Rick Santorum of Pennsylvania claimed: "Conservatism is common sense and liberalism is an ideology."[9]

In fact, conservatism now fits the definition of ideology quite aptly, according to the *HarperCollins Dictionary of American Government and Politics.** But regardless of how any of these terms is defined, asserting that conservatism is not an ideology is, of course, sophistry. Meyer's belief that conservatism is a "movement" by no means precludes

---

*Jay M. Shafritz (ed.), *The HarperCollins Dictionary of American Government and Politics* (1993) defines "ideology" as

(1) A comprehensive system of political beliefs about the nature of people and society; an organized collection of ideas about the best way to live and about the most appropriate institutional arrangements for society. . . . But the term has evolved to mean the philosophical bent of true believers of whatever belief. The mainstreams of American politics have never been rigidly ideological; only the extremes of both major parties—on the far Right and far Left—are much concerned with correct rules of thought for the party's most faithful. . . . But ideology seems to be making a comeback with the new Right. (2) Whatever one believes about the political process, whether it is articulated or not. (3) An interrelated set of ideas or a world view that explains complex social phenomena in a relatively simple way. (4) The selected and often distorted notions about how society operates. A group may adhere to such notions as a means of retaining group solidarity and of interpreting a world from which they have become alienated.

it from being an ideology; Kirk's reference to Adams's claim that ideology is idiocy has no substance; Oakeshott has inadvertently defined conservatism as an ideology rather than distinguishing the two concepts; Reagan's claim that the word "ideology" scared people indicates only his aversion to the term, not the notion that conservatism is not an ideology.

As is typical of conservatives' inconsistency, however, countless conservatives do refer to their set of beliefs as an ideology. In fact, numerous leading conservative publications, including the *National Review, Human Events, The America Spectator, The Weekly Standard,* and *The American Conservative,* have all called conservatism an ideology.[10]

No Classic Conservatism, Or Movement Moses

A classic is something accepted as definitive, never out of fashion (like a blue suit or a black dress), and whose excellence is generally agreed upon. Within that framework, there is no conservatism that can be considered classic. Conservatives can trace their history, but they don't always agree upon it when doing so. There have, from time to time, been periods when there was widespread agreement among conservatives, only to have this fleeting harmony later fall apart. There is no genuine founding father of American conservatism, although Edmund Burke, the British Member of Parliament, who set forth his conservative views in *Reflections on the Revolution in France* (in 1790), comes close. Burke's influence on American thinkers is indisputable (he favored the American Revolution but opposed the French Revolution), but his defense of monarchy and aristocracy never played well with American conservatives. Thus, Burke's conservatism is not, for Americans, classical.

Conservatism is a movement with no Moses, although William F. Buckley is sometimes considered to be an analogous figure, as John B. Judis's biography of him, subtitled *Patron Saint of the Conservatives,* would attest. Buckley's support of conservatism's latter-day saints, like

Richard Weaver, Frank Meyer, Friederich Hayek, Russell Kirk, and James Burnham, through his *National Review,* have certainly invigorated modern conservatism. Kirk and Burnham have always been the most significant among these formative voices, although by 1986, when Russell Kirk prepared his last edition of *The Conservative Mind,* young conservatives were already coming to consider his work as "Old Testament" conservatism, and his once well-known canons of conservatism now reside in the dustbin of history.* In retrospect the only things that tie all these early thinkers together are a dark view of human nature, their strong dislike of President Franklin Roosevelt's New Deal, and an outsized fear of communism. This is about as close to "classic" conservatism as it gets.

While Russell Kirk focused on theory and philosophy, James Burnham addressed practice and process. An exemplary scholar who taught philosophy at New York University, Burnham cofounded the *National Review* in 1955. His *Congress and the American Tradition,* which describes FDR's presidency overpowering Congress, has been called by a leading scholar of conservative intellectual history "one of the most penetrating works of political analysis produced by conservatives since World War II."[11] Burnham understood the ebb and flow of power between the legislative and executive branches, and he appreciated the expansion of the presidency under strong presidents such as Abraham Lincoln, Andrew Jackson, and Woodrow Wilson. He believed that FDR, however, overreached, by taking away every last vestige of Congress's power as a peer to the president and reducing the legislative branch to "a mere junior partner."[12]

Conservative columnist George Will wrote in 2005 that the "president's authorization of domestic surveillance by the National Security Agency [that] contravened a statute's clear language" was a striking

---

*Kirk's canons are concisely explained on the Web site of the Russell Kirk Center for Cultural Renewal, which is devoted to his thought. See http://www. kirkcenter.org/kirk/thought.html.

indication that conservatives had forgotten their roots. "For more than 500 years," Will noted, "since the rise of nation-states and parliaments, a preoccupation of Western political thought has been the problem of defining and confining executive power." Will, thinking like the conservative he is, invoked history as a reminder to other conservatives willing to listen. "Modern American conservatism grew in reaction against the New Deal's creation of the regulatory state and the enlargement of the executive branch power that such a state entails. The intellectual vigor of conservatism was quickened by reaction against the Great Society and the aggrandizement of the modern presidency by Lyndon Johnson, whose aspiration was to complete the project begun by Franklin Roosevelt." Will closed by drawing on the wisdom of the distant past. "Charles de Gaulle, a profound conservative, said of another such, Otto von Bismarck—de Gaulle was thinking of Bismarck not pressing his advantage in 1870 in the Franco-Prussian War—that genius sometimes consists of knowing when to stop. In peace and in war, but especially in the latter, presidents have pressed their institutional advantages to expand their powers to act without Congress. This president might look for occasions to stop pressing."[13]

In 1995, when the newly Republican-controlled Congress launched an assault on Bill Clinton, Will observed, contrary to the liberal shibboleth that government never contracts, "Well, it is contracting. It is contracting—and here we should honor the memory of James Burnham—because of congressional ascendancy. A traditional tenet of that fine man's conservatism has been re-established, to the point at which the current President is the least consequential President in Washington since Calvin Coolidge."[14]

To make his point, Burnham quoted the French historian and scholar, Amaury de Riencourt, who wrote in 1957 that "the President of the United States [was] not merely the Chief Executive of one of the Western democracies, but one already endowed with powers of truly Caesarian magnitude," and he feared that the American presidency could result in the destruction of freedom given its "concentration of supreme power in the hands of one man."[15] Caesarism, of course, is despotism, and Burnham urged conservatives to resist anything that enabled the rise of a potential Caesar, "that is to say, Napoleon, Mussolini, Stalin, Hitler, Peron, Franco, Khrushchev."

Unlike many of his successors, Burnham did believe that conservatism could be described and defined, and in 1959 he did so, which provides a record of how conservatism was perceived by a well-positioned insider in its early days. "We can define conservatism and liberalism by reference to certain philosophical principles," Burnham wrote, as he endeavored to bridge intellectual conservatism with real-world politics.[16] To define conservatism in its political context, Burnham drew a point-by-point comparison of conservative and liberal positions on specific issues that he believed distinguish each. With the caveat that "brevity brings a certain amount of distortion," he reduced his findings to thirteen statements, which he explained "hang together: that is, to occur as a group, not merely at random. Whether the cause of this linkage—which is not absolute, of course—is metaphysical, social or psychological we do not need to decide in order to observe that it exists."[17] Yet like Kirk's canons, Burnham's descriptions of the conservative approach today has little practical application.*

*Burnham found that conservatives believe: 1) there is a transcendent factor vital to successful government; 2) human nature is corrupt, and therefore conservatives reject all utopian solutions to social problems; 3) tradition must be respected, and when change is unavoidable it must be undertaken cautiously; 4) governmental power must be diffused and limited by adhering to the "separation of powers" and "checks and balances" of the Constitution; 5) direct democracy must be rejected because people are not well informed and are easily misled; 6) in states' rights; 7) each branch of government must be autonomous and must resist encroachment or usurpation by any other; 8) public support of limited government must be encouraged in order to keep government in check; 9) the Constitution's principles have permanent value; 10) government must be decentralized and localized so that power is diffused; 11) private enterprise should be encouraged; 12) morality begins with the individual; and 13) Congress should be more powerful than the executive branch. An expanded summary version of these statements are found at Appendix A.

The conservatism of Burnham and of an entire generation of conservative intellectuals has virtually disappeared as a functional political force, because it proved unable to stand up to the waves of demagogues, bigots, fanatics, malcontents, and assorted populists who have claimed the label for their own extremist aims. Leaders such as George Wallace, Strom Thurmond, Jesse Helms, and Pat Robertson—along with many more pedestrian politicians, political operatives, and social activists in pursuit of whatever narrow agendas—have easily overwhelmed and pushed aside the principles of conservative's founders.[18] Had conservatism been entrenched enough to prevent expediency from overtaking critical thinking, it might not have been so easily uprooted. But conservatism was built on an unstable ground, and was not sufficiently fortified to weather such political storms.

A Brief History of Modern Conservatism: Shallow and Twisted Roots

Numerous recent studies have traced the evolution of the conservative movement.[19] As these works show (but certainly do not concede), conservatism has too often been perverted by small minds, which has enabled any number of extremist forces to subvert its authentic principles. Unlike classic liberalism, which evolved slowly over centuries, modern conservatism was cobbled together, if not contrived, by a relatively small group of intellectuals during a brief period in the late 1940s and early 1950s. Modern conservatism was soon brought into elective politics in the 1950s; its followers then joined forces with Southern politicians in the 1960s, and began flirting with evangelical Christians in the 1970s. Conservatism's many factions were consolidated under Ronald Reagan's Republican Party in the 1980s. Less than satisfied with their lot under Reagan, however, evangelical Christians increased their religiously motivated political zealotry in the late 1980s, throughout the 1990s, and into the new century.

While modern conservatism is a post–World War II political phenomenon, its earliest adherents, sometimes labeled the "old right,"
date back to those Republicans who refused to follow former president Theodore Roosevelt and his progressive Bull Moose Party during
the 1912 presidential election campaign. This group nonetheless
chose to remain within the Republican Party ranks and support the reelection of President William Howard Taft. This, of course, resulted in
the ascendance of Woodrow Wilson, who was even more progressive
than TR, but in those days, conservative purity was paramount. Between the world wars, conservative Republicans played an obstruc-
tionist role, blocking Wilson's League of Nations, opposing American
intervention in foreign affairs, resisting non-European immigration,
and pushing laissez-faire economic policies. Republican Party historian Lewis L. Gold notes that when "discussing the failures of the United
States to intervene in World War I, or the difficulties of the League of
Nations in the 1920s, Republicans rarely point out how much their
[own] party did to sustain these now discredited policies."[20]

Early conservatives were groping for something more than a philosophy of opposing anything that departed from the status quo and
giving corporations the freedom they sought from government. They
were searching for ideas and found common cause in their opposition
to the New Deal. No factor did more to stimulate the growth of modern conservatism than the election of Franklin Roosevelt (with the
possible exception of the spread of communism). He is the man conservatives most dislike, for he embodies the big-government ideology
they most fear. Opposition to FDR's policies and programs resulted in
people like H. L. Mencken and former Republican president Herbert
Hoover's joining the conservative cause, adding stature to the nascent
movement.[21] In time, conservatives found political leadership in President Taft's son, Robert Taft, of Ohio, who became majority leader of
the Senate in 1953, but seven months later died of cancer.

Lionel Trilling, a leading voice of the left, observed in 1950 that in "the United States at this time, liberalism is not only the dominant but the sole intellectual tradition. . . . [T]here are no conservative or reactionary ideas in general circulation."[22] Trilling, for a while, was correct. Intellectual efforts, rather than political leadership, however, ultimately proved more significant for the initial growth of conservatism. The work of conservative scholars, which had commenced in the late forties, although inconsequential at first, did serve to create a foundation for modern conservatism, and a philosophy was developed from scratch. At first they looked to European thinking and tradition, but this seemed un-American to many of them, and they, accordingly, began developing an authentically American conservative heritage. This was not easy, given the liberal tradition of this country, and in fact, nothing in America's founding, or the creation of the United States, was of a conservative nature.

George H. Nash, himself a conservative, is the leading authority on this intellectual development, and his work *The Conservative Intellectual Movement in America* is considered a classic.[23] Nash's study, however, reveals the dubious analysis employed by early conservatives in constructing their philosophy. Nash reports that the post–World War II resurgence of conservatism resulted in three independent schools of thought, all of which developed concurrently. First, Nash explains, "classic liberalism" morphed into "libertarianism," which held that the expanding powers of the state threatened "liberty, private enterprise, and individualism." Second, "traditional conservatism" developed in reaction to the secularism among the totalitarian states during the aftermath of World War II. This brand of conservatism called for "a return to traditional religious and ethical absolutes," and rejected "relativism" as something corroding Western values. Third, Nash reports, there emerged a school of "militant, evangelistic anti-communism."[24]

The conspicuous weakness in Nash's work is his failure to report any of the inevitable conflicts among these three early schools of thought. Nash also does not establish any real connection between them other than anticommunism, which they all embraced (as did most progressives and liberals). Thus, he provides little historical insight into early fissures within conservatism, although these would develop into the factions which have yet to resolve their differences.

Early conservative scholars sought to establish the conservative tradition in America, often doing so by turning history upside down. They began with the Declaration of Independence, which involved an attempt to co-opt such profoundly liberal concepts of inalienable rights and equality. The Declaration, which formalized the end of colonial American allegiance to the monarchy of George III, has long been considered a classic statement of liberal political theory.[25] Echoing the words of the liberal philosophers like Jean-Jacques Rousseau and John Locke, Jefferson proclaimed as self-evident truths that "all men are created equal" and "are endowed by their Creator with certain unalienable rights," including "Life, Liberty and the pursuit of Happiness." These are concepts that are hardly articles of faith in conservative thought.

Nash admits that the Declaration was "troublesome" for the early conservatives, and reports that one scholar suggested conservatives should claim that, in fact, the Declaration's egalitarian ethos had not been carried over to the Constitution; rather, that the Declaration was just that, a declaration and not a governing document.[26] Nash explains that it was ultimately decided "to stress the compatibility" of both the Declaration and the Constitution with conservative views, although that compatibility was created by brazenly reinterpreting the founding events and documents.[27] Accordingly, for conservatives the clause "all men are created equal" would be construed to apply merely to equality under the law and not to "some misty 'pursuit of happiness' [as] the true foundation of our polity" and certainly not to the brand of egalitarianism favored by liberals. Most conservatives, in fact, oppose equality, and there is ultimately no clearer underlying distinction between conservatives and liberals than their views on this issue.* Nash concludes that in "a variety of ways, then, conservatives sought to drain the Declaration of its explosive [liberal] rhetorical potential."

Removing equality from the American tradition, however, created early divisions within conservative ranks, because deliberate tampering with history simply was not acceptable to everyone. In 1965, for example, conservative political scientist Harry Jaffa, a highly respected Lincoln scholar, concluded that no principle was more fundamental than the Declaration's assertion that "all men are created equal." This did not apply merely to equality under law, but to *political* equality. According to Nash, the gist of Jaffa's position was that "no man is by nature the ruler of another, that government derives its just powers from consent of the governed—that is from the opinion of the governed." Thus, majority rule could not be separated from *"the principle of the natural equality of political right of all men"* (italics in original).[28] Jaffa had no doubt, unlike some conservative scholars, that the "Founding Fathers adhered to the principles of the Declaration of Independence" when writing the Constitution.[29]

Another example of a conservative attempt to rewrite history is in the interpretation of the American Revolution. Because revolution is the antithesis of conservatism, Nash explained, conservatives relied "on the work of such conservative scholars as Daniel Boorstin," later head of the Library of Congress, who argued in *The Genius of American Politics* (1953) that the American Revolution was, unlike the French

*Princeton sociologist Douglas S. Massey, speaking for liberals, explains that what "distinguishes liberals from others is the belief that the rights and privileges outlined in the Declaration of Independence and enumerated in the U.S. Constitution are guaranteed to all people regardless of their characteristics, inborn or acquired. Thus, equality of opportunity should be offered to all persons resident in the United States, whether male or female, black or white, gay or straight, rich or poor, owner or worker; and liberals believe that equality of opportunity should exist not only in theory but in reality." Douglas S. Massey, *Return of the "L" Word: A Liberal Vision for the New Century* (Princeton, NJ: Princeton University Press, 2005), 12.

Revolution, not a cataclysmic upheaval, but rather a "limited war for independence" fought by colonialists to obtain the traditional rights of their forefathers. Others have pushed the argument even further, insisting that the American Revolution was merely an effort to place a check on Parliament and the out-of-control king of England. These conservatives "tended to stress that the American Revolution was a moderate and prudent affair—hardly a revolution at all," Nash reports.[30] Of course, a distinctly different reality is portrayed by almost all legitimate historical accounts of the American Revolution (whether written by conservatives or liberals), from David McCullough's highly praised *1776* (2005) to Merrill Jensen's *The American Revolution within America* (1974) and Bernard Bailyn's *The Ideological Origins of the American Revolution* (1967). The war for independence was America's longest war (lasting eight years) and its deadliest until the Civil War. Especially given its outcome, to call it a "moderate" or "limited" war borders on the absurd.[31] For example, McCullough wrote in *1776,* "The war was a longer, far more arduous, and more painful struggle than later generations would understand or sufficiently appreciate."[32]

In their efforts to present conservatism as an American tradition, conservatives have also reinterpreted the U.S. Constitution. One of the key elements of the Constitution is the establishment of a unique republic, in that a federal system would coexist with state and local governments. Before it was ratified many opponents attacked its progressive and innovative nature, for far from representing the status quo, the Constitution was dramatically liberal. James Madison defended it in *The Federalist Papers* by explaining that the founders "have not suffered a blind veneration for antiquity, for custom" but rather employed "numerous innovations . . . in favor of private rights and public happiness." Madison said that "precedent could not be discovered," for there was no other government "on the face of the globe" that provided a model.[33] Madison, the father of the Constitution, clearly saw his work as the opposite of conservatism. Far from venerating the principles of the past, or feeling bound by custom, our nation's founders relied on reason, which is anathema for many of today's conservatives.

By laying claim to the Constitution as part of their own antiliberal tradition, conservatives have, even Nash seems to believe, gone too far. "In sharp contrast with many (including some of the Founding Fathers) who believed that the Constitution was intended to set up a stronger national government than the one under the Articles of Confederation," Nash wrote with a tone of apology, "many conservatives stressed the powers of individuals and states under the federal system." Even more inexcusable is that some conservative thinkers "seemed to infuse an almost anti-Federalist understanding of the Constitution" into its interpretation.[34] Anti-Federalists, of course, opposed its ratification, so to take that line of thought its full distance would have us still operating as European colonies. Absurd? Apparently not, as one influential Southern conservative historian, Clyde Wilson, has argued that the anti-Federalists were the only true American conservatives.[35] Fortunately, such thinking did not carry the day, but it has been prevalent from the outset of the conservative movement.

Had conservative scholars of the 1950s conceded the nation's liberal legacy, and stated at the time that they were formulating a conservative philosophy based on a century and a half of history since the nation's founding, a legitimate conservative foundation could have been built on the American tradition. Nash isolated the key question facing the early conservatives: "How could a nation conceived in violence and dedicated to universal rights ever be called 'conservative'?" Political scientist Clinton Rossiter, considered one of the first neoconservatives, answered this question head-on, and unlike his peers, honestly, in his early study *Conservatism in America*, stating correctly that America's political roots were "progressive" and the United States was conceived out of "a Liberal tradition."[36]

Goldwater Conservatism Is Dead, R.I.P.

Barry Goldwater defined conservatism for my generation and several others. Incongruously, many former Goldwater conservatives have been instrumental in reshaping conservatism, but in doing so they have abandoned the senator's own philosophy and the sense of conscience that anchored his thinking. The senator explained that much of his own conservative thinking had come from his mother's "wonderful common sense" as well as his experiences as an Arizona businessman during the period that he and his brother ran their chain of successful department stores. Before Goldwater ran for Congress, Senator Everett Dirksen (R-IL) sent him speeches and background papers of his own, and had the Library of Congress gather a number of speeches by Senator Robert Taft (R-OH) for the candidate to study. Although he had never been much of a student as a young man, the senator became one, and spent the first ten years of his Senate career fascinated by books and reading, not to mention studying the workings of government. Herbert Hoover, who in 1932 was the first president for whom Goldwater had voted, became the senator's friend and mentor after he arrived in Washington, and he collected all of Hoover's published works to study them.

Senator Goldwater wrote a thrice-weekly column on conservatism for the *Los Angles Times* for almost four years.[37] He was frequently asked to define conservatism and did so over the course of several of those columns. *The Conscience of a Conservative* (1960) attempted to refine that definition, but it was over the next decade that he distilled it into its final form. In *The Conscience of a Majority* (1970) he defined conservatism as the belief that "the solutions to the problems of today can be found in the proven values of the past."[38] (He elaborated later, saying that "in its simplest terms, conservatism is economic, social, and political practices based on the successes of the past.")[39] As for the *conscience* of the conservative, he wrote that it was "pricked by anyone who would debase the dignity of the individual human being."[40]

When I asked him years later what now "pricked" the conservative conscience, he said that he should have written that the conservative conscience is "pricked by anyone or *any action*" that debases human dignity. "Doesn't poverty debase human dignity?" I asked. "Of course it does," he replied, and went on to say that if family, friends, and private charity cannot handle the job, the government must.* When I pressed him on conservatives being opposed to equality, he chuckled. "Those are the intellectual conservatives', who couldn't get themselves elected dog-catcher."[41] (Sadly, this once may have been true, but it is certainly not the case today.)

"Politics is the art of achieving the maximum amount of freedom for individuals that is consistent with the maintenance of social order," Senator Goldwater wrote, and in balancing between these forces, he argued, "the conservative's first concern will always be: *Are we maximizing freedom?*"[42]

I have always thought of these fundamentals—draw on the proven wisdom of the past; do not debase the dignity of others; and maximize freedom consistent with necessary safety and order—as conservatism's "paragon of essences," and have considered them broad enough to address a wide range of issues, from fiscal responsibility to libertarianism (toward which the senator was strongly inclined) to acknowledging the threat of communism (and today, terrorism) without getting hysterical about it. Distinctly absent from Goldwater's conservatism was any thought of the government's imposing its own morality, or anyone else's, on society. In other words, the values of today's social, or cultural, conservatism had no place in the senator's philosophy.

Philip Gold, who campaigned for Goldwater in 1964, argued in

---

*Other examples of his belief in equality are evident in his efforts on behalf of women pilots from World War II, who flew transport missions just as men had, but had not been treated equally; he got them the same pension and benefits men had received, assuring them equal treatment. And he quietly pushed for racial integration of the Arizona National Guard before the armed services had done so.

his meditative *Take Back the Right: How the Neocons and the Religious Right Have Betrayed the Conservative Movement* that conservatives should have retained a covenant with the fathers of conservatism, for "continuity across generations [is] the essence of conservatism." What has breaking that covenant, as has clearly occurred with Goldwater, meant? It is a serious loss, believes Gold, for Goldwater "cared deeply about civilization. . . . He also was humane, one of his party's few who took issues such as civil rights, women's rights and the environment seriously."[43]

Conservatism Today: A Dysfunctional Family

No doubt the adamancy with which some conservatives insisted on their interpretations, or views, of history led to the movement's eventual splintering into several factions. Whatever the origin of their disagreements, however, they remain a divided family. Today the Republican Party strives to contain conservatism's constituent groups, some of whom get along and others who do not. It is not possible to identify precise divisions within conservatism, because many conservatives identify with more than one dogma. William Safire cleverly made this point when he conducted a personal "depth-poll" of his own brain to find out what held together at least "five Republican factions." Safire, it appears, sees himself as an "economic," "social," and "cultural" conservative with "libertarian" impulses and the idealistic instincts of a "neoconservative." "If these different strains of thought were held by discrete groups of single-minded people," acknowledges Safire, "we would have a Republican Party of five warring bands." He concedes that all these varying attitudes cause him "cognitive dissonance," which he experiences as "the jangling of competing inclinations, with the owner of the brain having to work out trade-offs, suppressions and compromises until he or she achieves a kind of puzzled tranquility within." Safire said his dissonance is "forced into harmony by the need to choose one leader who reflects the preponderance of" his views.[44]

In 1996 the *Washington Times*'s magazine *Insight* examined "Who's Who in America's Conservative Revolution," an article that highlighted the remarkable degree of sectarianism in the right wing, a fact well known to most conservatives. *Insight* noted that there were thirteen print journals geared toward the various factions of conservative readers.[45] These journals represented "distinct, though overlapping, philosophies," which the magazine, a well-known conservative publication itself, divided into ten different species of conservatives. Here, in highly compressed, occasionally paraphrased, and updated form, is a glimpse of the modern conservative family tree:*

Austriocons: The paleoconservatives (paleocons), so called because they were conservatives back when most of the neoconservatives (neocons) were still Trotskyites, are split over the issue of free trade. Those paleos who are followers of the "Austrian" school of economics, i.e., the free-trade libertarians who honor Ludwig von Mises, were dubbed by *Insight* as "Austriocons."

Buchanocons: Paleos who have rebelled against free trade and the unaccountable global bureaucracies that they believe it is producing. Their political leader is Patrick Buchanan. Since 2002, they have had their own journal, *The American Conservative.*

Neocons: Intellectuals who drifted from the far left to the center to the right, carrying their flagship magazine, *Commentary,* with them. They are mostly Jewish, and mostly New York based. Neocons

---

*This breakdown does not include such factions as the so-called *South Park* conservative—a term credited to conservative blogger and pundit Andrew Sullivan. Marty Beckerman writes in *Playboy* (December 2005) that in addition to "low taxes and high times," the *South Park* conservatives "oppose the drug war, obscenity laws, abstinence education and marriage protection acts, but support" President Bush and the Republican party "with religious fervor." Jonah Goldberg of the *National Review* reportedly finds *South Park* conservatism a poisonous trend that kids will grow out of when they become parents. Goldberg is correct, I suspect, that *South Park* conservatism will be short-lived.

tend to be militant internationalists. They publish their own inside-the-Beltway weekly, *The Weekly Standard.*

Aquinacons: Neocons acquired a Christian wing when the Reverend Richard John Neuhaus founded his monthly magazine, *First Things,* patterned after *Commentary.* However, this is an increasingly distinct group, one that can be called "Aquinacons" because its members focus on the work of a rising generation of academic experts on the natural-law theories of Aristotle and Thomas Aquinas.

Radiocons: (Just kidding, says *Insight.*) This group includes talk-radio conservatives like Rush Limbaugh, Gordon Liddy, Mike Reagan, Blanquita Cullum, Dr. Laura Schlessinger, and other popularizers of the political and cultural right, if not their enormous middle America audiences.

Sociocons: Often lumped with the religious right, these social conservatives advance secular arguments for curbing abortion, divorce, illegitimacy, rights of homosexuals, and drugs. Its leading lights are the Family Research Council, the Institute for American Values, and columnist Cal Thomas.

Theocons: Conservatives who actually favor a more or less theocratic application of biblical law. Unlike Aquinacons, they reject natural law. In fact, this faction is far smaller than some in the news media believe, according to *Insight.*

Republicons: Young people who learned their conservative theory back in college and since have given themselves over to activism, either as Republican campaign strategists or as policy advocates. Newt Gingrich is their hero, and Grover Norquist (of the Americans for Tax Reform) is their leader. They have politically gold-plated résumés and no time for pessimism.

Catocons: Hard-core libertarians who recognize that even if your goal is to dismantle government, you have to play the Washington policy-wonk game to change things. Their leading think tank is the Cato Institute.

Platocons: Allied with, but different from, the Aquinacons, the Platocons are the disciples of the late Leo Strauss, who excited generations
of students at the University of Chicago about classical political
philosophy. Not all Straussians are conservatives, however. Still,
their belief that ideas are intrinsically important, and are not just
manifestations of class interest or historical prejudice, puts them
at odds with the academic left.[46]

There is almost no end to the ways in which the conservative factions can be sliced and diced.[47] Nonetheless, they all fall neatly within
three general categories, with their current significance determined by
poll numbers that indicate their relative size within the conservative
movement.[48] In February 2004 TechnoMetrica Institute of Policy and
Politics (TIPP) conducted a nationwide survey that gathered information across the left/right political spectrum. It found that conservatives constituted 43 percent of their respondents, with moderates at
35 percent and liberals at 18 percent. The TIPP poll sample revealed
a higher percentage of conservatives than has been the norm for other
polls. For example, the national election exit polls for eight elections
between 1976 and 2004 have fairly consistently shown conservatives
at 33 percent, moderates at 47 percent, and liberals at 20 percent.[49]
But the size of the conservative response to the TIPP poll provides an
excellent basis for the poll's follow-up question, which asked conservatives about the nature of their conservatism. In response, 52 percent of
conservatives described themselves as *social conservatives,* 49 percent as
fiscal conservatives, and 13 percent as *neoconservatives.* (The 114 percent total appears attributable to overlapping responses, for there is no
doubt that some social conservatives would also view themselves as
fiscal conservatives.)[50] Absent from this TIPP poll are breakdowns for
categories like traditional conservatives, religious conservatives, and
right-leaning libertarians, because these groups can easily fall within
social conservatism, fiscal conservatism, and neoconservatism.[51] Most
revealing in the TIPP poll is the strength of social conservatism.

Conservatism's Power of Negative Thinking

Given the rather distinct beliefs of the various conservative factions, which have only grown more complex with time, how have conservatives succeeded in coalescing as a political force? The simple answer is through the power of negative thinking, and specifically, the ability to find common enemies. The adherents of early conservatism—economic conservatives, traditional conservatives, and libertarians—agreed that communism was the enemy, a fact that united them for decades—and hid their differences. Today's conservatives—especially social conservatives, as opposed to intellectuals and the more thoughtful politicians—define themselves by what they oppose, which is anything and everything they perceive to be liberal. That category includes everyone from Democrats to anyone with whom they disagree, and can, therefore, automatically be labeled a liberal. Another group that has recently been designated as an enemy is "activist judges," regardless of their party or philosophical affiliation. Activist judges are best described as those whose rulings run contrary to the beliefs of a particular conservative faction.

Antipathy to liberalism has been present from the outset of the conservative movement but it only became a powerful unifying influence in the early 1980s. Sidney Blumenthal, when still a staff writer at the *Washington Post*, concluded that "conservatism requires liberalism for its meaning," for "without the enemy [of liberalism] to serve as nemesis and model, conservative politics would lack its organizing principle."[52] Blumenthal's observation, made two decades ago, is even more valid today. Leading conservative Web sites, including well-funded think tanks like the American Enterprise Institute, the Heritage Foundation, and the right-leaning libertarian Cato Institute, spend a lot of time and money criticizing or complaining with varying degrees of contempt about all matters perceived to be "liberal."[53] Important conservative opinion journals, like the *National Review* and *Human Events,* see the world as bipolar: conservative versus liberal.[54]

Right-wing talk radio could not survive without its endless bloviating about the horrors of liberalism. Trashing liberals is nothing short of a cottage industry for conservative authors. Take the "queen of mean," Ann Coulter, whose titles speak for themselves: *Slander: Liberal Lies about the American Right* (2002); *Treason: Liberal Treachery from the Cold War to the War on Terrorism* (2003); and *How to Talk to a Liberal (If You Must): The World According to Ann Coulter* (2004). *Slander*, for example, contains page after page of scorn, criticism, belittlement, and bemoaning of ideas she believes liberal. Her books have also generated a subsidiary cottage trade in fact-checking her work, which has amply demonstrated that Coulter apparently considers accuracy as something that needs only to be approximated.[55]

All the hyperventilating about liberalism by conservatives is surprising, because it is so unnecessary. Liberalism is a straw man conservatives love to attack, but there are not, in fact, enough liberals to be a true threat to conservatism. A recent Harris Poll found that only 18 percent of American adults call themselves liberals,[56] and the TIPP poll, cited earlier, found the figure to be 20 percent. Although then Speaker of the House Newt Gingrich unequivocally declared in 1998 that the "age of liberalism is over," condemnation of the liberal bogeyman continues to be a clarion call for most conservatives. In truth, conservatives attack liberals, or those they label or perceive as liberal, for several reasons. It is, of course, a handy means to rally the troops, for the conservative base enjoys it when their leaders and prominent voices attack those who do not share their views. It is also a means to raise money; fund-raising letters and drives regularly recount the horrors of liberalism. Many conservatives, however, are simply entertained by reading conservative authors or hearing conservative talk-show hosts rant about liberals. The exaggerated hostility also apparently satisfies a psychological need for antagonism toward the "out group," reinforces the self-esteem of the conservative base, and increases solidarity within the ranks.[57]

Law professor John Eastman described the contemporary conservative movement as "a bit of a three-legged stool."[58] Eastman wrote that conservatives find cohesion in their efforts to pack the federal judiciary with judges who will work at "recovering the original understanding of the Constitution—one that recognized the scope of federal power over matters truly national, such as national security, but that sought to revive the limits on federal authority in other areas of daily life, as the Constitution envisioned."[59] In short, the concerned effort to oppose so-called judicial activism is important to most all conservatives, and indeed, books, blogs, and essays on the subject have come from high-profile voices throughout the conservative factions.[60] Thus, when Bush nominated his White House counsel, Harriet Miers, for the Supreme Court, notwithstanding her stellar conservative credentials she was attacked relentlessly by other conservatives, who doubted she had the cerebral wherewithal to wage battle behind closed doors at the high Court on their behalf.[61] *National Review* writer John Derbyshire was a leader in the snarling pack chasing Miers, employing conservative rhetoric to do the job. After "reading her thoughts, messages and speeches," Derbyshire reported, "I mean, the sheer, dreary, numbing m—e—d—i—o—c—r—i—t—y of them." He concluded:

> This is a person who never had an original or interesting thought in her life. Reading Miers is like suffocating under a mountain of polystyrene packing blobbles. What on earth does it say about the President that, knowing, as he must have, how completely and irredeemably second-rate she is, he would put her name forward? The world, certainly in places like the Supreme Court, is a never-ending war of ideas. To ask which side of this war Ms. Miers would fight on is pointless. She doesn't know the war is underway; and if she knew, she'd probably think it could easily be brought to an end if we'd all just be nicer to each other.[62]

Notwithstanding a number of less than subtle signals from the White House that Ms. Miers, a born-again evangelical Christian, would indeed vote the way conservatives wished on issues like abortion, school prayer, sex education, and other social issues, she was eventually forced to withdraw her nomination.

A close study of conservatives reveals an interesting trait: These people do not see themselves as they actually are, but rather as something very different. In short, they seem to have little facility for self-analysis. Consider, for example, Derbyshire's mean-spirited remarks about Harriet Miers, and now listen to Derbyshire's take on himself, when he says he "started reading [the *National Review*] in the late 1970s, and it has always kept that agreeable, tolerant, gentlemanly tone, and as long as it keeps it, I shall be an *NR* reader (and, I hope, contributor). The tone comes, of course, from the personality of the founder, Bill Buckley, who is one of the most good-natured men I have ever met—a true American gentleman."[63] Could a man as intelligent as Derbyshire actually believe his comments about Ms. Miers were "gentlemanly"? Not surprisingly, the very conservatives who love to hurl invective against the ranks of their enemies prove to have the thinnest of skins when the same is done to them. Many of the examples are familiar: Ann Coulter, who can trash perceived liberals on national television but has been known to walk offstage when booed, or to start crying when she thinks she is being treated unfairly; Rush Limbaugh, who also makes his living saying unkind things about those with whom he disagrees, thought it unfair, as did his followers, when his addiction to OxyContin was reported, along with the dubious means he serviced his habit, despite his own attacks on others who use drugs. Similarly, Mr. Virtue, William Bennett, apparently found nothing ironic or contradictory in his preaching (and selling) virtue while being a compulsive gambler himself, and was angry when he was found out.

Conservatives Are Often Illogical,
Inconsistent, and Contradictory

Many conservatives, particularly those who are clearly authoritarians, are not aware of their illogical, contradictory, and hypocritical thinking. If made cognizant of it, they either rationalize it away, neglect to care, or attack those who reveal their human weaknesses. Because such thinking seems to be a reality of contemporary conservatism, anyone who operates from a logical mind, or has an inclination for reasoned judgment, can have trouble with it. Social conservatives are especially susceptible to irrational beliefs, as a few examples will show.

Evangelical Christian conservatives speak of their belief in a "culture of life," a concept drawn from the teaching of the Catholic Church that underlies the evangelicals' opposition to abortion. But for the Catholic Church, the culture of life also means opposition to the death penalty, which evangelical Christian conservatives fully support and strongly encourage. They are untroubled by the inconsistency of their beliefs, and when this is pointed out they explain it away. The unborn are innocent while those being executed are not, yet the culture of life believes it is God's wish to protect all life. As another example, social conservatives are deeply offended by atheists who want to remove the words "under God" from the Pledge of Allegiance, yet with great solemnity and earnestness they recite—as often as possible—that pledge and its words: "liberty and justice for all." For all but atheists, they mean. Ever since the U.S. Supreme Court prohibited prayer in public schools, Christian conservatives have been up in arms, with the most vocal being Christians who believe that the Bible is the inerrant word of God. Of course, those who truly know the Bible know that Jesus said, "And when you pray, do not be like the hypocrites, for they love to pray standing in the synagogues and on the street corners to be seen by men. I tell you the truth, they have received their reward in full. *But when you pray, go into your room, close the door and pray* to your Father, who is unseen. Then your Father, who sees *what is done in secret,* will reward you (Matthew 6:5–7; emphasis added). So illogical is much of the biblically driven political thinking of evangelical Christian conservatives, for whom faith appears to trump reason, that theologians like Episcopal bishop John Shelby Spong have written books with titles like *Rescuing the Bible from Fundamentalism* (1991).

Jonah Goldberg, writing for the *National Review,* has acknowledged the contradictions within modern conservatism. Rather than finding them a problem, though, he deems them a virtue. "The beauty of the conservative movement," he said, "is that we all understand and accept the permanence of contradiction" in thinking. One can envision George Orwell spinning in his grave in frustration at a remark like that, for it is pure "doublethink." Goldberg noted in passing that Jesus was not a conservative, which is certainly true, and is another fact ignored by the religious right. It does not take a particularly close reading of the New Testament, or the teachings of Jesus, to appreciate that the term "politically conservative Christian" has an oxymoronic quality. This is why conservatives have had to invent terms like "compassionate conservatism." But for those who believe that contradiction is a thing of beauty, the concept of compassionate conservatism will not tax credulity whatsoever.

Psychological Perspectives on Conservatism

Public criticism by conservatives greeted the work of New York University professor John T. Jost and his collaborators when they published a report entitled "Political Conservatism as Motivated Cognition."*[64] This study examines the psychology of political conservatism, basing

---

*Motivated cognition refers to thinking, or beliefs, that are based on factors other than pure reason or logic. As Dr. John Jost explained it: "Basically, the idea is that there are [normal] psychological reasons for why someone believes what he does, above and beyond the purely rational or informational reasons for believing

its findings on a mass of data: forty-four years of studies by social scientists investigating conservatism, using eighty-eight different techniques and involving over twenty-two thousand participants.[65] Because its results are founded on empirical information drawn from experiments and testing—and conservatism views itself as grounded in empirical thinking—the negative reaction seemed out of place. Indeed, conservative commentators devoted little serious attention to the study, rejecting its conclusions based on a press release.[66]

Jost and his collaborators developed their working definition of "conservative" by reviewing dictionaries and encyclopedias along with the literature of historians, journalists, political scientists, sociologists, and philosophers from the mid-1950s (which, according to most conservative scholars, generally marks the beginning of the modern conservative movement in the United States) through the end of the 1990s. The study placed apt parameters on its inquiry while focusing on those who would be considered conservative under most any characterization. Their survey of the usage of the term "conservative" over roughly a half century revealed "a stable definitional *core* and a set of more malleable, historically changing *peripheral* associations."[67] While its core meanings were considered to include "a resistance to change" and "an acceptance of inequality," its peripheral meanings were more complex, because not only did they change with time, but in some cases they overlapped the core meanings. For example, the study found the peripheral focus of "conservatism in the United States during the 1960s entailed support for the Vietnam War and opposition to civil rights, whereas conservatism in the 1990s had more to do with

---

something. People are motivated to believe that they are better than average drivers, that most of their opinions are correct, that their children are especially wonderful, etc. It wouldn't make too much sense to say that someone is "motivated" to believe that 2 + 2 = 4." (Interview with author. Unless otherwise stated, the comments about the study are based on my interpretations of it, not Dr. Jost's.)

being tough on crime and supporting traditional moral and religious values." In addition, the authors provide examples of people who became conservatives for reasons having nothing to do with the identified core meanings, yet who later accepted those aspects of conservatism "because of their association with likeminded others."[68]

The heart of Jost and his collaborators' findings was that people become or remain political conservatives because they have a "heightened psychological need to manage uncertainty and threat."[69] More specifically, the study established that the various psychological factors associated with political conservatives included (and here I am paraphrasing) fear, intolerance of ambiguity, need for certainty or structure in life, overreaction to threats, and a disposition to dominate others. This data was collected from conservatives willing to explain their beliefs and have their related psychological dynamics studied through various objective testing techniques. These characteristics, Dr. Jost said, typically cannot be ascribed to liberals.

Right-wing talk-radio hosts, conservative columnists, and conservative bloggers generally dismissed Jost's study, although apparently few could be bothered to read it. Jonah Goldberg of the *National Review* wrote a lengthy piece about it, but managed to focus on such irrelevancies as Alec Baldwin, Viagra, Napoleon, and what he calls "the left's medicalization of dissent." Goldberg described the study as "gassy, insubstantial, malodorous . . . cow flatulence."[70] Rush Limbaugh and Ann Coulter offered characteristic attacks, with Limbaugh mixing name calling with false and misleading information before dismissing it.[71]

After being hammered by conservatives for several months, Jost and his collaborators responded with a *Washington Post* op-ed piece, noting that their critics remained conspicuously less than familiar with the actual contents of their study. Notwithstanding commentary to the contrary, the Jost group pointed out that they had not, in fact, implied that conservatism was "abnormal, pathological or the result of mental illness." Nor had they claimed that conservatives themselves were insane, sick, or strange.[72] At the same time, they were not claiming their study was welcome news for conservatives.[73]

The difficulty of identifying in oneself such psychological factors as fear, intolerance of ambiguity, need for certainty or structure in life, overreaction to threats, and a disposition to dominate others does not mean that such dynamics can be summarily rejected. These characteristics are, in some cases, not only easily recognized by others but are discernible through psychological testing. A study published subsequent to Jost's confirmed the findings of his group. It is an unprecedented survey of nursery school children, commenced in 1969, that revealed the personalities of three- and four-year-olds to be indicative of their future political orientation.[74] In brief, this research suggests that little girls who are indecisive, inhibited, shy, neat, compliant, distressed by life's ambiguity, and fearful will likely become conservative women. Likewise, little boys who are unadventurous, uncomfortable with uncertainty, conformist, moralistic, and regularly telling others how to run their lives will then become conservatives as adults.[75]

Future Direction of Conservatism

Austin W. Bramwell, one of the best and brightest of the new generation of conservatives, laments the great quantity of information about conservatism that has little quality, as he explained in the magazine for traditional conservatives, *The American Conservative*. Bramwell says that "whereas 50 years ago the American Right boasted several political theorists destined to exert a lasting influence, today it has not one to its credit." He adds that "conservatism has reached an unacknowledged consensus about the outcome of the theoretical debates of the '50s and '60s. The consensus holds, first, that someone has discovered the Holy Grail that will vindicate conservatism once and for all, otherwise why be a conservative in the first place? Second, it holds that, whatever the Grail actually is, it does not do any good to describe it with too much specificity. These beliefs contradict each other, yet the conservative consensus has proved remarkably stable."[76] This is a highly accurate assessment of conservative thinking.

Who is Austin Bramwell? To begin with, he is Sarah Bramwell's husband.[77] Sarah is another well-credentialed young conservative, a former chairperson of the Conservative Party of the Yale Political Union, a former senior editor of a Yale University journal of conservative opinion, a former associate editor of the *National Review*, a former deputy press secretary to Colorado's Republican governor Bill Owens, and a featured speaker at the fortieth anniversary of the Philadelphia Society, which has been described by the *New York Times* as "a prestigious club for conservative intellectuals."[78] The Bramwells were married at the Episcopal Church of the Heavenly Rest in New York, so they do not appear to be conservative Catholics or evangelical Christians. Austin, at twenty-six, became the youngest member of the board of trustees of the *National Review*, taking his seat when founder Bill Buckley relinquished control of the journal in June 2004. Austin had written for *National Review* throughout his years as an undergraduate at Yale and at Harvard Law (2003), where he was an officer in the school's chapter of the Federalist Society. After clerking with Judge Timothy M. Tymkovich of the U.S. Court of Appeals for the Tenth Circuit (a Bush II appointee who sits on the bench in Denver), Austin joined the trusts and estates division of the prestigious New York City law firm Milbank, Tweed, Hadley & McCloy. The Bramwells' intelligence is conspicuous and their dedication to conservatism has been steadfast. The Bramwells are the future of American conservatism. Where do these young conservatives believe conservatism should be focusing its energy?

Sarah Bramwell shared her thoughts at the Philadelphia Society's national meeting. She began by noting that the early goals of modern conservatism were to "defeat Communism and roll back creeping socialism." Today neither remains relevant, she acknowledged. As for future foreign affairs, she explained that "articulating and defending some kind of international policy is *not* the major goal of conservatism in the next forty years." Domestically, conservatives can continue to "nibble away" at the administrative state (read: "creeping socialism"), but she accepts the fact that the administrative state is "here to stay." So what comes next? "Well, since the 1960s, the conservative movement took on a third goal, namely winning the culture wars," by which she means, "everything from preserving traditional morality, to passing on the Western inheritance, to preserving a distinctly American common culture, to resisting the threat posed by biotechnology to human nature itself." And what must conservatives do to win these wars? Sarah believes they must continue to "make the case against such things as gay marriage, stem-cell research, open borders, and our hideous suburban sprawl." Because her time was limited, she focused on the terrible job conservatives were doing on "*the* cultural battle of our age"—gay marriage.[79] Sarah left no doubt where she sees the battles, and her husband is of like mind.

During a 1999 forum at Yale on free speech and homosexuality, as the chairman of the Yale Political Union's Conservative Party chapter, Austin Bramwell claimed that "principled objections to homosexuality and to the gay movement can rarely be voiced on [the Yale] campus."[80] In 2004, Austin wrote in the *National Review* on why those who oppose gay rights should not use the argument "If homosexuality is okay, what's wrong with incest?" The better question is "If homosexuality is okay, what's wrong with self-mutilation?" Austin again took the cudgel against gay marriage in the January 2005 issue of the *American Conservative,* advising gay marriage opponents not to despair, for the people were on their side, and all they needed was the right strategy.* He explained that the strategy was simple, for no constitutional amendment was needed. A simple act of Congress, based on the Fourteenth Amendment, would do the job, based on his rather

---

*Most recent Gallup Poll figures show about 53 percent of Americans oppose gay marriage. See http://www.pollingreport.com/civil.htm/.

tortured reading of the U.S. Supreme Court ruling in *Loving v. Virginia,* which struck down antimiscegenation laws.[81] It is unsettling that a young conservative would today rely on the same approach employed by an uglier version of conservatism in a past era: white supremacy.[82]

Austin does not hold out much hope for new thinking. He recently wrote about how today's young conservatives "rarely come to right-wing ideas through any kind of epiphany. Rather they inherit their conservatism from parents or grandparents. Through generously funded seminars and think tank internships, they study the canon of conservative thought . . . almost all written in the 1940s, '50s and '60s."[83] (I would add that the earlier teachings are largely irrelevant in today's conservative politics.) Austin appears to be speaking for himself, his wife, his friends, and his own associates in explaining how they came to conservatism.

So What Exactly *Is* Conservatism?

Cut through all the smoke of conservatism and what is really left? David Horowitz—an intellectual who was once active with the radical left but had second thoughts and moved to the right—has described it as well as any amorphous thinking can be analyzed. Horowitz's shift in outlook appears to have given him unique insight, and he has offered a concise definition of conservatism vis-à-vis liberalism. In 1992, as part of a lecture series at the Heritage Foundation, Horowitz said that "conservatism [is] an attitude about the lessons of the actual past. By contrast, the attention of progressives [is] directed toward an imagined future. Conservatism [is] *an attitude* of caution based on a sense of human limits and what politics [can] accomplish" (emphasis added). In his response to the question being addressed by this Heritage Foundation conference—whether contemporary conservatism was truly conservative—Horowitz candidly answered, "No," acknowledging that today's conservatives are "rebels against the dominant liberal culture."[84]

In later updating his Heritage lecture, Horowitz wrote that conservatism "begins as an attitude, and only later becomes a stance," and noted "that conservative attitudes derive from pragmatic consideration."[85] This, clearly, is a highly conceptual view of conservatism, but an accurate one.

To further clarify the elusive nature of conservatism, and the elemental attitudes it encompasses, let us turn to political science professors Kenneth Janda of Northwestern University, Jeffrey M. Berry of Tufts University, and Jerry Goldman of Northwestern University, who discuss this political philosophy in their textbook, *The Challenge of Democracy: Government in America.* They provide a remarkably simple yet sophisticated chart that graphically shows the distinction between political conservatism and other ideologies (liberalism, libertarianism, and communitarianism) from both historical and contemporary vantage points, and the dynamics of these conflicting points of view.*

Their graphic (reproduced on page 37) requires a little explanation, since it addresses four ideologies. It depicts their conflicts along with their relationships to "freedom," "order," and "equality." Freedom in this context means liberty, as in the freedom of speech, religion, and association. Order refers to the use of the government's police powers to maintain or protect public health, safety, welfare, and morals. Equality, at minimum, envisions one-person one-vote political equality. But there is more to political equality than voting, for

---

*I do not believe I know any communitarians, but I am not unfamiliar with their outlook, which here is helpfully illustrated. Communitarianism is defined by Janda, Berry, and Goldman, who rely on the *Oxford English Dictionary,* as an ideology that envisions "a community formed to put into practice communistic or socialistic theories." While this philosophy is beyond the focus of my study, it should be noted that Janda, Berry, and Goldman use the term in its more restricted sense, as reflective of the movement founded in 1990 by sociologist Amitai Etzioni, and it nicely completes their chart for its juxtaposition with liberalism, libertarianism, and conservatism. For anyone seeking more information on communitarianism see Amitai Etzioni, *Rights and the Common Good: The Communitarian Perspective* (New York: St. Martin's Press, 1995).

those with wealth, public prominence, or political connections can in-fluence the political system to a much greater degree. If the system is to be fair, all citizens would have equal influence regardless of wealth, education, and status. Stated differently, modern liberals argue that there should also be social equality, including both equality of oppor-tunity and equality of outcome, thereby giving every person the same chance to succeed. The Janda-Berry-Goldman chart (following) is as good a visual representation as any of the conflicts and the fundamen-tal dynamics of conservatism vis-à-vis other political ideologies.*

Given the growing dominance of social conservatism and its trans-formative impact, along with the influence of neoconservatism on American foreign policy, "definitions of conservatives now have to be entirely rewritten," explained Lewis Gould, University of Texas emer-itus history professor and author of the most complete single-volume study of Republicans available.[86] I would phrase this a bit differently: Both social conservatives and neoconservatism have overwhelmed the conservative movement and the Republican Party, and to gauge their influence, and its consequences, it is essential to understand authori-tarian thinking and behavior. Social conservatism and neoconser-vatism have revived authoritarian conservatism, and not for the better of conservatism or American democracy. True conservatism is cau-tious and prudent. Authoritarianism is rash and radical. American democracy has benefited from true conservatism, but authoritarian-ism offers potentially serious trouble for any democracy.

*To fully understand the Freedom-Order-Equality dynamics, I urge you to visit the Web site that Ken Janda and Jerry Goldman have created. It provides a tutorial, and a self-test that will show you where you fall on their chart. See http://idealog.org. For comparison, you might also visit a libertarian site that also offers a self-test at http://www.self-gov.org/quiz.html.

Liberals	Communitarians
Favor: Government activities that promote equality, such as affirmative action programs to employ minorities and increased spending on public housing.	*Favor:* Government activities that promote equality, such as affirmative action programs to employ minorities and increased spending on public housing.
Oppose: Government actions that restrict individual liberties, such as banning sexually explicit movies or mandatory testing for AIDS.	*Favor:* Government actions that impose social order, such as banning sexually explicit movies or mandatory testing for AIDS.
Libertarians	**Conservatives**
Oppose: Government activities that interfere with the market, such as affirmative action programs to employ minorities and increased spending on public housing.	*Oppose:* Government activities that interfere with the market, such as affirmative action programs to employ minorities and increased spending on public housing.
Oppose: Government actions that restrict individual liberties, such as banning sexually explicit movies or mandatory testing for AIDS.	*Favor:* Government actions that impose social order, such as banning sexually explicit movies or mandatory testing for AIDS.

THE MODERN DILEMMA

Equality · Freedom

Freedom ◄——————————————► Order

THE ORIGINAL DILEMMA

CHAPTER TWO

CONSERVATIVES WITHOUT CONSCIENCE

ANSWERS TO QUESTIONS such as why so many conservatives are hostile and mean-spirited, why they embrace false history, and why they take on a cause like attempting to impeach President Clinton despite public opposition to the undertaking are not found in any traditional conservative philosophy—however that attitude might be defined or described. Nor does conservatism explain the truly radical policies and governing of the Bush and Cheney administration. It certainly does not explain conservatives' engaging in conspicuously unconscionable activities. I am not referring here to their practice of defaming perceived enemies, or to the corruption that has infected the K Street to Congress corridor. Rather, I have in mind more consequential activities, like taking America to war in Iraq on false pretenses, and the blatant law breaking by countless executive branch departments and agencies that, directed by the president or with his approval, torture our perceived enemies or spy on millions of Americans to look for terrorists. These activities have been acquiesced to by the Republican-controlled Congress, and by millions of conservatives who are tolerating, if not encouraging, this behavior.

Why is this happening? How can young American men and women working for the CIA or armed forces ignore their consciences to carry out orders that defy well-known international laws? How do employees who go to work every morning at the National Security Agency, the most powerful electronic spying machine in the world, illicitly turn their awesome surveillance powers on fellow Americans? Is it merely a matter of dutifully following the president's instructions? What was going through the heads of Justice Department lawyers as they sifted through the law to create dubious arguments justifying torture of our enemies? Where are the consciences of the conservatives who are now running the government, and where are the consciences of the countless conservative voters who tolerate, and in many cases actively support, this behavior? Or are these activities, in fact, reflective of their consciences?

I found answers to these and many other questions primarily in two places. During the years following Watergate, when I was looking for explanations of what had gone so wrong with Nixon's presidency, I encountered the work of Stanley Milgram. Later, when writing this book, I discovered the research of Bob Altemeyer. Both have conducted studies so important that it is dangerous to ignore their findings.

In the aftermath of Watergate a significant number of studies were undertaken by political and social psychologists, in fields of inquiry with which I was not familiar but which I found extremely revealing. Many seemed right on the mark and were helpful in understanding the dynamics of what had transpired. Some of these studies examined the mind-set within the Nixon White House that produced Watergate, and to assist in them I frequently shared my insider knowledge. One such study resulted in my encountering the classic experiments developed by social psychologist Stanley Milgram, who invited me to be the featured speaker at a gathering of psychologists in New York not long after I had published my book about Watergate, *Blind Ambition*. The purpose of the conference was to discuss Watergate as it related to Milgram's pioneering work on obedience to authority.

Obedience is "the psychological mechanism that links individual action to political purposes," Milgram explained, and he called it "the dispositional cement that binds men to systems of authority."[1] Without it many organizations simply would not work; with it, they could also run amuck. Because I had witnessed obedience facilitate both good and bad in government, I believed Milgram's work was both relevant and important. Today I think the implications of that research should be known by everyone working in Washington, if not in governments everywhere.

Obedience to Authority

To his surprise, and to the amazement and dismay of others, Milgram's classic experiments revealed that 65 percent of seemingly ordinary people were willing to subject what they believed to be protesting victims to painful, if not lethal, electric shocks (450 volts of electricity). They did so simply because they were instructed to by a scientist dressed in a gray lab coat in the setting of a scientific laboratory. This apparent authority figure ordered that the jolts of electricity be administered to determine if the "learner" would memorize word pairings faster if punished with increasingly painful electric shocks when he failed to accomplish the task. Actually, this experiment was designed to test not learning but rather the willingness of those administering the electric shocks to obey the authority figure. The subjects were not told of the ruse—that the "learner" was only pretending to experience pain and, in fact, was not being shocked—until the end of the experiment.[2]

When Milgram invited me to speak at his conference, he explained that it was because the Watergate probes had established that I was not a person who blindly followed the commands of authority figures. To the contrary, I had disobeyed an ultimate and powerful authority figure, the president of the United States, as well as his senior aides. Milgram noted that my breaking ranks and testifying about the Watergate cover-up placed me at the opposite end of the spectrum from people like Gordon Liddy and Chuck Colson, who compulsively obeyed authority. The conference proved to be a learning experience for me, because I discovered things about myself I had not really thought about.[3] More importantly, Milgram's work provided a compelling explanation for why many people obey or disobey authority figures, and the role of conscience in their behavior.

Conscience and Obedience

Milgram described conscience as our inner inhibitory system—part nature, part nurture, and necessary to the survival of our species.* Conscience checks the unfettered expression of impulses. It is a self-regulating inhibitor that prevents us from taking actions against our own kind. Because of conscience, Milgram says, "most men, as civilians, will not hurt, maim, or kill others in the normal course of the day." Conscience changes, however, when the individual becomes part of a group, with the individual's conscience often becoming subordinated to that of the group, or to that of its leader. In an organizational setting few people assess directions given by a higher authority against their own internal standards of moral judgment. Thus, "a person who is usually decent and courteous [may act] with severity against another person . . . because conscience, which regulates impulsive aggressive action, is per force diminished at the point of entering the hierarchical structure." Those who submit to an authoritarian order, and who adopt the conscience of the authority figure that issues the order, are in what Milgram called an "agentic state." They have become an agent of the authority figure's conscience.

Milgram devised various methods to test and measure points of individual resistance to authoritative commands. He discovered that most people who resist those commands go through a series of reactions, until they finally reach the point of disobeying. The decision of whether to follow an order is not a matter of judging it right or wrong,

---

*I have provided only a brief summary of Milgram's key thoughts on conscience. See Stanley Milgram, *Obedience to Authority: An Experimental View* (New York: Harper Perennial, 1969), 588, 127–34, which I have either paraphrased or quoted.

he learned, but rather a response to the unpleasantness of "strain" (a natural reaction, for example, to the moaning and eventual screams of a putative victim). When "a person acting under authority performs actions that seem to violate his standards of conscience, it would not be true to say that he loses his moral sense," Milgram concluded. Rather, that person simply places his moral views aside. His "moral concern shifts to a consideration of how well he is living up to the expectations of the authority figure."

Milgram believed that Hannah Arendt's book *Eichmann in Jerusalem* (1963) was correct in its analysis. She took issue with the Israeli war crimes prosecutor's efforts to depict Eichmann as a sadistic monster for his horrific role in exterminating Jews during World War II. She in turn described Eichmann as "an uninspired bureaucrat who simply sat at his desk and did his job,"[4] a compliant cog who had set aside his conscience. "Arendt's conception of the banality of evil comes closer to the truth than one might dare imagine," Milgram observed. In fact, the lesson of his work was that "ordinary people, simply doing their jobs, without any particular hostility on their part, can become agents in a terribly destructive process." Stated a bit differently, Milgram revealed that for a remarkable number of people, it is very difficult to disobey authority figures, but quite easy for them to set aside their conscience.

Milgram's research explained how someone like Chuck Colson was able to set aside his conscience when Nixon wanted a break-in at the Brookings Institution, and Colson became a dependable and unquestioning lieutenant for following orders.[5] Colson, a former Marine, was a click-the-heels, salute, and get-the-job-done type. But after he had left the White House, had become a born-again Christian, and had acknowledged Nixon's disgraceful conduct, the Milgram model became less than satisfactory in explaining Colson's efforts to promote a bogus history of Watergate.

Milgram's notion of an agentic conscience, however, appears to explain how, under Bush and Cheney, National Security Agency employees can turn their powerful electronic surveillance equipment on other Americans without objection. It can also account for CIA employees' and agents' willingness to hide so-called enemy combatants (that is, anyone they suspect of terror connections) in secret prisons, not to mention engage in torture—all contrary to law. Gordon Liddy, in contrast, pretends that he is obedient to the orders of his superiors, when exactly the opposite is the truth, as a close reading of his semiconfessional autobiography reveals. When in the FBI Liddy made illegal entries—"black-bag jobs"—searching for clues in an auto theft case, even though such activity was authorized (under the Fourth Amendment) only for certain national security cases, and even then had to be approved by FBI headquarters in advance. Liddy describes his illegal activity as "a simple extrapolation from FBI procedure in security cases." Rather than follow orders, he has consistently "extrapolated" and regularly disobeyed and deceived superiors.[6]

Milgram's work does not explain Liddy's behavior, or for that matter the obedience of the conservative Republicans who agreed to vote to impeach Clinton because their leaders instructed them to do so. And it does not even begin to illuminate the question of what drives authority figures, for Milgram focused only on those who compliantly follow orders, not on those who issue them. To really understand the conscience of contemporary conservatism we must turn to the study of authoritarianism, which explores both those who give orders in a political setting, as well as those who obediently follow such orders.

Linguistics expert George Lakoff reports in *Moral Politics: How Liberals and Conservatives Think* that the language and thinking of contemporary conservatism is, essentially, authoritarian. The conservative's worldview draws on an understanding of the family that follows "a Strict Father model." (By way of comparison, he noted, the liberal worldview draws on a very different ideal, "the Nurturant Parent model.") Lakoff contends that the organizing ideal of conservatism is the strict father who stands up to evil and emerges victorious in a highly competitive world. In the terms of this model, children are born bad and need a strict father to teach them discipline through punishment.[7] Chris Matthews of MSNBC's *Hardball* has made similar observations, and describes today's Republicans as the "Daddy" party and Democrats as the "Mommy." There is no doubt in my mind, based on years of personal observation, that contemporary conservative thinking is rife with authoritarian behavior, a conclusion that has been confirmed by social science. An examination of the relevant studies provides convincing support for the argument that authoritarian behavior is the key to understanding the conservative conscience, or lack thereof.

Authoritarianism

Social psychologists have spent some sixty years studying authoritarianism.* A decade before Milgram produced his startling findings, those most likely to comply with authority figures were identified as a personality type in *The Authoritarian Personality,* a study undertaken at the University of California, Berkeley. This work was part of the effort of leading social scientists to understand how "in a culture of law, order and reason . . . great masses of people [could and did] tolerate

---

*It is important to appreciate that the term "authoritarianism" as used by the social and political psychologist is different from the authoritarianism of the political scientist or the typical journalistic reference. Political scientists and journalists typically view authoritarianism as a form of government. This authoritarianism is not what is meant by political and social psychologists who use the term, and it is not how the term is used in this chapter. When an "authoritarian personality" prevails, authoritarianism can exist in a home, in a classroom, in a church, or in a courtroom. Theoretically, a very unauthoritarian person could function as head of an authoritarian government, although that would be unusual; likewise, an authoritarian leader could easily be head of a democracy. As I point out in the next chapter, authoritarian personalities can also push democracy toward political authoritarianism. In this chapter, however, authoritarianism refers to the thinking and behavior of authoritarian personalities.

the mass extermination of their fellow citizens," a question that was of some urgency after the horrors of World War II.[8]

The Berkeley study introduced the idea of "the authoritarian type"—people with seemingly conflicting elements in their persona, since they are often both enlightened yet superstitious, and proud to be individualists but live in constant fear of not being like others, whose independence they are jealous of because they themselves are inclined to submit blindly to power and authority.[9] For good reason, alert observers of American democracy are again expressing concern, as they had after World War II, about the growing and conspicuous authoritarian behavior in the conservative movement. Alan Wolfe, a professor of political science at Boston College and the director of the Boisi Center for Religion and American Public Life, suggests that *The Authoritarian Personality* be retrieved from the shelves. "The fact that the radical right has transformed itself from a marginal movement to an influential sector of the contemporary Republican Party makes the book's choice of subject matter all the more prescient," Wolfe wrote in the *Chronicle of Higher Education*.[10]

Although *The Authoritarian Personality* is not without critics, Wolfe believes that despite its flaws it deserves a reevaluation. Public officials "make good subjects for the kinds of analysis upon which the book relied; visible, talkative, passionate, they reveal their personalities to us, allowing us to evaluate them," he observes. A good example, he suggests, is United Nations ambassador John R. Bolton. At Bolton's Senate confirmation hearings (after which the Senate refused to confirm him; Bush nonetheless gave him a recess appointment), his contentious personality was exposed, with one former State Department colleague calling him "a quintessential kiss-up, kick-down sort of guy." Wolfe notes, "Everything Americans have learned about Bolton—his temper tantrums, intolerance of dissent, and black-and-white view of the world—step right out of the clinical material assembled by the authors of *The Authoritarian Personality*." Wolfe also finds Republican senator John Cornyn of Texas and former House majority leader Tom DeLay in its pages as well.[11]

During the past half century our understanding of authoritarianism has been significantly refined and advanced. Leading this work is social psychologist and researcher Bob Altemeyer of the University of Manitoba. Altemeyer not only confirmed the flaws in the methodology and findings of *The Authoritarian Personality*, but he set this field of study on new footings, by clarifying the study of authoritarian followers, whom he calls "right-wing authoritarians" (RWA). The provocative titles of his books—*Right-Wing Authoritarianism* (1981), *Enemies of Freedom* (1988), and *The Authoritarian Specter* (1996)—and a few of his many articles found in scholarly journals—such as "Highly Dominating, Highly Authoritarian Personalities" in the *Journal of Social Psychology* (2004) and "Why Do Religious Fundamentalists Tend to Be Prejudiced?" in the *International Journal for the Psychology of Religion* (2003)—indicate the tenor of his research and the range of his interests.*

Halfway through Altemeyer's *The Authoritarian Specter* I realized that I should get guidance to be certain I understood the material correctly, because the information he had developed was exactly what I needed to comprehend the personalities now dominating the conservative movement and Republican Party. For instance, he asked a very troubling question at the outset of *The Authoritarian Specter:* "Can there really be fascist people in a democracy?" His considered answer, based not on his opinion but on the results of his research, was: "I am afraid so."[12] Altemeyer's studies addressed not only those people mentioned by Alan Wolfe, along with my muses Chuck Colson and Gordon

---

*Throughout this chapter I have quoted or paraphrased Altemeyer, and so noted in the text. This material is based on an extensive exchange of e-mails over a seven-month period, and to not excessively clutter this chapter, I have not added endnotes or footnotes in each instance. However, when I have relied on other material by Altemeyer, I have provided a citation.

Liddy, whose behavior had provoked my inquiry, but all conservatives. Altemeyer graciously agreed to assist me in understanding his work and that of his colleagues.[13]

To study authoritarians Altemeyer and other researchers have used carefully crafted and tested questionnaires, usually called "scales," in which respondents are asked to agree or disagree with a statement such as "Our country desperately needs a mighty leader who will do what has to be done to destroy the radical new ways and sinfulness that are ruining us," or, "A 'woman's place' should be wherever she wants to be. The days when women are submissive to their husbands and social conventions belong strictly in the past."[14] As a professor of psychology Altemeyer has tested (usually anonymously) tens of thousands of first-year students and their parents, along with others, including some fifteen hundred American state legislators, over the course of some three decades. There is no database on authoritarians that even comes close in its scope, and, more importantly, these studies offer empirical data rather than partisan speculation.

Authoritarianism Vis-à-Vis Conservatism

Since the "authoritarian type" was first introduced in 1950, the question of the relationship of authoritarianism to ideology has been an ongoing investigation. Extensive research, and overwhelming evidence, shows "that authoritarianism is consistently associated with right-wing but not left-wing ideology."[15] To underscore the fact that his questionnaire does not address the left, Altemeyer specifically calls his scale a survey of *right-wing* authoritarianism. "I have tried to discover the left-wing authoritarian, whom I suspect exists, but apparently only in very small numbers," he told me. He is *not* testing for political conservatism per se, however. Nonetheless, he finds that those who score highly on his right-wing authoritarian scale are by and large "conservatives," as journalists and the general public understand that term. Other social scientists have reached the same conclusions.[16]

In one of Altemeyer's recent articles—"What Happens When Authoritarians Inherit the Earth? A Simulation"—he describes right-wing authoritarians as "political conservatives (from the grass roots up to the pros, say studies of over 1500 elected lawmakers)." He explained what can be a confusing distinction between a right-wing authoritarian and a political conservative:

> When I started out, and ever since, I was not looking for political conservatives. I was looking for people who overtly submit to the established authorities in their lives, who could be of any political/economic/religious stripe. So in the Soviet Union, whose Communist government we would call extremely "left-wing," I expected right-wing authoritarians to support Communism because that was what the established authorities demanded, and they did. So when I use "right-wing" in right-wing authoritarianism, I do not mean the submission necessarily goes to a politically "right-wing" leader or government, but that it goes to *established* authorities in one's life. I am proposing a psychological (not political) meaning of right-wing, in the sense that the submission goes to the psychologically accepted "proper," "legitimate" authority. That's the conceptualization.
>
> Now it turns out that in North America persons who score highly on my measure of authoritarianism test tend to favor right-wing political parties and have "conservative" economic philosophies and religious sentiments. This is an empirical finding, not something that conceptually has to be, that was conceptually assumed or preordained. So my statement about authoritarians being political conservatives is a statement of what turns out to be true according to the studies that have been done. To put it in a nutshell: Authoritarianism was *conceptualized* to involve submission to established authorities, who could be anyone. But *it turns*

out that people who have "conservative" leanings tend to be more authoritarian than anyone else. (Incidentally, I put all those tiresome quotation marks around "conservative" and "liberal" because I don't want people to think I know what I'm talking about. Good definitions are very difficult here, especially from place to place and era to era.)

While there is no question that a satisfactory definition of conservatism is elusive, it is not surprising that right-wing authoritarians are conservatives under almost any current definition, based on the items found in the principal tool for measuring authoritarianism, the RWA (right-wing authoritarian) scale.[17] For example, in the RWA scale (see a full sample in Appendix B), the following questions would surely be answered in varying affirmatives (strongly agree or agree as opposed to disagree or strongly disagree) by social conservatives, particularly Christian conservatives:

- Our country desperately needs a mighty leader who will do what has to be done to destroy the radical new ways and sinfulness that are ruining us.
- The only way our country can get through the crisis ahead is to get back to our traditional values, put some tough leaders in power, and silence the troublemakers who are spreading bad ideas.
- "Old-fashioned ways" and "old-fashioned values" are the best guide for the way to live.
- God's laws about abortion, pornography, and marriage must be strictly followed before it is too late, and those who break them must be strongly punished.
- Once our government leaders give us the "go-ahead," it will be the duty of every patriotic citizen to help stomp out the rot that is poisoning our country from within.

Social conservatives would just as likely *very strongly* disagree with these statements from the RWA scale:

- Gays and lesbians are just as healthy and moral as anybody else.
- Atheists and others who have rebelled against the established religions are no doubt every bit as good and virtuous as those who attend church regularly.
- There is absolutely nothing wrong with nudist camps.
- There is nothing wrong with premarital sexual intercourse.

Altemeyer explains the conservative-liberal dimension of his research in *The Authoritarian Specter.* "I submit that when journalists, educators, and politicians themselves talk about liberals and conservatives on the issues of our day," he wrote, "they are usually talking about the dimension measured by the RWA scale." He noted,

> When I hear Rush Limbaugh, Jesse Helms, or Pat Buchanan say that liberals favor guaranteeing equal rights for homosexuals, I say to myself, "Actually, *Low RWAs* do, and it connects to much else in their thinking." And when I hear Gary Trudeau, Edward Kennedy, and Barbara Jordan say that the conservatives oppose abortion and favor the death penalty, I say to myself, "Actually, if you understand that it's *High RWAs* who do these things, you'll realize why and a lot, lot more." When people are "conservatives"— politically, religiously, economically—the odds are pretty good that they are High RWAs. That is not an opinion, but a scientifically established fact.[18]

A recent study employing the RWA scale, conducted by another researcher, showed it to be quite prescient in predicting voting patterns for Republican candidates in the 1996 and 2000 elections.[19] While the right-wing authoritarian scale does not measure either conservatism or Republican party identification, this recent research again confirms Altemeyer's findings that those who score high on the scale are, more than likely, both.

Early in our exchanges on authoritarians Altemeyer related, "The biggest thing that has happened recently has been the discovery that there are two, not one, authoritarian personalities." He explained that the Berkeley group's research, like that of other social scientists and his own, focused on "authoritarian *followers,* persons who submit too fast, too long to established authorities." (Emphasis added.) These people are RWAs. More recently social psychologists have "developed a measure to identify authoritarian *leaders,* persons who want to be submitted to." (Emphasis added.) These individuals, because of their social dominance orientation (SDO), are take-charge types. Not unaware of my background at the Nixon White House—since Watergate was one of several events he had examined that demonstrated "that many citizens in a democracy will support high-handed, repressive, and antidemocratic policies" that obviously were not envisioned by the nation's founders—Altemeyer suggested that I was no doubt personally familiar with these types of personalities. After learning more about them, I found he was correct, and, in addition, I have discovered them in my recent studies of the Bush White House and Washington political culture. And all of them are hard-right conservatives.

Working my way through Altemeyer's books and journal articles, along with the writings of others in the field, I began to understand the particular categories within the authoritarian personality classifications. First there are the followers, the right-wing authoritarians. Then there are the leaders, the social dominators. And finally, there are those who uniquely combine the worst personality traits of both types and appear to be best positioned to become leaders of right-wing movements and undertakings, a group Altemeyer describes as "scary." While many conservatives seem willing to set aside their consciences, it is not clear this last group possesses a conscience. But let us move forward one step at a time, first examining the nature of each of these authoritarian personalities.

Right-Wing Authoritarians: The Followers

Altemeyer characterizes right-wing authoritarians as "especially sub-missive to established authority"; as showing "general aggressiveness" toward others when such behavior "is perceived to be sanctioned" by established authorities; and as highly compliant with "social conven-tions" endorsed by society and established authorities. All these atti-tudes must be present in significant if varying degrees if an individual is to fall within Altemeyer's well-honed definition. Both men and women may score high on the RWA scale. These three elements of the right-wing authoritarian personality, while not elusive, still call for a little further explanation.

SUBMISSIVE TO AUTHORITY

By "submissive," Altemeyer means these people accept almost without question the statements and actions of established authorities, and they comply with such instructions without further ado. "Authorities" include parents (throughout childhood), religious officials, govern-ment officials (police, judges, legislators, heads of government), mili-tary superiors, and, depending on the situation, other people like "bus drivers, lifeguards, employers, psychology experimenters and count-less others." High-scoring right-wing authoritarians are intolerant of criticism of their authorities, because they believe the authority is unassailably correct. Rather than feeling vulnerable in the presence of powerful authorities, they feel safer. For example, they are not trou-bled by government surveillance of citizens because they think only wrongdoers need to be concerned by such intrusions. Still, their sub-mission to authority is not blind or automatic; these authoritarians believe there are proper and improper authorities (good judges and bad judges, good presidents and bad presidents), and their decision to submit is shaped by whether a particular authority is compatible with their views.

AGGRESSIVE SUPPORT OF AUTHORITY

Authoritarian aggression, according to Altemeyer, is "a predisposition to cause harm to" others when such behavior is believed to be sanctioned by an authority. This harm can be physical, psychological, financial, and social, or "some other negative state which people would usually avoid." When the public tolerates right-wing authoritarian aggression, it too may be considered aggressive in its tacit approval of such conduct. An aggressive predisposition does not always result in aggressive action, however, since fear of retaliation or even social pressure may prevent it. Authoritarians are inclined to control the behavior of others, particularly children and criminals, through punishment. They have little tolerance for leniency by courts in "coddling" criminals. Targets of right-wing authoritarian aggression are typically people perceived as being unconventional, like homosexuals. Research finds that authoritarian aggression is fueled by fear and encouraged by remarkable self-righteousness, which frees aggressive impulses.

CONVENTIONALITY

Right-wing authoritarians accept and follow the traditional norms of society. In religious matters they tend to be fundamentalist. Because authorities have already determined what is right and wrong, they reject moral relativism. Religion influences their attitudes toward sex— other than for reproduction it is considered sinful, if not perverse. They embrace the ideal of the traditional family, with the woman serving as child rearer and subservient wife. They are "straight and narrow" in their dress and behavior, and believe themselves the country's true patriots.

Altemeyer's data provides additional information about the dispositions of right-wing authoritarians. Here are a few examples that provide further perspective. These have not been deliberately isolated as negative characteristics; rather, they are traits that authoritarians believe to be positive.

- They travel in tight circles of like-minded people.
- Their thinking is more likely based on what authorities have told them rather than on their own critical judgment, which results in their beliefs being filled with inconsistencies.
- They harbor numerous double standards and hypocrisies.
- They are hostile toward so many minorities they seem to be equal-opportunity bigots, yet they are generally unaware of their prejudices.
- They see the world as a dangerous place, with society teetering on the brink of self-destruction from evil and violence, and when their fear conflates with their self-righteousness, they appoint themselves guardians of public morality, or God's Designated Hitters.
- They think of themselves as far more moral and upstanding than others—a self-deception aided by their religiosity (many are "born again") and their ability to "evaporate guilt" (such as by going to confession).

It is authoritarian followers who filled churches across the United States on "Justice Sunday" to lobby for right-wing judges in federal courts; who can be seen on C-Span seated at dinner tables, after paying ten times the cost of their meals, to listen to Bill Frist or Karl Rove give a speech at the Federalist Society; who are the well-scrubbed young people who join college Republican clubs, whose parents or grandparents are delegates at GOP presidential conventions. By and large these Americans have never been troubled by the execution of a prisoner, and there has never been a war in which the United States engaged that they did not support. If they work inside the Beltway, you can recognize them by the American flag pins on their suit lapels or dresses, and you can be relatively certain they are carrying a copy of the U.S. Constitution in their pocket or pocketbook. According to Bob Altemeyer,

Authoritarian followers, in all probability, trusted President Bush's justifications for invading Iraq—when all those who had been in

Iraq searching for weapons of mass destruction said there was no evidence they existed. The High RWAs were likely the Americans who told pollsters they believed such weapons *had been found* after the invasion, when none had been found. They were probably the ones who accepted without pause the administration's revised claim that the war had been necessary to remove Saddam Hussein from power. Because of their high levels of dogmatism, most of them will probably never realize that this war was unjustified, an enormous error with horrendous costs. They will find someone else to blame for the war's costs other than themselves and the leaders they follow. Many of them would attack France, Massachusetts, or the moon if the president said it was necessary "for freedom." And authoritarian followers formed the rock core of the millions who marched to the polls in November 2004, often at the instruction of their church, and re-elected George Bush.

Social Dominance Orientation and "Double Highs": The Leaders

While the term "social dominance orientation" (SDO) may sound like academic jargon, it is highly descriptive of the personalities of many who run social and political situations and organizations—the leaders who insist on running the show. The word "social," of course, refers to the general organization of society; "dominance" relates to control or command over other people; and "orientation," as used here, means their inclination or disposition. These are people who seize every opportunity to lead, and who enjoy having power over others.

Altemeyer explained that his "RWA scale has never been a good measure of authoritarian dominance; it was constructed more to capture the psychology of the submissive crowd."[20] It was Felicia Pratto of the University of Connecticut and Jim Sidanius of the University of California, Los Angeles, who developed social dominance theory, and a social dominance orientation scale. Building on their work, Alte-meyer cross tested for other traits as well, research that revealed the so-called Double Highs, those few who score high on both the RWA and SDO scales. First, a look at the social dominators.

For a half century, the study of authoritarian personalities focused primarily on followers, on understanding how such large numbers of people were taken in by Hitler and Mussolini. It was only a decade ago, and largely by accident that social dominance orientation theory was discovered to be such a powerful tool to study authoritarian lead-ers. According to the *Oxford Handbook of Political Psychology,* the SDO scale measures not only dominance but economic conservatism and another hallmark of the ideology, belief in inequality.[21] The social dominance scale focuses on questions relating to equality. For exam-ple, it seeks agreement or disagreement with statements like the fol-lowing: "Some people are just more worthy than others"; "this country would be better off if we cared less about how equal all people were"; "to get ahead in life, it is sometimes necessary to step on others"; and "all humans should be treated equally." The SDO scale even asked to what extent people being tested agreed or disagreed with the very con-cept of equality. Social dominance orientation suggests an underlying personality that is "characterized by . . . traits of being hard, tough, ruthless, and unfeeling toward others, as opposed to compassionate, generous, caring, and altruistic." (For a complete sample of the SDO survey see Appendix C.)

A person with a social dominator/leader personality has a world-view that is related to but different from that of a right-wing authoritarian/follower. Authoritarian leaders see the world as a com-petitive jungle in which the fittest survive; authoritarian followers see the world as dangerous and threatening.[22] Men are more typically so-cial dominator types. Testing shows that social dominators believe equality is "a sucker word in which only fools believe." Dominators see themselves as realists, maintaining that "complete equality is probably impossible; that natural forces inevitably govern the worth of individuals; and that people should have to earn their place in society."[23] Employing other tests on social dominators, Altemeyer found that

> [h]igh SDOs tend to agree with statements such as, "Do you enjoy having the power to hurt people when they anger or disappoint you?" "If you have power in a situation, you should use it however you have to, to get your way," and "I will do my best to destroy anyone who deliberately blocks my plans and goals"; while disagreeing with "It is much better to be loved than feared," and "Would it bother you if other people thought you were mean and pitiless?"

Equality, Altemeyer explained, "is antithetical to dominance, and social dominators want to dominate."[24] In an e-mail, he added that one of the more telling findings regarding social dominators is their responses to his equality scale, which reveal that their typical arguments against greater equality are a cover for much baser, selfish motivations.

Dominators are prepared to "proceed with relatively little moral restraint," for they agree with statements like "There really is no such thing as 'right' and 'wrong'; it all boils down to what you can get away with," and "basically, people are objects to be quietly and coolly manipulated for your own benefit." They disagree with statements like "Do unto others as you would have them do unto you, and never do anything unfair to someone else," and "Since so many members of minority groups end up in our jails, we should take strong steps to make sure prejudice plays no role in their treatment by the legal system."[25] Other social scientists have similarly found that high-scoring social dominators are "potentially ruthless in their pursuit or maintenance of their desires" and they do not believe that their "actions should never cause harm to others." And dominators believe "that the end does justify the means."[26] Today it is recognized that such authoritarian dominators are attracted to "status-inequality-enforcing occupations," like prosecuting attorney or a job in law enforcement, and that they are "over-represented in positions of political power."[27]

In his description of social dominators, Altemeyer poses a rhetorical question: "Do you know such people: relatively intimidating, unsympathetic, untrusting and untrustworthy, vengeful, manipulative, and amoral?" While Altemeyer admits that it may seem "unsympathetic to describe those who score highly on the Social Dominance Orientation scale" in this manner, such terms have been used by these individuals to describe themselves. Empirical data bears out such qualities as "relatively power hungry, domineering, mean, Machiavellian and amoral, and hold[ing] 'conservative' economical and political outlooks."[28] These people know exactly where they want to stand. Experiments reveal that right-wing authoritarian followers are particularly likely to trust someone who tells them what they want to hear, for this is how many of them validate their beliefs. Social dominators, on the other hand, typically know exactly what song they want to sing to followers.

Unfortunately, there are people who, when given tests for social dominance and right-wing authoritarianism, score high on both. Altemeyer calls them "Double Highs." These dominating authoritarian leaders are the individuals whom Altemeyer refers to with good reason as "particularly scary."

The Double High Authoritarians

Social dominators whom tests show to be Double Highs seem full of contradictions. They score high as both leaders and as followers, an apparent anomaly that Altemeyer accounts for by explaining that Double Highs respond to questions relating to submission not by considering how they submit to others, but about how others submit to them. They inevitably see the world with themselves in charge.

Altemeyer provided a number of examples of Double High behavior. Ordinary social dominators and ordinary authoritarian followers *both* tend to be highly prejudiced against ethnic and racial minorities.

Double Highs, however, possess "extra-extra unfair" natures, and they can be ranked as the most racially prejudiced of all groups. It seems that two authoritarian streams converge in them to produce a river of hostility, particularly regarding rights for homosexuals and women. Another example of their prejudice has to do with religion. Typical social dominators are not particularly religious, but Double Highs resemble right-wing authoritarians in their strong religious backgrounds. Like right-wing authoritarians, Double Highs tend to be Christian fundamentalists.[29] But Double Highs generally do not attend church out of any sense of religious commitment, because religion provides no moral compass for them. "They may think of themselves as being religious and they go to church more than most people do, but they believe in lying, cheating, and manipulating much more than the rest of the congregation does," Altemeyer's research shows. They agree with statements like "The best reason for belonging to a church is to project a good image and have contact with some of the important people in your community."[30] They also reveal their parochialism by agreeing with statements like "If it were possible, I'd rather have a job where I worked with people with the same religious views I have, rather than with people with different views"; "all people may be entitled to their own religious beliefs, but I don't want to associate with people whose views are quite different from my own"; and "non-Christian religions have a lot of weird beliefs and pagan ways that Christians should avoid having any contact with."[31]

Double Highs are also dogmatic. While an average social dominator does not typically embrace "grand philosophies or creeds," Double Highs do. Altemeyer ran a Global Change Game* simulation with fifty-five university students, all of whom scored high as right-wing authoritarian followers, and seven of whom also scored high on social dominance. As their profiles suggested, the seven Double Highs either directly or indirectly took charge, and the others followed. During the

*See http://www.mts.net/~gcg/.

two-session simulation, Double Highs engaged in nuclear blackmail, made themselves wealthy by dubious means, provoked a worldwide crisis by destroying the ozone layer, allowed 1.9 billion people to die of starvation and disease, and sent the poor regions of the world "down the tubes." Simulations, and students, of course, are a long way from reality, yet their performance further suggests the potentially dangerous natures of Double Highs.[32]

Altemeyer observed that if Double Highs were "in control of a school prayer, or anti-homosexual, or anti-immigration, or anti-feminist, or anti-abortion, or anti-gun-control movement—not to mention a military force," they could pose a serious threat. This is not only because of their own ideology and nature, but because "they lead people who are uninclined to think for themselves"—submissive, gullible right-wing authoritarian followers, who "are brimming with self-righteousness and zeal, and are fain to give dictatorship a chance." Altemeyer warned, "We have seen them in action before, to our sorrow. We might be wise to develop an understanding of their psychological makeup."[33] Not given to hyperbole in his scholarly work, Altemeyer has nevertheless repeatedly likened the traits of Double Highs to those of Hitler, and to those who are "most likely to mobilize and lead extremist right-wing movements" in the United States.

Conservatives Without Conscience

A striking revelation found within these studies is the fact that both right-wing authoritarians and social dominators can be accurately described as conservatives without conscience.[34] Needless to say, conscience itself cannot be measured directly. But stated beliefs and expressed behavior often reflect the workings of a conscience.[35] For example, social dominators freely admit on tests that measure moral issues of right and wrong behavior that such matters are irrelevant to them. That suggests little conscience, a fact which is often corroborated by behavior. Altemeyer noted that "social dominators believe that a really good skill to develop is the ability to look someone straight in the face and lie convincingly. Obviously, that person has no conscience." Nothing shows lack of conscience better than bold-faced lying. Altemeyer pointed out that lying, however, is not a uniquely social dominator skill; it is also easy for right-wing authoritarians to do because of their remarkable self-righteousness.

Examining the consciences of right-wing authoritarian followers, however, is slightly more complicated than doing so for social dominators, because their actions are often different from their words, and they are not able to reflect about themselves easily because of their incredible self-righteousness. They are, however, even more important than the dominator, because there are more followers than leaders, and leaders cannot retain power without followers. A striking aspect of these followers is their limited self-perception. "If you ask right-wing authoritarians, they will say they have very strong consciences indeed, which is one of the reasons they are so good compared to others," Altemeyer said. "But empirical studies have shown that they are not as good as they believe themselves to be when compared to others. When tested for cheating, right-wing authoritarians, notwithstanding their protestation to the contrary, did not prove themselves to be so principled."[36] Similarly, it might be expected that right-wing authoritarians who are extremely religious evangelicals would have strong consciences directed by moral precepts or ethical restraints. That, however, does not seem to be the case. "Whether the issue is divorce, materialism, sexual promiscuity, racism, physical abuse in marriage, or neglect of a biblical world view," wrote evangelical theologian Ronald J. Sider in *The Scandal of the Evangelical Conscience*, "the polling data point to widespread, blatant disobedience of clear biblical moral demands on the part of people who allegedly are evangelical, born-again Christians. The statistics are devastating."[37]

How can this paradox be explained? Right-wing authoritarians employ "a number of psychological tricks and defenses that enable them to act fairly beastly," Altemeyer explained, all the while thinking they are "the good people." To begin with, they have relatively little self-understanding: "For instance, they do not realize they are more prejudiced and hostile than most people. In fact, they do not realize *any* of the many undesirable things that research has discovered about them."* Second, right-wing authoritarians have very compartmentalized minds, and "they can just pull off a Scarlett O'Hara ('I'm not going to think about it!') whenever they want." Altemeyer found the fact that so many others are able to detect their hypocrisies while they themselves are oblivious demonstrates how effective they are at ignoring their shortcomings. Third, he said, "right-wing authoritarians shed their guilt very efficiently when they do something wrong. Typically they turn to God for forgiveness, and as a result feel completely forgiven afterwards. Catholics, for example, use confession. Fundamentalist Protestants use a somewhat different mechanism. Many who are 'born-again' believe that if you confess your sins and accept Jesus as your personal savior you will go to heaven—no matter what else you do afterwards. (This is called 'cheap grace' by those within fundamentalism who hold its members to higher standards.)" In brief, "When a great deal of misbehavior is engaged in by born-again Christians it troubles their fundamentalist consciences very little, for after all, they are the Saved. So by using their religious beliefs effectively, right-wing authoritarians have high moral standards in many regards, but pretty ineffective consciences."

This analysis can account for how someone like the born-again Chuck Colson can go about his hatchet work on people today without troubling his conscience just as he did at the Nixon White House. And how Christian conservatives like Pat Robertson can openly call

---

*However, "right-wing authoritarians openly admit their hostility when they perceive strong social support for being aggressive—for example, against homosexuality. They also admit to a bit more hostility when they feel safe doing so, as when they are anonymous. But their social comparison process may prevent them from learning how relatively aggressive they really are." Bob Altemeyer, *Enemies of Freedom* (San Francisco: Jossey-Bass Publishers, 1988), 190.

for the assassination of foreign leaders, despite the Ten Command-ments that he holds so dear. It is as if these individuals had worn down their consciences with cheap grace—a remarkable and frightening process. "One of the things a conscience is supposed to do is make us act better, but when you have a means of eliminating guilt, there is not much incentive to clean up your act. You can see how conscience gets short-circuited," Altemeyer noted. He added, "Bad behavior may pro-duce guilt, but it is easily washed away. So then more bad behavior can result, again, and again, each time getting removed very easily through religion. There is a terrible closing to this reality. The lack of guilt over things he has done in the past can actually contribute to the self-righ-teousness of the authoritarian. And this self-righteousness has proven, in experiments, to be the main factor that unleashes the right-wing authoritarian's aggressive impulses."[38] He concluded, "I have called them 'God's designated hitters.' We end up with the irony that the people who think they are so very good end up doing so very much evil, and, more remarkably, they are probably the last people in the world who will ever realize the connection between the two." There is no better explanation for the behavior of many Christian conserva-tives, for it accounts for their license to do ill, Christian beliefs notwith-standing.

Certainly, not all authoritarian conservatives are without conscience. There is no better example of an authoritarian conservative with a high political profile than Pat Buchanan. Lance Morrow, writing in the *National Review,* observed: "Buchanan emerged from Gonzaga [High School in Washington, DC] an authoritarian and dogmatist, possessing something of the Jesuit's fierceness and delight in argu-ment. I cannot see that he has changed in the 40-odd years since then. About America he has instincts of a sometimes paradoxical dynamic: aggressively defensive, militantly wistful."[39] Likewise, in a less than flattering piece, the *New Republic* claimed, "In many ways, Buchanan's authoritarian personality—although far less complex than Nixon's tortured motivations—was a perfect political instrument for the dark, polarizing side of Nixon." Its authors added that "Buchanan's authoritarian mania was the key to high ratings for shows like 'Crossfire,' 'The McLaughlin Group,' and 'The Capitol Gang.'"[40] While such characterizations are fairly typical assessments of Buchanan, he has in fact shown himself to have a strong and consistent set of principles. During Watergate, Buchanan was part of the Nixon White House defense team but since the Nixon tapes emerged, he has acknowledged, "I think what Nixon did, clearly, was wrong. And he made terrible mistakes. And partly as a result of his mistakes, he was destroyed, but he was destroyed also by his political enemies. . . . We weren't saints."[41]

Nixon White House chief of staff Bob Haldeman, along with John Ehrlichman and Chuck Colson, had asked Buchanan to create what would become known as the Plumbers Unit to investigate the leak of the Pentagon Papers and to drive the prosecution of Dan Ellsberg, both criminally and in the court of public opinion. Buchanan refused to take the assignment, but had he accepted it, it is difficult to imagine his hiring Gordon Liddy or Howard Hunt, who together incubated the mentality behind the Watergate break-ins and ensuing cover-up. When testifying before the Senate Watergate Committee Buchanan made this telling statement: "Charles Colson was quoted as saying, 'I would do anything the President of the United Sates would ask me to do, period.' I would subscribe to that statement for this reason: The President of the United States would not ask me to do anything unethical, improper, or wrong, or illegal." (Nixon's tapes later confirmed Buchanan's testimony.) Committee counsel pressed Buchanan, asking, "What tactics would you be willing to use?" To which he responded, "Anything that was not immoral, unethical, illegal, or unprecedented in previous Democratic campaigns." He did not hesitate to describe dirty politics he considered unacceptable. "Now there is a line across which political tricks should not go, quite clearly. One of them obviously was in Florida. The salacious attack on Senator Jackson and Senator Humphrey." (This dirty campaigning had in fact been sponsored by the Nixon White House, which was unknown at the time by Buchanan.)[42]

Profile of Authoritarians

No question hovered at the front of my mind more, reading through Altemeyer's studies of authoritarian behavior, than, why are right-wingers often malicious, mean-spirited, and disrespectful of even the basic codes of civility? While the radical left has had its episodes of boorishness, the right has taken these tactics to an unprecedented level. Social science has discovered these forms of behavior can be rather easily explained as a form of aggression.

Altemeyer's studies of authoritarian aggression are groundbreaking and have been recognized by the American Association for the Advancement of Science.* Altemeyer discovered that the aggression of right-wingers seems to be not merely instrumental—that is, expressed for some political purpose—but engaged in for the pure pleasure of it. Torture is an extreme example, yet apparently authoritarians can find even that enjoyable, as the Abu Ghraib photos tragically illustrate. But on a more pedestrian level, he found it difficult for most right-wingers to talk about any subject about which they felt strongly without attacking others. This heightened level of aggressiveness has a number of psychological roots. Right-wing authoritarians, as we have seen, are motivated by their fear of a dangerous world, whereas social dominators have an ever-present desire to dominate. The factor that makes right-wingers faster than most people to attack others, and that seems

---

*In 1986, the American Academy for the Advancement of Science awarded Altemeyer its prize for behavioral science research for his essay "Authoritarian Aggression." The prize encouraged development and application of verifiable empirical research methodologies in the social sciences. This is a highly prestigious recognition by scientific peers, and no higher accolade is given to social scientists. See http://archives.aaas.org/awards.php?a_id=24.

to keep them living in an "attack mode," is their remarkable self-righteousness. They are so sure they are not only right, but holy and pure, that they are bursting with indignation and a desire to smite down their enemies, Altemeyer explained.

When one examines authoritarians closely, their propensity to attack others by any means fair and foul is not surprising, for they are fundamentally fierce people. Yet Altemeyer's studies indicate that if they could see themselves as others do, which they are seldom able to, they might gain perspective on their conduct. Their blinders, however, help make them who they are. Because there is so little information available for the general reader about authoritarians, notwithstanding literally reams of scientific reports that have accumulated since 1950 when this work commenced, it is as if the public has been hindered in understanding authoritarians by its own set of blinders. This is risky, for authoritarianism, which is a key but overlooked reality of contemporary conservatism, can be ignored only at our collective peril. Social scientists would do well to make more of their work in this area accessible to the general public, and journalists and political writers should avail themselves of this data.

"Typologies" are a controversial methodology, yet some types are simply too obvious not to recognize, particularly when decades of scientific research have established and confirmed them. Princeton political scientist Fred I. Greenstein has cautioned about the uses of personality in analyzing political activity, and employment of "typologies"; in fact, he directly addressed "the tangled history of studies of authoritarianism." He noted, however, that what once seemed to be at a "dead end" in studying authoritarian personalities has proven not to be the case. Rather, "in the 1980s an ingenious and rigorous program of inquiry by Altemeyer (1981, 1988) furnished persuasive empirical evidence that the original authoritarian construct was an approximation of an important political-psychological regularity—the existence in some individuals of an inner makeup that disposes them to defer to authority figures."[43] Since Greenstein made these observations the science has, as noted, significantly progressed. Not only has Altemeyer added to his empirical data, but a significant number of social scientists have confirmed his findings.

In closing, what follows is a summary of types of traits typically found in social dominators and right-wing authoritarians, based on extensive testing. Although these collations of characteristics of authoritarians are not attractive portraits, they are nonetheless traits that authoritarians themselves acknowledge. An asterisk indicates the traits that are essential for a person to fall within the definition, but not every person who meets the definition will have all the traits, even though many do. If you add these key definitional traits, you will have a portrait of Double High authoritarians; people who display all the traits of both types are likely to be the particularly alarming Double Highs:

Social Dominators—Leaders:

- typically men
- dominating*
- opposes equality*
- desirous of personal power*
- amoral*
- intimidating and bullying
- faintly hedonistic
- vengeful
- pitiless
- exploitive
- manipulative
- dishonest
- cheats to win
- highly prejudiced (racist, sexist, homophobic)
- mean-spirited
- militant
- nationalistic

- tells others what they want to hear
- takes advantage of "suckers"
- specializes in creating false images to sell self
- may or may not be religious
- usually politically and economically conservative/Republican

Right-Wing Authoritarian—Followers:

- men and women
- submissive to authority*
- aggressive on behalf of authority*
- conventional*
- highly religious
- moderate to little education
- trust untrustworthy authorities
- prejudiced (particularly against homosexuals, women, and followers of religions other than their own)
- mean-spirited
- narrow-minded
- intolerant
- bullying
- zealous
- dogmatic
- uncritical toward chosen authority
- hypocritical
- inconsistent and contradictory
- prone to panic easily
- highly self-righteous
- moralistic
- strict disciplinarian
- severely punitive
- demands loyalty and returns it
- little self-awareness
- usually politically and economically conservative/Republican

A few closing thoughts about authoritarian personalities. As distasteful as these qualities may appear, for authoritarians they can be (secretly or even openly) very attractive. While these traits may, or may not, be found in all persons who are social dominators or right-wing authoritarians, they are characteristics of those who test high. People who test low tend to have fewer of these traits, but it is not possible to say which ones they do possess. Although most authoritarians will deny they are such, often failing to recognize these qualities in themselves, low testers may, in fact, be justified in their denials. The good news is that when some high-testing right-wing authoritarians do become aware of their characteristics they actually do work to change their outlook and behavior. Social dominators, however, do not seem able to make such adjustments. Authoritarianism is not a pathology; nor is the term pejorative, for it is descriptive.

However one views authoritarians, their behavior is not without significance, for they have played a major role in developing the contemporary conservative movement, and now they are taking conservatism increasingly toward *political* authoritarianism. Many are appropriately described as conservatives without conscience. What distinguishes conservatives with conscience from those without? The summary table below highlights a few distinctions, based upon information developed by social scientists and upon my own broad application of that information to government and politics at the national level.

Conservatives *Without* Conscience	Conservatives *With* Conscience
They have a high authoritarian personality with a host of negative traits.	They have a low authoritarian personality with few negative traits.
They pretend to honor the past while often drawing on its worst.	They draw on the wisdom of the past and not the worst.

Order and safety always trump freedom when government needs to balance them.

Freedom always trumps order and safety when government needs to weight them.

A "unitary executive" branch operates under the president, who has virtually exclusive and unlimited powers in foreign affairs as commander-in-chief.

They insist that the separation of powers in government be maintained, along with checks and balances in all areas.

If conservatives control Congress they run it their way and exclude others from having a say.

They believe Congress must be a deliberative body free from tyranny of the majority.

Federal courts should be staffed by judges who think and act like good conservatives, and if they do not, Congress should take jurisdiction away from lower courts, which it controls.

They oppose packing federal courts with ideologues and interfering with judicial independence.

Because most of the public does not really understand politics, elites must run the government, and equality goes to those who earn it.

They oppose elitism and encourage equality for all.

Government secrecy is necessary in an age of terror, and transparency makes it difficult to run the government.

They reject government secrecy and seek as much transparency as possible.

Terrorism has created an indefinite war, and, as Winston Churchill said, "In wartime, truth is so precious that she should always be attended by a bodyguard of lies."

They believe honesty is not merely the best policy, it is the only policy. And terrorism must be viewed realistically.

America was founded on Judeo-Christian principles, the Bible is an indisputable guide for government, and there is nothing in the Constitution creating a "wall of separation" between church and state.

Religious dogma is personal and private, and the Bible is not a basis for government policy; separation of church and state is essential in our pluralistic society.

Big government is here to stay, deficits do not matter, and if liberal social programs can be choked by cutting taxes, that is even better.

The national government should be limited, and should be fiscally responsible.

Voters who are kept anxious by fears of terrorism will become or remain conservatives and keep Republicans in power; it is time—and smart politics—to go back to a Department of War to deal with terrorists.

The politics of fear have no place in a democracy. A strong defense is the best offense, and the military-industrial complex should not control the Department of Defense.

So long as America remains the strongest nation, it can control the world and maintain peace by preemptively going to war to prevent the proliferation of weapons of mass destruction.

America cannot police the world unilaterally and needs the good will and cooperation of other nations to prevent the spread of terrorism and WMD.

Tough times demand tough talk, and it is an unfortunate reality that mudslinging works in politics.

Civility is a sign of strength not weakness, and democracy cannot survive without it.

It should surprise no one that when conservatism and authoritarianism are joined together the result is authoritarian conservatism. Here too are found right-wing authoritarian followers and social dominators, as well as conservatives without conscience. With science to assist as an analytical tool, the growing authoritarian conservatism can be more deeply probed.

CHAPTER THREE

AUTHORITARIAN CONSERVATISM

POLITICAL AUTHORITARIANISM in America still pales in comparison with that in countries like China and Russia, or in any of the many semidictatorial or quasi-totalitarian governments. This is as it should be; America's founders rejected political authoritarianism when they rejected monarchy and it has no place in our history. But democracy is not simply the antithesis of political authoritarianism, for any government has an inherently authoritarian nature. The United States is a republic, meaning that authority resides with the people, who elect agents to represent them in making day-to-day political decisions. Our founding fathers understood that republics were vulnerable; they knew that "many republics in history, such as the Roman republic, had been replaced by despots," political scientist Jay Shafritz of the University of Pittsburgh pointed out. Shafritz noted that when Benjamin Franklin was asked what sort of government had been created at the Constitutional Convention, he suggested that weakness in his reply, "a republic, if you can keep it."[1] The vehicle that despotism rides is authoritarianism, and we have been fortunate that authoritarianism, until recently, existed only at the fringes of our government.

In fact, authoritarian conservatism has been present in American politics in some form since America's founding. There has always been an authoritarian element in modern conservatism (which developed post–World War II), but only recently has it found widespread adherence, overpowering libertarian and traditional thinking. Nonetheless, there exists a symbiotic relationship between authoritarianism and conservatism, which today is concentrated in social conservatism and the policies of neoconservatism. Its presence in these factions is no small matter, though, for it is they who largely control the current political agenda in the United States. Keeping the authoritarian influence of conservatism in check, however, is vital to maintaining our republican form of government, and it can only be checked if it is recognized and its implications understood.

Early Authoritarian Conservatism

Alexander Hamilton, the monarchist-leaning founding father, can justifiably be considered America's first prominent authoritarian conservative. Political scientists Charles W. Dunn and J. David Woodard reported in their study *The Conservative Tradition in America* that Hamilton's "brand of conservatism may be properly labeled authoritarian conservatism." Dunn and Woodard trace the ideology of authoritarian conservatism to Joseph de Maistre, a French nobleman and political polemicist who became an outspoken opponent of Enlightenment thinking, and who favored a strong central government.[2] Maistre's writing provides an all too vivid glimpse at his rather dark worldview, such as this from his appreciation of executioners.

> A prisoner, a parricide, a man who has committed sacrilege is tossed to [the hangman]: he seizes him, stretches him, ties him to a horizontal cross, he raises his arm; there is a horrible silence; there is no sound but that of bones cracking under the bars, and the shrieks of the victim. He unties him. He puts him on the wheel; the shattered limbs are entangled in the spokes; the head hangs down; the hair stands up, and the mouth gaping open like a furnace from time to time emits only a few bloodstained words to beg for death. [The hangman] has finished. His heart is beating, but it is with joy: he congratulates himself, he says in his heart "Nobody quarters as well as I." . . . Is he a man? Yes. God

receives him in his shrines, and allows him to pray. He is not a criminal. Nevertheless, no tongue dares declare that he is virtuous, that he is an honest man, that he is estimable. No moral praise seems appropriate for him, for everyone else is assumed to have relations with human beings: he has none. And yet all greatness, all power, all subordination rest on the executioner. He is the terror and the bond of human association. Remove this mysterious agent from the world, and in an instant order yields to chaos: thrones fall, society disappears.[3]

Conservative scholar Peter Viereck examined authoritarian conservatism in his work *Conservatism: From John Adams to Churchill,* in which he analyzed the "rival brands" of early conservatism, dividing them into two founding schools: that of Edmund Burke and that of Maistre.[4] Viereck characterized Burkean conservatism as "the moderate brand" while Maistre's as "reactionary."* Burkean conservatism was not authoritarian but constitutionalist, while Maistrean conservatism was "authoritarian in its stress on the authority" being granted to "some traditional elite."[5] Although most conservative scholars choose to ignore Maistre, treating him as an unwelcome member of the family,[6] his work is significant in that it suggests that authoritarianism was an integral component of conservatism at the time of its founding. Authoritarian conservatism had subsided by the time Andrew Jackson was elected president in 1828, and in the ensuing years (literally from

---

*Joseph de Maistre's conservatism (and his Catholicism) was, in fact, brutally authoritarian. However, Owen Bradley's work, *A Modern Maistre: The Social and Political Thought of Joseph de Maistre* (Lincoln: University of Nebraska Press, 1999) seeks "to make of Maistre the ambiguous, equivocal, un-decidable figure . . . rather than a monster plain and simple" (viii). According to the book's editor, "Bradley makes a convincing argument that, far from wallowing in a morbid fascination with violence, as is often suggested, Maistre sees ritual sacrifice as spiritualizing and minimizing violence needed to maintain social order" (*American Historical Review* [December 2000] at http://www. historyco operative.org/cgi-bin/justtop.cgi?). However Maistre is viewed, his authoritarianism raises troubling questions for any modern democracy.

the age of Jackson until recently) it was quiescent.[7] Today, however, a neo-Maistrean brand of conservatism is on the rise.

Dunn and Woodard paused in their study of the American conservative tradition to compare authoritarian conservatism with libertarianism and traditional conservatism. They provided an illuminating contrast.

> Authoritarian conservatism begins with basic conservative beliefs—order, distrust of change, belief in traditional values—and branches in the direction of favoring state power to protect these beliefs. Libertarianism has an entirely different set of core beliefs which are based upon nineteenth-century liberalism. Those beliefs subordinate the order of a community to the desire for individuality and stress personal rights over personal responsibilities. Libertarians move away from state power to secure maximum liberty for the individual. Authoritarian conservatives are like traditional conservatives in their belief in established values, while libertarians are like traditional conservatives in their desire for limited government. Traditional conservatives and libertarians, however, differ in the degree of their belief in limited government. Libertarians are extreme in their opposition to state power while traditional conservatives are more moderate in their opposition. Traditional conservatives are much more likely to accept some state power than are libertarians.[8]

Two factions of conservatism currently embrace a contemporary adaptation of authoritarian conservatism: neoconservatives and social conservatives.* Neoconservatives are a relatively small group of social-

---

*There appears to be no national poll of Republicans indicating how many identify themselves as "authoritarians." I did, however, locate an informal poll taken by libertarians at the Texas GOP conventions in 2002 and 2004. While less than scientific, it is suggestive. Some 339 attendees at the 2004 convention indicated whether they were: "conservatives" (like George W. Bush, Ronald Reagan, and Jack Kemp), "social conservatives" (like Dan Quayle and Pat Robertson), dominance authoritarians, with significant, if not disproportionate, influence. Social conservatives, whose core members are Christian conservatives, comprise the largest and most cohesive faction of conservatism. They are, by and large, typical right-wing authoritarian followers. Both neoconservatives and social conservatives include countless conservatives without conscience within their ranks.

Authoritarian Policies of Neoconservatism

Neoconservatism first surfaced in the public during the Reagan administration. More recently its interest in, and influence on, American foreign policy has drawn a great deal of attention. One of the more colorful (and accurate) descriptions of the typical neoconservative comes from Philip Gold, who justifiably described himself as having "impeccable conservative credentials and long experience in the national-security field," as well as being "a grumpy old Marine (a former intelligence officer), who has grown infuriated with and appalled by the conservative embrace of disaster" served up by neoconservatives. Gold, a former Georgetown University professor, described neoconservative foreign policy wonks as "a new aristocracy of aggression that combines 19th-century Prussian pigheadedness with a most un-Prussian inability to read a man or a ledger book, and a near total lack of military—let alone combat—experience. Ask these people to show you

---

"authoritarian conservatives" (like Pat Buchanan and Bill Bennett), "liberals" (like Kennedy, Clinton, Kerry, Gore, and Gephardt—it seems liberals do not have first names in Texas), "centrists" (like Colin Powell, John McCain, and Ross Perot), or "moderate libertarians" (like Milton Friedman, Jeb Bush, Jesse Ventura, Steve Forbes, and Barry Goldwater). The examples provided for each category make the poll less than accurate, because some of the examples do not necessarily match their labels. The poll revealed, however, that 6.8 percent of those responding declared themselves "authoritarian," with 9.9 percent of these being women and 4.6 percent being men. Very similar scores were recorded at the 2002 convention. See: "The Republican Liberty Caucus of Texas" at http://tx.rlc.org/events/2004_06_04_result.htm.

their wounds and they'll probably wave a *Washington Post* editorial at you."*

The *Christian Science Monitor* describes neoconservatives as mostly liberal Jewish intellectuals who became disenchanted with the left in the 1960s and 1970s. By the 1980s they had become Republicans, having found a home for their aggressive policies in the Reagan administration. According to the *Monitor,* what distinguishes neoconservatives from other conservatives is their desire for militarily imposed nation building. They believe the United States should "use its unrivaled power—forcefully if necessary—to promote its values around the world." Neoconservatives do not trust multilateral institutions to keep world peace; rather they believe the United States must do it.[9] An American empire is a perfectly plausible scenario for neoconservatives; containment is a policy they believe is outmoded. Neoconservatives view Israel as "a key outpost of democracy in a region ruled by despots." They want to transform the Middle East with democracy, starting with Iraq. Today the foreign policies of neoconservatives and of the Bush administration are fundamentally synonymous.

I. Lewis "Scooter" Libby, Vice President Dick Cheney's former chief of staff and national security adviser—and he was also an assistant to the president—is an überneoconservative, a personification of the true believer who has been involved with neoconservatism since its arrival in Washington during the Reagan administration. Libby is also

---

*In 2004 Gold published *Take Back the Right: How the Neocons and the Religious Right Have Betrayed the Conservative Movement* (New York: Carroll & Graf, 2004), where he refers to the neocons as "the America-must-lead-because-America-must-lead; let's-go-thump-somebody crowd," and the religious right as "the Christ-died-so-we-could-tell-you-what-to-do brigades." His book is a lament for today's conservatism by a man who spent much of his life promoting a conservative agenda. "It would be many years before I realized that conservatism was content with the lowest common denominator, and that, in the end, conservatism would rather complain than create," he concluded.

an exemplary authoritarian.* Until he was indicted by special counsel Patrick Fitzgerald for perjury, false statements, and obstruction of justice relating to the investigation of the leak of CIA operative Valerie Plame's covert status, Libby was relatively unknown, a "behind the throne" man with unique influence within the Bush/Cheney White House. Libby worked with Cheney when he was Secretary of Defense under Bush I, and while at the Defense Department he assisted his former Yale professor Paul Wolfowitz in drafting a defense policy guidance paper calling for unilaterally preemptive wars and the invasion of Iraq—a decade before the 9/11 terror attacks. (When this highly controversial document was leaked to the press, Bush I had the policy withdrawn, assuring the world that this was not the way Americans were thinking.) Later Libby would help draft a report for the neoconservative Project for the New American Century entitled "Rebuilding America's Defenses—Strategy, Forces, and Resources for a New Century," which was merely a restatement of the early policy paper, but

---

*I discussed with Bob Altemeyer the applications his findings to persons who had not been tested anonymously, and while authoritarian traits may be obvious in their behavior, precisely categorizing them can be difficult. Altemeyer advised, "We know about right-wing authoritarians, and social dominators, *in general,* based upon how *most* of them have acted in various studies. But in every study some authoritarians acted differently, and when you take an individual person, you can expect he too will act differently some of the time—just as it is much easier to predict where a herd of cattle is heading than to predict whether any particular steer is presently going this way or that, frontward or even backward. Then social sciences produce generalizations, which a lot of people find useful information. But any generalization means there will be exceptions, and you will almost always run into some when you study the complexity of an individual. Almost all generally authoritarian people thus will have some nonauthoritarian wrinkles in their behavior." Accordingly, I have not attempted to get too precise in labeling the conspicuous authoritarian behavior of people like Scooter Libby and others. On the other hand some authoritarian behavior is too obvious not to label appropriately.

under Bush II it became the blueprint for the administration's defense policy.

Libby has been extremely aggressive in promoting the aims of neoconservatism. Reportedly:

> It was Libby—along with Paul Wolfowitz, Doug Feith, and a handful of other top aides at the Pentagon and White House— who convinced the president that the U.S. should go to war in Iraq. It was Libby who pushed Cheney to publicly argue that Saddam Hussein had ties to al Qaeda and 9/11. It was also Libby who prodded former Secretary of State Colin Powell to include specious reports about an alleged meeting between 9/11 terrorist Mohammed Atta and an Iraqi intelligence official in Powell's February 2003 speech to the United Nations.[10]

This, of course, turned out to be extremely bad advice but typical of authoritarian aggression. Libby no doubt took whatever steps were necessary to further the cause he believed in, even pushing dubious information with great self-righteousness.

The skulduggery that led to Libby's indictment is likewise characteristic of authoritarian behavior. Libby had sought to discredit the visit to Africa, by former ambassador Joseph Wilson, to determine if Niger was supplying yellowcake uranium to Iraq. Bush and Cheney had been claiming that Iraq's pursuit of uranium was evidence of their development of a nuclear capacity, thus providing a justification for a preemptive war. Wilson found the yellowcake report not true (in fact, it had been based on forged documents), and after the president made a contrary statement in his 2003 State of the Union address, Wilson publicly corrected the record. Libby was outraged and apparently believed that by claiming that Wilson's wife, Valerie Plame, a CIA operative involved in monitoring the proliferation of such weapons, had been involved in sending her husband to Niger, the trip would be perceived as some kind of boondoggle. In fact, she was not involved in the CIA's decision to ask her husband to make the trip, but Libby leaked her covert identity to members of the news media anyway. Under some circumstances it is a violation of the law to reveal the covert status of CIA operatives, for it not only places the agents themselves in jeopardy, but also their contacts. Surely Libby knew this, given his long experience with national security. When special counsel Patrick Fitzgerald investigated her exposure, Libby gave FBI agents and the grand jury false statements about the newspeople to whom he had revealed her name. As Altemeyer's work shows, authoritarians have little if any conscience when pursuing their causes, and reason gives way to expediency.

Many conservatives view the grandiose plans of neoconservatives and their aggressive implementation by people like Scooter Libby as overzealous and loaded with potentially terrifying consequences. By way of comparison, more traditional conservatives call for "realism" in foreign policy that they feel is more appropriate in this age of terrorism. Henry Kissinger and Brent Scowcroft champion this school of thought, and the *American Conservative,* a publication launched by Pat Buchanan, has urged that American self-interest be the controlling consideration in national security. "Realists take seriously the threat from international terrorism but keep it in historical perspective," a lead article reported. "They are also skeptical of the administration's claim that we face a more dangerous adversary now in al Qaeda than we did with the Soviet Union during the Cold War. After all, the Soviets had a huge nuclear arsenal, while our worst-case fears today are that al Qaeda might get one or two crude radiological 'dirty bombs.' Realism counsels prudent caution but not panic in our approach to the global War on Terror."[11]

Libertarians are likewise counseling prudence in responding to terror attacks, and they have urged the Bush administration to reign in its post-9/11 authoritarianism. The libertarian Cato Institute has asked government officials to "demonstrate courage rather than give in to their fears. Radical Islamic terrorists are not the first enemy that

America has faced. British troops burned the White House in 1814, the Japanese navy launched a surprise attack on Pearl Harbor, and the Soviet Union deployed hundreds of nuclear missiles that targeted American cities. If policymakers are serious about defending our freedom and our way of life, they must wage this war without discarding our traditional constitutional framework of limited government."[12] Similarly, economic conservatives, who favor free trade and elimination of government restraints and regulations, are also wary of granting the president unlimited power to deal with terrorism. They are uncomfortable with the unchecked and unbalanced Bush/Cheney presidency, and the conspicuously right-wing authoritarian Congress that compliantly cedes to the executive branch. For example, Norman Ornstein, a longtime student of the U.S. Congress who works for the economically conservative American Enterprise Institute, noted that the key oversight committees of Congress "shuttered their doors" at the outset of the Bush administration and that "the Bush Justice Department is to checks and balances what Paris Hilton is to chastity."[13] Most economic conservatives understand that authoritarianism is as faulty a strategy in government as it is in business.[14]

Neoconservatism's authoritarian strategies and its militarism have taken us into a preemptive war in Iraq, have encouraged us to wage war in Iran and North Korea as well, and have been the foundation for a foreign policy that has made America loathed all over the world.[15] It does not take the National Security Council but common sense to understand that the blowback for these actions may well be terror attacks on our children and grandchildren, not to mention ourselves. Many people believe that neoconservatives and many Republicans appreciate that they are more likely to maintain influence and control of the presidency if the nation remains under ever-increasing threats of terrorism, so they have no hesitation in pursuing policies that can provoke potential terrorists throughout the world.[16] Indeed, this is precisely the type of amoral, Machiavellian behavior that socially dominant personalities are known to employ.

Most conservatives have not publicly objected to the neoconservative, militaristic foreign policy of the Bush/Cheney administration,* a predictive failure in light of the fact that social scientists have established that authoritarians as followers tend to be relatively submissive to and unquestioning of presidential authority, particularly when they perceive the president's beliefs to be consistent with their own views— beliefs which they are expressing their support for. Thus, when the Bush/Cheney presidency adopted neoconservative policies and made them their own, they also became the policies subscribed to by their unquestioning authoritarian followers, the largest bloc of which is made up of Christian conservatives. American-style despotism is possible only if it has a large and influential base, and that potential exists in the religious right's active role in the political arena.

Authoritarian Origins of Social Conservatism

Appropriate recognition is seldom given to the authoritarians who launched social or cultural conservatism and made it an increasingly significant influence on conservative thinking. (As noted earlier, I believe the terms can be used interchangeably, notwithstanding efforts by some to define them separately.) Any representative list of the major players in launching this movement should include J. Edgar Hoover, Spiro T. Agnew, Phyllis Schlafly, and Paul Weyrich. Each, in his or her way, has made significant contributions by adding to the work of their

---

*We may never learn the full extent of the objections expressed by "realist" Republicans. For example, it is only reluctantly that former Bush I national security adviser Brent Scowcroft has spoken out, because he is a close friend of the former president Bush. But because none of his old friends, who now control American foreign policy, were listening, he wrote an August 15, 2002, *Wall Street Journal* op-ed, "Don't Attack Saddam: It would undermine our antiterror efforts." James Risen writes in *State of War: The Secret History of the CIA and the Bush Administration* (New York: Free Press, 2006) that the president "angrily hung-up the telephone" on his father, when he was expressing concerns about the "neoconservative ideologues" controlling the Bush II foreign policy.

predecessors; all are authoritarians. These individuals took what was but a thread within conservatism, and collectively their influence made it into the rope that now controls conservatism and Republican politics.*

J. EDGAR HOOVER

As the director of the Federal Bureau of Investigation, Hoover ruled like a despot. At each stage of his career, he also worked methodically at terrifying Americans and he appears to have been well aware that fear is a wonderful manipulator, particularly with authoritarian followers. Hoover ran the FBI from 1924, during the time of Coolidge, until he died in 1972 during Nixon's presidency. One FBI historian observes that "Hoover's conviction of his own righteousness and his insistence on compliance with his personal idiosyncrasies is graphically captured in his first manual of instructions, which he prepared immediately after becoming Director. Unlike later manuals, which were prepared with assistance, this one exudes Hoover's vigorous authoritarianism, his exaggerated sense of his own importance, his intolerance of individuality, and his extreme narrowness of vision."[17] Hoover biographies in fact reveal him to be a classic Double High authoritarian, a manipulative demagogue, with the worst traits of both right-wing authoritarians and social dominators.[18]

I myself witnessed Hoover successfully manipulate Attorney General John Mitchell, during one of my own more memorable meetings

---

*Social and religious elements, however, have been present from the outset. When writing *The Conservative Mind,* Russell Kirk, it will be recalled, declared "the essence of social conservatism is preservation of the ancient moral traditions of humanity." And Kirk's first canon called for belief in "a transcendent order, or body of natural law, which rules society as well as conscience." Inherent in Kirk's conservatism is the Burkean notion "of the state as ordained by God." George Nash, in *The Conservative Intellectual Movement in America,* explained that one segment of the modern conservative movement "urged a return to traditional religion and ethical absolutes and a rejection of the 'relativism' which had allegedly corroded Western values" (xv).

with the director. We had gathered in the attorney general's conference room following the death of four students and the wounding of nine others at Kent State University, when Ohio National Guardsmen opened fire during a noontime antiwar demonstration on May 4, 1970. Our agenda that day was to assess whether the Department of Justice should investigate aggressively what had happened at Kent State and why, but it became clear quickly that Hoover wanted to keep the FBI out of it, for reasons that were astounding. Hoover held forth at some length about how one of the young girls who had been killed was a "slut," and indeed he seemed to know more about her sex life than the events that had transpired during the shootings. His harangue was so disturbing that after the meeting I spoke with an attorney friend in the Civil Rights Division, which had jurisdiction over the situation. Hoover, he said, did not know what he was talking about, and many in the FBI were aware that he was trying to give President Nixon and Attorney General John Mitchell a way of avoiding a federal investigation.* Without Hoover's approval nothing happened at the bureau. His associate director, William Sullivan, later reported that Hoover was the only person "who could make decisions in the FBI." Sullivan added, "All the well-meaning people in the bureau did exactly what he told them, for if they didn't, they'd be pounding the pavement. They had to carry out his orders if they didn't want to sell their homes and take their children out of school."[19] After studying Hoover's behavior and activities, Dr. Harold Lief, Professor Emeritus of Psychiatry at the University of Pennsylvania, concluded he was "what is known as an Authoritarian Personality. Hoover would have made a perfect high-level Nazi."[20]

For decades, particularly in the 1950s and 1960s, Hoover was a

---

*While there have been several excellent books, not to mention a President's Commission on Campus Unrest, addressing the Kent State shootings, the facts remain contested as to exactly what happened that spring day. Hoover's slanders reveal a great deal about the man who should have sorted the facts out when memories where fresh by undertaking a full investigation.

public presence to be reckoned with in America. Presidents, who came and went, protected the nation from foreign invasion; Hoover, who held his post for almost a half century, protected the nation's "internal security" from mobsters, Nazis, communists, hippies, and antiwar protesters. He intimidated (and blackmailed) members of Congress and presidents (about whom he gathered information); and he helped foster McCarthyism by feeding often dubious information to the maniacal red-hunting senator. Hoover influenced the Supreme Court by using background investigations to disparage potential nominees he did not like and to promote those he did. He also aided Nixon's efforts to remove Justice Abe Fortas from the Court, and hoped to do the same (but failed) with Justice William O. Douglas. Hoover trained his FBI agents in the black arts of burglary and other surreptitious skills, and had them employed at his whim. He was a racist who sought to disable the civil rights movement; he refused to hire black FBI agents; and he tried to get Martin Luther King, Jr., to commit suicide. He rigged the Warren Commission investigation in a manner that still colors the nation's understanding of President Kennedy's assassination. How many innocent people were framed by Hoover's FBI— a prototype of authoritarian government—will never be known.

The peak of Hoover's career—the period when conservatives almost genuflected at the mention of his name—was during his crusade against communism. Conservative historian Paul Johnson describes McCarthyism, in which Hoover was deeply involved, as a time "when the hysterical pressure on the American people to conform came from the right of the political spectrum, and when the witch hunt was organized by conservative elements."[21] It was a time when Hoover preached a terrifying gospel about communism. His FBI hacks cranked out endless articles (regularly placed in national as well as local publications) and speeches (for FBI agents, members of Congress, Justice Department lawyers, and other government officials) explaining how communists, if they managed to infiltrate, would destroy the American family—its lifestyle, its homes, its ability to provide food for the table, and even the time parents had to dote on their children. And because the godless communists sought to destroy America's religions, Hoover warned that no American dare lose faith in God, for should they do so, communism would fill the void, and this would place them in hands worse than those of the devil. But luckily for his beleaguered countrymen, Hoover had solutions. For example, his ghost-written *Masters of Deceit; The Story of Communism in America and How to Fight It,* published in 1958, offered a six-point defense for defeating communism.* Hoover called for "[t]he sanctity of the individual, the need for mutual responsibility among Americans, a life transcending materialism, responsibility to future generations, that humans and not political parties should establish moral values, and that love triumph over hate," which all should be "part of a larger value system that guided the thoughts and actions of upstanding, moral Americans."[22] So loyal were Hoover's conservative followers that neither John F. Kennedy nor Richard Nixon dared to fire him, fearing conservative wrath.[23]

Now, however, Hoover has become so tarnished that both Republicans and Democrats in Congress have introduced legislation to remove his name from the FBI headquarters in Washington, the most visible remnant of his legacy.[24] Hoover's true legacy, however, is more subtle and insidious, for it was he with his fanaticism who planted the seeds from which contemporary social and cultural conservatism has grown. Hoover's focus on the American family and Christianity attracted an earlier generation of adamant anticommunists, who have become today's zealous social conservatives.

SPIRO T. AGNEW

One particularly enthusiastic Hoover admirer was Nixon's vice president, Spiro T. Agnew. His charismatic style and high office gave him a

---

*Given what is known about Hoover it is difficult to believe that he actually believed much of what he preached.

certain marquee appeal, and he was an early leader of the cultural war.[25] As governor of Maryland, Agnew had been a moderate, but by the time he became vice president he had moved toward the hard right. He appears to have been a solid right-wing authoritarian with social domination tendencies.* He certainly was not a Double High authoritarian like Hoover. At the Nixon White House Agnew had the job of currying conservative favor. Employing the rabble-rousing rhetoric of Pat Buchanan, Nixon dispatched Agnew to fight the cultural war, and the vice president delighted in unloading depth charges and assorted munitions assembled by Buchanan and others. In the fall of 1969, the war was escalated, and Agnew became the first high-profile conservative to go after the mainstream news media. For a half hour the vice president tore into the unaccountable power of the unelected newspeople, who decided what forty to fifty million Americans would learn of the day's events.[26] Nixon later wrote in his memoirs, with some delight, that "at the networks, there was pandemonium; all three decided to carry the speech live."

Agnew loved his work. "My mission is to awaken Americans to the need for sensible authority, to jolt good minds out of the lethargy of habitual acquiescence, to mobilize a silent majority that cherishes the right values but has been bulldozed for years into thinking those values are embarrassingly out of style."[27] His recurring themes and targets were "avowed anarchists and communists," "elitists," the "garbage of society," "thieves, traitors, and perverts," "radical liberals," and, of course the news media, whom he called "an effete corps of impudent snobs, a tiny fraternity of privileged men elected by no one and enjoying a monopoly sanctioned and licensed by the government. They are nattering nabobs of negativism." (They were also, for Agnew, the "hopeless, hysterical hypochondriacs of history.") Agnew's avowed

---

*The Eastern liberal establishment is not an "established authority" for an authoritarian conservative like Agnew, so his attacks were not against what he believed acceptable authority.

aim was "dividing the American people," which he called "positive polarization." He was delighted when he caused a ruckus. "I not only plead guilty to this charge, but I am somewhat flattered by it."[28] Conservative media loved Agnew's authoritarian aggression as well. A *Wall Street Journal* editorial approvingly noted that "Mr. Agnew's targets—the media, war protesters, and rebellious youth—are representative of a class that has enjoyed unusual moral and cultural authority through the 1960s." (The editors proceeded to detail the failings of these authorities, the "highbrows, the intellectual—the beautiful people—Eastern liberal elite.")[29] Thus, with Nixon in charge and taking the high road, the early skirmishes of the cultural war were launched by Agnew taking the low one. But the forced resignations of both men put the cultural war on hold. Others, meanwhile, quietly went about the work of building an army and drawing up future plans.

PHYLLIS SCHLAFLY

The Equal Rights Amendment passed Congress on March 22, 1972, and was sent to the states for ratification, with a seven-year deadline. Within the first year, it was quickly approved by twenty-two of the necessary thirty-eight states.[30] Then came Phyllis Schlafly. Whether one agrees or disagrees with her politics, she is a remarkable woman.* She appears to have a moderately right-wing authoritarian personality,

---

*Schlafly graduated from college in 1944 at nineteen years of age with a Phi Beta Kappa key, and received her master's degree in government from Harvard a year later. She twice ran unsuccessfully for Congress. She has long been involved in Republican politics at the state and national levels, once chairing the Illinois Federation of Republican Women. Ms. Schlafly obtained a law degree at Washington University Law School, and worked with her husband in a legal assistance (ACLU-type) organization for conservative causes. To date, she has written over twenty books; her monthly "The Phyllis Schlafly Report" to conservative activists is now in its thirty-eighth year; her syndicated column appears in about 100 newspapers; her radio commentaries are heard daily on some 460 stations; and her radio talk show on education, called *Phyllis Schlafly Live,* appears on 45 stations. She has also raised six children.

but she does not carry much of the unpleasant baggage that many of these authoritarians do. Her authoritarianism is more akin to that of the strict schoolmarm.

With miraculous managerial skills, Schlafly assembled and trained women in key remaining states to block ratification of the ERA. In a standard authoritarian ploy, she relied on fear, claiming that the ERA would deny women the right to support by their husbands, that it would eliminate privacy rights and result in unisex public toilets, that it would mean that women would be drafted into the military and sent into combat, and that it would fully protect abortion rights and homosexual marriages. None of this was true, but her powerful propaganda got the attention of a lot of women who had never been particularly interested in politics. The authoritarian leader's use of misleading information to gain control is a consistently successful technique for them. As a *New Yorker* profile observed of Schlafly's style, "While Ann Coulter and Laura Ingraham were still playing tea party, she recognized that deliberation was no match for diatribe, and logic no equal to contempt. She was, in this way, a woman ahead of her time."[31]

Schlafly did not just organize women, but also persuaded businesses (like the insurance companies) and various religious groups to join her effort.[32] By 1980 Schlafly had successfully killed the ERA and had given birth to an antifeminist, so-called profamily movement that supported other social conservative causes. Schlafly's activism evolved way beyond her allegiance to the "Goldwater-Reagan" (her term) school of conservatism (which she sums up as "lower taxes, limited government, fiscal integrity—and American military superiority, because everybody is safer that way"), and provided a corps of trained volunteers whose grassroots efforts have changed conservatism.

Not unlike Pat Buchanan, however, and notwithstanding her authoritarian conservatism, Phyllis Schlafly regularly takes issue with radical Republican proposals relating to domestic policy and foreign affairs. She also attacks the Bush/Cheney big-government policies and fiscal irresponsibility. Importantly, she remains a guardian of civil liberties at a time when other conservative authoritarians have willingly and unquestioningly trusted "the authorities'" claim that only the terrorists need worry. She has tried to correct abuses in the USA Patriot Act, explaining that "the problem that confronts America today is **foreign-sponsored** terrorism, and we must draw a bright line of different treatment between U.S. citizens and aliens. Our government should monitor the whereabouts of aliens, but **not** require U.S. citizens to relinquish our freedom"[33] (bold emphasis is in her original). To oppose the extension of the Patriot Act, Schlafly joined with former Republican congressman Bob Barr of Georgia and the ACLU in forming Patriots to Restore Checks and Balances. Schlafly's example illustrates that authoritarians can be effective leaders without being social dominators.

Paul Weyrich

The same cannot be said of Paul Weyrich, whose early work complemented that of Phyllis Schlafly in the development of social conservatism. Both Schlafly and Weyrich were once strident anticommunists, Hoover's vigilant Americans. They continued the culture war that Agnew and Nixon had started, and their principal contribution was mustering the troops, working from the bottom up.

Weyrich has been described by friendly observers as "the Lenin of social conservatism—a revolutionary with a rare talent for organization," and while his stature within social conservatism is waning, it remains significant.[34] Weyrich is a master of the art of direct-mail fund-raising and is best known as the "funding father" of modern conservatism. He believed conservatives needed a Washington-based think tank comparable to the once liberal (now moderate) Brookings Institution, so along with a colleague from Capitol Hill, Edwin Feuler, Weyrich established the Heritage Foundation in 1973. Today Heritage is the wealthy granddaddy of conservative think thanks.[35] These organizations have become the marketing arms of contemporary conservatism, providing various factions an imprimatur of scholarship, and none more than social conservatives. Much of their "thinking" supports their particular "authority," and in this sense they are efficient authoritarian tools. They devote significant resources, and intellectual firepower, to demolishing policies and programs on the liberal agenda.[36]

Barry Goldwater described Weyrich as "a bull-headed, stubborn, son-of-bitch," and observed that "Weyrich doesn't really understand how Washington works, but he thinks he does."[37] In his memoir he worried that Weyrich and other social conservatives were "pushing [their] special social agendas . . . at the risk of compromising constitutional rights," an agenda that threatened to splinter Republicans. Weyrich "preached little or no spirit of compromise—[no] political give-and-take." He "failed to appreciate that politics is the ordinary stuff of daily living, while the spiritual life represents eternal values and goals." Goldwater added, "Public business—that's all politics is—is often making the best of a mixed bargain." Social conservatives, nonetheless, stressed "the politics of absolute moral right and wrong. And, of course, they are convinced of their absolute rightness."[38] The senator was addressing the second phase of Weyrich's activism, when the latter helped organize the religious right. In a profile that recognized his authoritarian influence, the *Washington Times* noted that Weyrich "helped bring [conservatism] structure, discipline and, gradually, dominance" over the Republican Party.[39] Weyrich may be a Double High authoritarian, and his authoritarianism is, at times, brutal.

Weyrich once admitted, and many believe only half in jest, that "to gather all of [his] enemies together" would require "RFK Stadium."[40] He calls himself a "cultural conservative," and in doing so he explains that what is important to him is opposition to legal abortion, stricter divorce laws, and prayer in public schools. *Washington Post* reporter E. J. Dionne described Weyrich's outlook as a "dour, almost medieval, pessimism."[41] Not unlike many Christian authoritarians, Weyrich has not hidden his anti-Semitism. At the outset of the Bush administration, Weyrich published an Easter message in which he stated, "Christ was crucified by the Jews. . . . He was not what the

Jews had expected so they considered Him a threat. Thus He was put to death."[42] (It is impossible to believe that Weyrich, a deacon in the Melkite Catholic Church, does not know that the Romans crucified Jesus, and that his libel has been responsible for the persecution of Jews throughout history.)

During the 1980s and early 1990s the news media frequently turned to Weyrich for the conservative Catholic view of the religious right, and with typical authoritarian aggressiveness, mixed with much self-righteousness, he minced no words in denouncing conservatives who failed to live up to his standards.[43] In 1995 the *New York Times* listed Weyrich in the top twenty-five individuals of the conservative "attack machine," which it described as "specialists in bare-knuckle attacks on political opponents."[44] But his most significant influence on conservatism was the role he played in bringing fundamentalist Protestants and conservative Catholics into the political arena. These Christian conservatives almost by definition are right-wing authoritarians.* Unhappy in the late 1970s, when the Heritage Foundation's financial backers did not wish to get into social issues, Weyrich turned his organizing skills and energy to drawing Christian conservatives into the movement. He remains active in that effort to this day, and the Heritage Foundation later joined the fold.

The Religious Right: The Great Army of Authoritarian Followers

"The Christian Right," one scholar observed, "owe[s] its existence to two Catholics and a Jew. Richard Viguerie, Paul Weyrich and Howard Phillips. . . . They believed that . . . there were many socio-moral is-

---

*"Acceptance of traditional religious beliefs appears to have more to do with having a personality rich in authoritarian submission, authoritarian aggression, and conventionalism, than with beliefs per se. . . . Authoritarians just absorb whatever beliefs their authorities teach." Bob Altemeyer, *The Authoritarian Specter* (Cambridge, MA: Harvard University Press, 1996), 146–47.

sues that could serve as the basis for an organized conservative movement"; accordingly, in 1979, they "persuaded Jerry Falwell, a popular
fundamentalist Baptist preacher from Lynchburg, Virginia, to lead an
organization they named the 'Moral Majority.'"[45] This was the birth of
the modern religious right. It had not escaped the notice of Viguerie,
Weyrich, and Phillips that in 1976 long-dormant Christian fundamentalists had been attracted to the presidential campaign of born-
again presidential candidate Jimmy Carter, and their vote helped the
former Georgia governor defeat the incumbent president, Gerald
Ford. After having their beliefs ridiculed during the 1925 trial of John
Scopes for teaching evolution in the classroom in violation of a law
fundamentalists had persuaded the Tennessee legislature to adopt, they
had withdrawn from any and all political activity. Jimmy Carter's
evangelicalism kindled the interest of many of these fundamentalists,
who like Carter called themselves evangelicals.

Following Carter's election as president, the news media, strug-
gling to understand the evangelical phenomenon, began blurring Christian fundamentalists with evangelicals, with neither group happy to
be lumped in with the other. Considerable confusion still exists about
the terms "Christian fundamentalist" and "evangelical Christian," and
even those who fall within these ranks use the terms loosely, and often
interchangeably. In fact, not until the reelection of the second evangelical president did even religion scholars fully sort the matter out.[46]
In December 2004, after George Bush's success the nonpartisan *National Journal* decided it was time to clarify a confusion that had gone
on far too long, and they were successful in distinguishing the two, as
explained below.

Fundamentalist Christians retreated from politics and much of
modern life after the Scopes trial in 1925, but their children, when
they reached adulthood in the early 1940s, wanted to return to a more
active public existence. This new generation called themselves "neo-
evangelicals," and in 1942, they founded the National Association of

Evangelicals, dropping the "neo."* Unlike their parents, who "practiced extreme forms of separation, refusing to cooperate in common ventures with others who did not believe as they did," the evangelicals "were bridge builders and were more willing to give some credit to, and treat with charity, those with whom they disagree." The evangelicals, however, continued to share their parents' tenets of faith. "Both believed in a literal interpretation of the Bible and hold that Christians must individually accept Christ and be born again, according to Christ's words in John 3:5–8: 'Verily, verily, I say unto thee, Except a man be born of water and [of] Spirit, he cannot enter into the kingdom of God. That which is born of flesh is flesh; and that which is born of Spirit is spirit. Marvel not that I said unto thee, Ye must be born again.'"[47] Thus, in a broad sense, the term "fundamentalist" covers evangelicals, but evangelicals in fact distinguish themselves from fundamentalists, and vice verse. (Except as noted, I have distinguished them. I use the term "conservative Christians" or "Christian conservatives" to cover both Protestants and Catholics.)

By 1978 increasingly politically active evangelicals had grown disenchanted with Jimmy Carter, whom they had helped put in office. They did not like his progressive Democrat policies, in general, but, in particular, they were offended by a proposal by the Internal Revenue Service to deny tax-deductible status to *all* private schools, including private Christian ones. Carter's apparent acceptance of the IRS proposal caused uproar within the evangelical community. Reverend Tim LaHaye, the best-selling Christian author and one of the founders of the Moral Majority, met with Carter at the White House to discuss the measure, along with other concerns conservative Christians had about his progressive policies. Following their meeting, LaHaye reportedly left the Oval Office, lowered his head, and prayed: "God, we

---

*Today the National Association of Evangelicals claims to represent an astounding thirty million members and to speak for over forty million evangelicals in the United States. See: http://www.nae.net.

have got to get this man out of the White House and get someone in here who will be aggressive about bringing back traditional moral values."[48] That is exactly what conservative Christians did. They worked like bees—literally millions of them devoted themselves to this task— and by 1981 they had significantly helped to put Ronald Reagan in the Oval Office.

Today evangelicals comprise the core of the religious right, and white Protestant evangelicals, depending on the poll, range from a quarter to a third of the electorate. A Zogby poll reported that conservative Christians account for an astounding 58 percent of all Republicans.[49] In 2000, 68 percent of white Protestant evangelicals voted for Bush and Cheney. In 2004 that statistic rose to 78 percent.[50] But it is not at the presidential level that conservative Christians have their greatest impact. "The religious right's power lies in the lower parts of the Republican machinery, in precinct meetings and the like," the *Economist* reported.[51] Without the support of Christian conservatives Republicans cannot even get nominated to local, state, and national offices, because they have become the filter through which all Republicans must pass today. Christian conservatives have a virtual lock on state and local Republican politics, and have totally outmaneuvered their opposition. "In American politics," wrote Joel Rogers of the University of Wisconsin, "who controls the states controls the nation. The right understands this, and for a generation has waged an unrelenting war to take over state government in America. It has succeeded, in large part because it hasn't faced any serious progressive counter effort."[52]

Who are these people? In 2004 the Pew Trust sponsored a two-day seminar for leading journalists, calling the gathering "Toward an Understanding of Religion and American Public Life." Religion historian Mark Noll, an evangelical who has authored several books on the subject, led a discussion about contemporary evangelicals. He explained their core religious beliefs, and noted that these religious commitments by themselves have not resulted in a cohesive, institutionally compact, or clearly demarcated group of Christians. There is, in reality, a large network of churches, voluntary societies, books and periodicals, and personal connections, as well as varying levels of belief and practice that fall under the evangelical label.[53] Noll pointed out that although certain Supreme Court rulings had caused evangelicals to become increasingly politically active, *Roe v. Wade* had been the tipping point. Before *Roe,* evangelicals were no more political than Billy Graham, thus either apolitical or unobtrusively political, and not active in politics. After *Roe,* self-appointed leaders within the evangelical movement became militant activists. "Baptists [ministers] Jerry Falwell and Timothy LaHaye, and the lay psychologist James Dobson, entered politics with a vengeance during the 1970s and 1980s," said Noll. They "created the new religious right and have made conservative evangelical support so important for the Republican Party since the campaigns of Ronald Reagan." Pat Robertson's 1988 presidential campaign, albeit unsuccessful in even coming close to getting the Republican nomination, further politicized a large segment of the evangelical community, Noll added.

Noll candidly acknowledged the authoritarian nature of evangelicals. Speaking as an evangelical and a historian of evangelicalism, he noted its incompatibly with the give-and-take of politics because of the rigidity of its beliefs. Noll said he wants evangelicals to learn "new ways of being present in the public space without believing that [they] have to *dominate* the public space" (emphasis in original transcript). Evangelical Christianity, he explained, is an intolerant religion, unable to say "your religion is fine with you; my religion is fine with me." Rather "evangelical religion is offensive. It claims forthrightly that there is one, and only one, way to God," and that is their way. The world has evolved, and Noll realized that evangelicals, so far, have not.[54]

Several attendees at the Pew conference referred to the work of a University of North Carolina sociologist, Christian Smith, who has studied how rank-and-file evangelicals think. One conferee said of Smith's work that it showed that the rank-and-file is "a lot nicer than their leaders!"[55] Smith's work supports the notion that the religious right's political thinking and behavior may be less than uniform, and that the leaders of the Christian right do not necessarily speak for evangelicals as a whole.[56] While this may be true of the segment of the population investigated by Smith and his collaborators, their sample appears unrepresentative.[57] In the end, I found that the observations of Mark Noll—who deals with a wide array of evangelical brothers and sisters, day in and day out—as well as those of politically attuned observers such as Cal Thomas, a conservative syndicated columnist and Fox News commentator, and former president Jimmy Carter seemed more insightful and revelatory. All of these individuals have been critical of Christians in politics while remaining true to their faiths.*

Cal Thomas, a conservative Christian who once served as vice president of communications for Jerry Falwell's Moral Majority, has joined journalist and evangelical minister Ed Dobson in making "a strong case for the church to lay down its impotent weapons of political activism."[58] Based on his experience at the heart of Christian right politics, Thomas said he believes that all the evangelical energy now devoted to politics could be better directed toward living and sharing the gospel. He has concluded that neither "our individual or collective cultural problems can be altered exclusively, or even mainly, through the political process." Thomas found that "the marriage of religion and politics almost always compromises the gospel," for "[p]olitics is all about compromise." The conflation of church and state has resulted in the church's getting "its theological pocket picked." "Whenever the

---

*The observations of evangelicals like Noll, Thomas, and Carter are corroborated in studies such as John C. Green's *The Christian Right in American Politics: Marching to the Millennium* (Washington, DC: Georgetown University Press, 2003) and Geoffrey Layman's *The Great Divide: Religious and Cultural Conflict in American Party Politics* (New York: Columbia University Press, 2001). The latter scholarly study drops the rhetoric and uses the best polling data available to analyze exactly what its title describes. Layman illustrates the religious right's polarizing impact on the nation, and correctly, it appears, predicts this will continue into the new millennium.

church cozies up to political power," he continued, "it loses sight of its all-important mission to change the world from the inside-out."[59]

Not surprisingly, Thomas does not approve of the political tactics employed by Christian conservatives. For example, when fund-raising, "they identify an enemy: homosexuals, abortionists, Democrats, or 'liberals' in general," he explained. Then, these enemies are accused, falsely, of being out to "get us" or "impose their morality on the rest of us or destroy the country." An action plan is offered—"We will oppose the enemies and ensure that they do not take over America"— and a plea for funds follows.[60] The focus is inevitably negative, and often the claims are outrageous, such as Pat Robertson's claim that God wanted him "to help usher in the Second Coming." Robertson denied making such a statement, and when Thomas produced a copy of the fund-raising letter in question, he was immediately vilified. Thomas noted that Robertson and others "must constantly have enemies, conspiracies, and opponents as well as play the role of righteous victim in order to get people to send in money." Understandably, Thomas is troubled by the irony that the Bible calls on Christians to love their enemies, "whether they be homosexuals, abortionists, Democrats, or liberals."[61]

Former president Jimmy Carter speaks with unique insight about mixing politics and religion. In *Our Endangered Values: America's Moral Crisis,* Carter wrote that this nation's leaders once "extolled state and local autonomy, attempted to control deficit spending, avoided foreign adventurism, minimized long-term peacekeeping commitments, preserved the separation of church and state, and protected civil liberties and personal privacy." However, today's leaders—he does not mention Christian conservatives because it is obvious to whom he is referring—have placed far more divisive issues at the center of their platform: "abortion, the death penalty, science versus religion, women's rights, the separation of religion and politics, homosexuality." These debates, he noted, have divided the nation and threatened America's traditional values. Carter said he believes the most important factor in that divisiveness is that "fundamentalists have become increasingly influential in both religion and government, and have managed to change the nuance and subtleties of historic debate into black-and-white rigidities and the personal derogation of those who dare to disagree." He added, "Narrowly defined theological beliefs have been adopted as the rigid agenda of a political party."[62]

The former president went on to describe religious fundamentalists based on his personal observations and experiences. (Carter appeared to use the term "fundamentalists" as including highly conservative evangelicals.) He said that, invariably, "fundamentalist movements are led by authoritarian males who consider themselves to be superior to others and, within religious groups, have an overwhelming commitment to subjugate women and to dominate their fellow believers." He found that these people believe the past is better than the present; they draw clear distinctions between themselves, as true believers, and others; they are "militant in fighting against any challenges to their beliefs"; and they are "often angry" and sometimes resort "to verbal or even physical abuse against those who interfere with the implementation of their agenda." Carter summarized the characteristics of fundamentalism as "rigidity, domination, and exclusion,"[63] a description that would apply equally to the authoritarian personalities introduced in the last chapter.

While neoconservatives are not religious fundamentalists, Carter said he believes that they hold related views. He had observed firsthand how neoconservatives evolved from criticizing his foreign policy—when he attempted to "impose liberalization and democratization" on other countries—to embracing his goals but to achieving them by employing very different means. Carter sought to spread democracy through diplomacy, while the neoconservatives "now seem to embrace aggressive and unilateral intervention in foreign affairs, especially to advance U.S. military and political influence in the Middle East."[64]

A long-tenured Sunday school teacher, Carter also adroitly uses his King James Bible to show how conservative Christians quote selectively from scripture to attack homosexuals and women, to oppose the separation of church and state, and to support other issues on their political agenda. Carter demonstrated that the Bible actually supports a much kinder, more loving, and more progressive ethos, but in the end, he said, he believes Bible quoting in politics is fruitless. "There is no need to argue about such matters, because it is human nature to be both selective and subjective in deriving the most convenient meaning by careful choices from the 30,400 or so biblical verses."[65]

Former senator John Danforth of Missouri (who served from 1976 until 1995) is an ordained Episcopal minister and a partisan Republican, and has made points similar to those of Jimmy Carter. Danforth has been called a "right-wing zealot in moderate's clothing."[66] Certainly he was to the right of Goldwater on the issue of abortion when they were colleagues in the Senate. Danforth cosponsored a proposed amendment to the Constitution that would guarantee legal protection to unborn children and overturn *Roe v. Wade*. Even he believes that conservative Christians have crossed the line.

Danforth wrote an op-ed for the *New York Times* in response to the insistence of Christian conservatives that the federal government intervene to save the life of Terri Schiavo. Speaking on behalf of mainstream Christians, Danforth observed, "When, on television, we see a person in a persistent vegetative state, one who will never recover, we believe that allowing the natural and merciful end to her ordeal is more loving than imposing government power to keep her hooked up to a feeding tube." He went on to describe in some detail (a selection of his statements are quoted and bulleted below) how conservative Christians operate and the impact they are having at the national level:

• [C]onservative Christians have presented themselves as representing the one authentic Christian perspective on politics . . .

[when] equally devout [mainstream] Christians come to very different conclusions.

- Many conservative Christians approach politics with a certainty that they know God's truth, and that they can advance the kingdom of God through governmental action. So they have developed a political agenda that they believe advances God's kingdom.

- In the [past] decade . . . American politics has been characterized by two phenomena: the increased activism of the Christian right, especially in the Republican Party, and the collapse of bipartisan collegiality. [It is not] a stretch to suggest a relationship between the two.

- [Mainstream Christians] reject the notion that religion should present a series of wedge issues useful at election time for energizing a political base. [Rather they] believe it is God's work to practice humility, to wear tolerance on our sleeves, to reach out to those with whom we disagree, and to overcome the meanness we see in today's politics.[67]

Religious Authoritarianism

When Christian conservatives take their religious beliefs into the political arena, they also carry their authoritarianism with them. Studies (cited earlier in a footnote) show that the "acceptance of traditional religious beliefs appear to have more to do with having a personality rich in authoritarian submission, authoritarian aggression, and conventionalism, than with the beliefs per se."[68] Bob Altemeyer offers a convincing explanation for why right-wing authoritarians are characteristically religious. Authoritarian parents transfer their beliefs to children through religious instruction. Christian conservatives tend to emanate from strict religious backgrounds, and often prevent their children from being exposed to broader and different views by sending them to schools with like-thinking children, or by home schooling them. This, in turn, results in an authoritarian outlook that remains strong during adolescence—the period when authoritarian personalities are formed and then taken into adult life.

Christian conservatives' primary tool in reinforcing authoritarianism is preaching fear, and no one does so more consistently than the head of the Christian Coalition, Pat Robertson. I met Robertson in 1982, when he invited me to appear on his television program, *The 700 Club*, the ostensible reason being to promote my recently published book, *Lost Honor*. I was told that his Christian Broadcasting Network reached over one hundred million homes, and that *The 700 Club* had a large following. While authors do not pass up such opportunities, I knew the book was not exactly normal fare for his audience, and I had little doubt that I was being checked out, for it was subtly suggested there was a place for me in this politically active Christian world. For my part, I certainly gave no sign that I was interested in the politics of Christian conservatism, for I had long believed that both religion and politics suffer when they are mixed. Robertson was a congenial and engaging host who wears his Cheshire cat grin both on and off camera. Even back in 1982 it was apparent that CBN was a substantial operation that was likely to grow, for viewers kept sending Robertson money. I was given a tour and saw a small army opening mail to retrieve five dollars here and five hundred dollars there, which arrived daily by the truckload. In the end, all that came of my appearance on *The 700 Club* was that Pat Robertson, of whom I had been only vaguely aware, was now on my radar. I have now been observing him for over two decades.

The Americans United for Separation of Church and State has also long been monitoring Robertson's assorted publications and *The 700 Club*. In 1996 Robert Boston, assistant director of communications for Americans United for Separation of Church and State, published *The Most Dangerous Man in America? Pat Robertson and the*

Rise of the Christian Coalition. From this account, and from my own knowledge, Robertson seems to possess all the key characteristics of a Double High authoritarian.*

According to Boston, Robertson's domineering personality was apparent from the earliest days of his born-again experience, when he headed off to a month-long religious retreat in Canada while his wife was seven months pregnant. Despite the fact that she had another small child to care for and the family was desperately poor, Robertson insisted on taking the trip. Later, when he went to purchase the UHF television station that would become the base of his operation, "with considerable bluster, Robertson confronted the owner . . . with the announcement, 'I'm Pat Robertson. God has sent me here to buy your television station.'"⁶⁹ Since 1987, Robertson has been calling for the government to assassinate foreign leaders he does not like. For example, he has said, "I know it sounds somewhat Machiavellian and evil, to think that you could send a squad in to take out somebody like Osama bin Laden, or to take out the head of North Korea. But isn't it better to do something like that, to take out Milosevic, to take out Saddam Hussein, rather than to spend billions and billions of dollars on a war that harms innocent civilians and destroys the infrastructure of a country? It would just seem so much more practical to have that flexibility."⁷⁰

As with most Double Highs, Robertson does not view women as equals. On one occasion he proclaimed, "There's never been a woman Grandmaster chess player. And if, you know, once you get one, then I'll buy some of the feminism, but until that point," he was having nothing to do with the female mind.** He contemporaneously issued

*While Robertson has many traits of social dominators and right-wing authoritarians, I am focusing only on those directly relating to the defining elements of social dominance, and indirectly to his right-wing authoritarianism. These elements are domination, opposition to equality, desire for personal power, and amorality.

**At the time he made the statement, however, Zsuza Polgar, at twenty-one years of age, had already become the first woman ever to earn the designation

a fund-raising letter declaring that the "feminist agenda is not about equal rights for women. It is about a socialist, anti-family political movement that encourages women to leave their husbands, kill their children, practice witchcraft, destroy capitalism, and become lesbians."[71] Robertson has an unequivocal view of a woman's true role: "The woman should be in submission to the man," he declared flatly. On racial equality, Robertson remains silent. His father, Willis Robertson, who served fourteen years in the House of Representatives and twenty in the Senate, made a career of blocking civil rights legislation. He was one of nineteen senators to sign the infamous Southern Manifesto criticizing the Supreme Court's ruling in *Brown v. Board of Education*. Pat, a bit less blatantly, "supported the apartheid government in South Africa until the very end."[72]

The most compelling evidence of his desire for personal power is his bid to become president of the United States. After purportedly being told by God, "I want you to run for president," Robertson launched a somewhat less than heavenly campaign, but one certainly befitting a Double High. Boston reported that only days after he announced his candidacy, the "*Wall Street Journal* broke a story reporting that Robertson had been lying about the date of his wedding for years in an effort to conceal that his wife was more than seven months pregnant when the ceremony occurred."[73] Robertson managed to sidestep the matter, though, excusing his own premarital sexual activity because it took place before he was born again. Robertson faced a similar criticism regarding inconsistent claims about his IQ, which at various times was announced as 159, then 139, and then 135, and many wondered how this Yale Law School graduate had been unable to pass the bar exam. When he lost his presidential bid—badly—Robertson formed what has become the most important of the religious right's

---

Grandmaster, the World Chess Federation's title for top-ranked players. She was followed the next year by Pia Cramling, and then by Zsuza's little sister, who became the youngest Grandmaster at age fifteen.

organizations, the Christian Coalition. He operated largely behind the scenes, hiring the less controversial Ralph Reed to run day-to-day operations. But Robertson's desire for personal power has never waned, and with the Christian Coalition claiming millions of members and almost two thousand state and local branches, he now has a chokehold on the Republican Party.

Robertson again achieved dubious notoriety as a result of the statement he made about Ariel Sharon, shortly after Israel's prime minister suffered a stroke. Robertson told his *700 Club* viewers that the "prophet Joel makes it very clear that God has enmity against those who 'divide my land.' God considers [Israel] to be his." Robertson insisted that Sharon's withdrawal of troops and settlers from the Gaza Strip and parts of the West Bank "was dividing God's land. And I would say woe unto any prime minister of Israel who takes a similar course to appease the EU, the United Nations, or the United States of America. God says, 'This land belongs to me. You better leave it alone.'"[74] His remarks were met with understandable outrage. *Time* magazine, among others, suggested that Robertson issue an apology because he was undermining the efforts of a group of evangelicals who were planning to build a $50 million Evangelical Heritage Center on the Sea of Galilee. Israel has agreed to provide the land and infrastructure for the project, with the funding and the center's details left to the evangelicals. *Time* explained that it is potentially a highly lucrative deal for both Israel and the evangelicals, for it is anticipated that the center will host as many as a million visitors a year, who will generate $1.5 billion in revenues.[75] Robertson apologized.

Although Robertson has long supported Israel, he has a history of making anti-Semitic remarks. "In Robertson's evangelical end-time scenario, Jews are simply pawns who help usher in the second coming of Christ," Robert Boston wrote. Robertson "believes that a mass conversion of Jews to Christianity will occur before Jesus returns to usher in the end of the world. In Robertson's view, the creation of Israel was a necessary component in this eschatological drama."[76] Robertson's anti-Semitism surfaced in his *New World Order* book. In typical Robertson—and Double High Authoritarian—fashion, he has claimed on one occasion that the book was ghosted, and on another that he wrote it himself. Whichever the case, he has never disavowed the book's contents. It is a bizarre tale of conspiracy, in which Robertson claims there is a secret plot afoot by the Freemasons, the Illuminati, the Trilateral Commission, the Council on Foreign Affairs, the Federal Reserve, and unidentified European bankers to create a world government under the United Nations. This new government will be taken over by the Antichrist, resulting in Armageddon, with half the world's population being eliminated. The book made the *New York Times* best-seller list. Michael Lind wrote a two-part review of it in the *New York Review of Books* exposing the book's anti-Semitic sources, which put Robertson on the defensive, and without explanation for his anti-Semitism. Maybe the most suitable review of *New World Order* was from Joe Queenan in the *Wall Street Journal:*

> The *New World Order* is a predictable compendium of the lu-
> natic fringe's greatest hits. . . . Mr. Robertson weaves a wild tale
> of international and extraterrestrial conspiracies, involving every-
> one from deposed Nicaraguan dictator Anastasio Somoza to Al-
> ger Hiss to Woodrow Wilson—an unwitting tool of Satan, whose
> role in the establishment of the Federal Reserve eventually re-
> sulted in the nation's abdication to the most Machiavellian crea-
> ture of all time: Paul Volcker. . . . Still, as paranoid pinheads with
> a deep distrust of democracy go, he's a bit of a disappointment. . . .
> Where, for example, is the stuff about JFK's secret meeting with
> Martin Borman in the Bermuda Triangle? Where is the stuff
> about extraterrestrials visiting the Mayans and telling them to
> give the Spear of Longinus to Elvis?[77]

To dismiss Pat Robertson as a loony crank, however, would be a mistake, for he takes his mission all too seriously. Realizing that he is never going to be the president of the United States himself, nor ever fully control a president regardless of how much assistance Christian conservatives provide to get a leader of their choice elected, he exercises his considerable influence in negative ways. He and his followers can block candidates for Republican nominations at the local, state, and national level, and no issue is more important in their filtering process than a candidate's position on judicial nominations, especially at the federal level. Of late, Robertson has focused much of his energy on the federal courts, and on the Supreme Court in particular. There is no question about his goals, which he has detailed in *Courting Disaster: How the Supreme Court Is Usurping the Power of Congress and the People* (2004), a cooperative writing effort with the lawyers at his American Center for Law and Justice—a sister organization he created that litigates continuously to expand the reach of religion and chip away at the wall separating church and state. The book castigates every Supreme Court decision that the Christian right does not like—those that are preventing it from imposing its religiosity on others—and was clearly written with the 2004 presidential election in mind. After describing doom and gloom, Robertson said, "[T]hings simply cannot continue as they are. Either they will get better or immeasurably worse, and in either case those who believe in the founding vision of this nation cannot afford to be passive any longer." If George W. Bush is reelected and conservatives get more seats in Congress, said Robertson, "we may be able to accomplish some of our more important goals." At the top of that list are "two and perhaps three" seats on the Supreme Court.[78] His prayers are being answered.

Packing Federal Courts with Judges Who Will Do God's Work

The agenda of Christian conservatives is, relatively speaking, limited, and they believe much of it can be accomplished through the federal courts. Broadly speaking, they want to control the right of women to have abortions; to ban all forms of gay marriage; to prevent the teaching of safe sex in schools; to encourage home schooling; to ban the use of contraceptives; to halt stem cell research with human embryos; to stop the teaching of evolution and/or to start the teaching of intelligent design; to bring God into the public square and eliminate the separation of church and state; to overturn the legality of living wills; to control the sexual content of cable and network television, radio, and the Internet; and to eliminate an "activist" judiciary that limits or impinges on their agenda, by placing God-fearing judges on the bench who will promote their sincerely held beliefs.

Because they do not want to lose the support of evangelicals, or to see them withdraw from politics as their parents or grandparents did in the 1920s, Republicans must take this agenda seriously. Reagan and Bush I gave promises but failed to fully deliver; Bush II, who became one of them, has delivered. An unspoken quid pro quo has developed for their support. Republicans appoint judges and justices whose views are compatible with Christian conservatives to do what neither Congress nor the president can accomplish: to make the agenda of Christian conservatives into the law of the land. Thus the effort that began under Reagan, and was continued by Bush I, has been most aggressively pursued by Bush II, who has undertaken a deliberate and concerted effort to pack the federal judiciary with conservative judges from top to bottom. Bush II has been more successful with lower courts than with the Supreme Court, with only two appointments, but that, too, may change soon, given the age and health of several of the justices.

Seven of the nine justices currently serving on the Supreme Court have been appointed by Republicans, but three of those seven are not nearly conservative enough to satisfy Christian conservatives. Many of them consider Justices John Paul Stevens (a Ford appointee), Anthony Kennedy (a Reagan appointee), and David Souter (a Bush I appointee) to be liberals. They are not, and, in fact, there is not a single true liberal on the high Court. Clinton appointed two moderates, Justices Ruth Ginsburg and Stephen Breyer, because he did not wish to spend

his political capital with the Senate on trying to get a liberal confirmed. While today's Supreme Court is more conservative than any
since before the New Deal, lower federal courts are more conservative
than they have ever been. By the end of 2005 "about 60 percent of the
federal appeals courts were appointed by Republican presidents," and
of "the 13 circuit courts of appeal, 9 have majorities of judges named
by Republican presidents."[79] It is at the federal appellate court level
that most law is made, and with the exceptions of the Second Circuit
(Connecticut, New York, and Vermont) and the Ninth Circuit (Arizona, Alaska, California, Hawaii, Idaho, Nevada, Montana, Oregon,
and Washington), the federal circuits are more conservative than the
Supreme Court. The Fourth Circuit (North Carolina, South Carolina, Virginia, and West Virginia), Fifth Circuit (Mississippi, Louisiana, and Texas), and Eleventh Circuit (Alabama, Georgia, and Florida)
especially have become strikingly so.

By constitutional design the federal judiciary is authoritarian,
with lower court judges bound to follow higher court rulings. Thus,
any five conservatives on the Supreme Court can make the law of the
land, because all lower federal judges are bound by their decisions.
George Bush won the support of social conservatives in 2000 and
2004 by promising he would appoint justices who thought like Justices Antonin Scalia and Clarence Thomas, the most conservative members of the Supreme Court. Bush delivered with the nominations of
Chief Justice John Roberts (who replaced the conservative William
Rehnquist) and Associate Justice Samuel Alito (who replaced the moderate swing vote of Sandra Day O'Connor). Theoretically, citizens
should have no concern about the political affiliation of judges whom
they expect to rule fairly and objectively. As a practical matter, however, ideology does make a difference. One can now predict with a fair
degree of certainty the outcome of a wide variety of legal rulings based
on the party affiliation of the judge, or judges, involved in the case. A
partisan judiciary does not deliver justice, and conservative Republicans are again acting as authoritarians in packing the federal courts.

As the federal judiciary becomes a legal phalanx of conservative judges, and as Congress becomes increasingly conservative, it is worth pondering what would happen if a liberal or progressive president won the White House in 2008, and refused to enforce a Supreme Court ruling. Hypothetically, say the ruling required prayer in all public proceedings or the posting of the Ten Commandments in all federal buildings. Say that liberal or progressive president claimed, "I have taken an oath that is as valid as that taken by members of the Court. The Court's ruling violates the United States Constitution. The Court has no constitutional authority to require enforcement of such a ruling; therefore, I order the Justice Department and the federal marshals not to enforce it." Needless to say, for a president to do so would be an extreme measure. Yet this is precisely what Pat Robertson and other Christian conservatives believe a conservative president should do, and that he should act as he sees the law, not as the high Court has seen it.[80] This, of course, is the way authoritarians think.

If this scenario were just one of Pat Robertson's more outrageous demands, it could be safely ignored. In fact, though, such thinking is widespread among Christian and social conservatives. For example, in 1997, Chuck Colson wrote in *Christianity Today* about his displeasure with the Supreme Court's ruling in *Boerne v. Flores,* which held that the Religious Freedom Restoration Act, passed by Congress to address the standard under which religious practices could be curtailed by government, was unconstitutional. Colson raised the question of who determines what the Constitution means: the Supreme Court, the Congress, or the president? Colson claimed that "contrary to what most Americans think, the Constitution does not give the Supreme Court final say on constitutional questions." He further asserted that in 1803, in *Marbury v. Madison,* "the Court assumed the power of judicial review," yet "three presidents have resisted Court orders: Thomas Jefferson refused to execute the Alien Imposition Act; [Andrew] Jackson spurned a Court order in a banking case; [and] Lincoln rejected the Dred Scott decision."[81] Colson, like Robertson and others on the religious right, is seeking, in effect, to nullify Supreme Court decisions of which he does not approve. Because such arguments are being made increasingly in lengthy law journal articles, which are later cited by conservative judges, it is worth taking a look at conservative scholarship in this area, and Colson is considered a scholar by his contemporaries.[82]

First, contrary to Colson's suggestion, the practice that is now called "judicial review" (the ability of federal courts to overturn acts of Congress) did not start with *Marbury*, but was already well established by 1803 and the *Marbury* ruling. In fact, the Court noted in *Marbury* that "[t]he question, whether an act, repugnant to the constitution, can become the law of the land" was to be resolved by relying on "long and well established" principles.[83] Even before the Constitutional Convention, high state courts had held legislative acts unconstitutional in several states, and references in the constitutional debates suggest that the delegates to the convention assumed federal courts would have such review authority. Members of the First Congress certainly understood that Supreme Court justices would decide constitutional questions. For example, Abraham Baldwin of Georgia stated during a debate of the First Congress, when speaking of the judiciary, that "it is their province to decide upon our laws; and if they find them unconstitutional, they will not hesitate to declare it so." During the same debate, Peter Sylvester of New York added, "It is certain that the Judiciary will be better able to decide the question of constitutionality in this way than any other. If we are wrong, that can correct our error."[84] Also long before *Marbury*, the newly created federal circuit courts, with Supreme Court justices presiding, reviewed the constitutionality of acts of federal officials and scrutinized federal statutes on no less than twenty occasions. Justice James Wilson, appointed by President George Washington and one of the more scholarly of the first justices, prepared a series of now famous lectures in 1790 and 1791 in which he explained that the courts must decide constitutional questions as a check on the legislature. In 1794 the Supreme Court declared a law passed by Congress in 1792, the Pension Act, was unconstitutional.[85] In short, the Court has had this power from the outset, and contrary to Colson's claim, it did not suddenly "assume" it in 1803.

Colson's historical examples, suggesting that presidents and Congress need not be bound by Supreme Court rulings, are red herrings. His claim that Thomas Jefferson did not execute "the Alien Imposition Act" is incorrect, for there is no such law. If Colson is referring to the infamous Alien and Sedition Act of 1798, it had nothing to do with a court order, and the example is therefore very misleading. When Jefferson was vice president, President John Adams asked him for his legal opinion of the sedition act (which made seditious libel a crime); Jefferson replied that he believed it to be unconstitutional. Nonetheless, Federalist judges upheld the law, and John Adams prosecuted under it—to his everlasting historical shame. When Jefferson became president he pardoned those who had been convicted. Because the act expired on March 3, 1801, and Jefferson was not inaugurated until March 4, 1801, he could not execute it anyway, since the law no longer existed.

Colson's claim that President Andrew Jackson "spurned a Court order in a banking case" is also misleading. Presumably, Colson is referring to Jackson's veto in 1832 of a bill to recharter the Bank of the United States. In taking this action, Jackson relied on the constitutional argument that Chief Justice John Marshall had rejected in *McCulloch v. Maryland* two years earlier, when the court upheld the constitutionality of the bank. President Jackson's veto, however, was not in defiance of a court order, for the Supreme Court had not said it was unconstitutional to not have a bank, so Jackson was under no obligation to recharter a national bank.[86]

Finally, in regard to his claim that Lincoln rejected the *Dred Scott* decision: Colson added in his commentary that "Lincoln even asked Congress to overrule the Court—which it did; passing a law that reversed *Dred Scott*." That is a stunning summation, not to mention distortion, of history. What actually occurred was that the Supreme Court issued its abominable opinion in *Dred Scott v. Sanford* in 1857, asserting that slaves were neither citizens nor persons under the Constitution; that Congress could not prohibit slavery in the territories; and that the Declaration of Independence's statement that "all men are created equal" referred only to white men. In 1858, during the famous Lincoln-Douglas debates when Lincoln was running for the Senate, *Dred Scott* was discussed. Lincoln, who later lost the race, argued that the Court had misread both the Constitution and the Declaration of Independence. He believed *Dred Scott* to be a political ruling, and rejected its politics, arguing, "We propose so resisting it as to have it reversed if we can, and a new judicial rule established upon this subject." Seeking reversal is not defiance of the law. Not until the outbreak of the Civil War did Lincoln actually defy the Supreme Court, when he suspended the writ of habeas corpus.* As for the *Dred Scott* decision, contrary to Colson's inference, it would take more than a law passed by Congress to overturn the decision. In fact, it required two amendments to the Constitution: the Thirteenth and Fourteenth. Lincoln, as it happened, asked for neither, although some historians believe he encouraged Senator John B. Henderson to introduce the joint congressional resolution to abolish slavery that eventually became the Thirteenth Amendment.[87] The Fourteenth Amendment was not proposed until June 13, 1866, over a year after Lincoln had been assassinated.

---

*Military authorities had arrested a number of suspected secessionists, including John Merryman. Chief Justice Robert Taney, who had written the *Dred Scott* opinion, ordered the Army commander holding Merryman to produce him, but the Army commander, under orders from Lincoln, ignored the Court's order. In holding the commander in contempt, Taney wrote in *Ex parte Merryman* that he had done all he could do by issuing his order, and that he believed Lincoln now had no constitutional power to suspend the writ. Lincoln disagreed, and on July 4, 1861, gave a full explanation to Congress of why he had suspended the writ: to preserve the Union.

Colson's baseless arguments are unfortunately typical of those that authoritarian conservatives insist on making, using facts that are irrelevant or misleading, if not demonstrably wrong. The self-righteousness of authoritarians, particularly of Double Highs like Colson and Pat Robertson, has become so pronounced that at times it seems as if they believe themselves actually to be speaking ex cathedra. Their contention that the president of the United States is not bound by rulings of the Supreme Court, or, for that matter, by the laws of Congress, when these rulings or laws relate to the functions of the presidency has gained increasing currency with authoritarian conservatives, both leaders and followers. As I will show in the close of the following chapter, this claim is truly frightening in its implications.

CHAPTER FOUR

TROUBLING POLITICS
AND POLICIES OF
OUR AUTHORITARIAN
GOVERNMENT

WHILE AUTHORITARIAN CONSERVATISM was growing in force in Washington for a decade before Bush and Cheney arrived at the White House, their administration has taken it to its highest and most dangerous level in American history. It is doubtful they could have accomplished this had authoritarian conservatism not already taken hold on Capitol Hill, but it might have ended in the legislative branch had this Republican presidency not given it a new legitimacy. Meanwhile, the federal judiciary has largely acceded to the status quo, for when Republican judges and justices are comfortable with those leading the charge, they embrace the fiction that "political questions" should rightfully fall to the political branches—as if they themselves were not political. The changes in policies and procedures that have taken place because of authoritarianism are quite dramatic. I entered politics at a time when there was good reason to worry whether the country was tilting too far left; but as I have grown older I am finding I have good reason to be anxious about the United States government's tilting too far to the right. It has always struck me that the country runs best when it stays close to the center.

Congressional conservatives first displayed their authoritarian colors when they reorganized the U.S. House of Representatives in 1995 to make it a monocratic operation. The House is being "run like a plantation," Senator Hillary Clinton recently observed, explaining that "nobody with a contrary point of view has had a chance to present legislation, to make an argument."[1] Authoritarians, under the leadership of Newt Gingrich and Tom DeLay, have successfully concluded a conservative revolution on the House side of Capitol Hill. With the possible exception of the hosts of right-wing talk radio, it is difficult to think of anyone who has done more to poison national politics—as part of that process—than Gingrich and DeLay. Both men are textbook examples of authoritarians, and their behavior and its consequences represent conservative authoritarianism at its most ruthlessly efficient. While Gingrich and DeLay are gone, the house they built remains.

Gingrich's Authoritarian House

Newt Gingrich's life story is well known. After earning his doctorate in modern European history from Tulane University, Gingrich—who had grown up on military bases around the world as the adopted son of a career soldier—began an undistinguished career teaching history and environmental studies at West Georgia College. His years as an academic were interrupted by unsuccessful bids for Congress in 1974 and 1976. His first wife, Jackie, raised their two daughters while putting her husband through graduate school. During his third run for Congress in 1978, Jackie traveled hundreds of miles campaigning for Gingrich; at his request, when it became an issue during the campaign, she announced that, unlike her husband's opponent, they would keep their family together if he won by moving to Washington rather than staying behind in Georgia. Members of Gingrich's staff knew what Jackie did not, and were betting one another on how long the marriage would last. Eighteen months after winning his seat in Congress, the man who had campaigned on keeping his family united asked for a divorce. Jackie, who was in the hospital recovering from a second cancer operation, was confronted by her husband carrying a yellow legal pad filled with a list of his wishes regarding how the divorce should be handled. He wanted her to sign it, then and there, even though she was still groggy from surgery. When Gingrich abandoned his family he left them near destitute, and it was Jackie's friends at her church who raised money to help her and her daughters survive.

Gingrich arrived in Washington just as Phyllis Schlafly's STOP ERA fight was revealing the power of social conservatives, for she had all but defeated the proposed amendment by this time. Paul Weyrich was simultaneously organizing Christian conservatives through the Moral Majority, and anyone as politically astute as Gingrich recognized the potential of the Christian right. In 1974 Republicans had experienced a post-Watergate wipeout in the Congressional elections, and in 1976 Carter's victory had cost Gingrich his race. But by 1978 Republicans were starting to regain some strength in Congress with the help of Schlafly's volunteers, who assisted in countless congressional contests. Abortion proved a successful wedge issue in 1978, separating liberal Democrats from conservative Democrats in the same way the issue of "family values" had in Gingrich's own election. In addition, conservatives had figured out how to get around post-Watergate election reform laws by establishing political action committees (PACs). By the time Gingrich arrived in the House, Republicans had gained thirty-three seats, narrowing the margin to 292 Democrats versus 277 Republicans. Gingrich, a person who sees himself as a visionary with endless ideas, began thinking about how Republicans could win control of the House, and how he could make his own mark on history. David Maraniss and Michael Weisskopf write that "during his freshman term in Congress, Gingrich had pestered the National Republican Congressional Committee (NRCC) brass into letting him run their long-range planning committee." Once given the job he "visited the NRCC offices day and night, proposing one grand idea after another . . . filing cabinets loaded down with 'Newt's Ideas.' One lonely cabinet in the corner was labeled 'Newt's Good Ideas.'"[2]

People who knew Gingrich early in his political career have described him—and because he is a man who still wants to be president of the United States such assessments remain relevant—in less than glowing terms. David Osborne spoke with many of them when he was preparing his telling profile for *Mother Jones* magazine, and he was given information descriptive of an authoritarian leader. Osborne reported that Gingrich was dominating, opposed to equality, desirous of personal power, and amoral; he can be a bully, hedonistic, exploitive, manipulative, a cheater, prejudiced toward women, and mean-spirited, and he uses religion for political purposes; he also wants others to submit to his authority and is aggressive on behalf of authority. A number of Gingrich observers described his nature:

- Lew Howell (a former press secretary): "Gingrich has a tendency to chew people up and spit them out, and when he doesn't need you anymore he throws you away. Very candidly, I don't think Newt Gingrich has many principles, except for what's best for him."
- Chip Kahn (who managed Gingrich's first two campaigns): "Ambitious bastard."
- Mary Kahn (a reporter who covered Gingrich before marrying Chip): "Newt uses people and then discards them as useless. He's like a leech. He really is a man with no conscience. He just doesn't seem to care who he hurts or why."
- L. H. Carter (once a close friend and adviser) on returning to Georgia after Newt was elected: "[H]e turned in my car and looked at me and he said, 'Fuck you guys. I don't need you anymore.'" Carter added, "The important thing you have to understand about Newt Gingrich is that he is amoral. There isn't any right or wrong, there isn't any conservative or liberal. There's only what will work best for Newt Gingrich. He's probably one of the most dangerous people for the future of this country that you can possibly imagine. He's Richard Nixon, glib."[3]

Gingrich eventually organized a small group of like-minded House Republicans, which included a fellow he did not particularly like, Texas congressman Tom DeLay. Gingrich's antipathy for DeLay was understandable, because DeLay is another social dominator authoritarian, and when social dominators are not convinced they can use each other, it is like trying to force the negative ends of magnets together. DeLay was not buying into Gingrich's strategy, which historian Donald Critchlow described as an effort to "undermin[e] the established order in the House."[4] In 1984 Gingrich began lining up Republicans to give speeches at night on the House floor when the House was no longer in session, but C-Span cameras were still on. Members of Congress are permitted to say anything about anyone other than fellow members of Congress (they try to protect their own) with no fear of being sued for defamation or invasion of privacy, or of being otherwise held accountable, because such speech is constitutionally privileged. Newt and company took full advantage of that privilege. For example, in one speech he accused Democrats of "being blind to communism," and he announced he was going to file charges against them for writing a letter to communist leader Daniel Ortega of Nicaragua. It was never clear what those charges might be, but that hardly mattered: This was all a show for a growing C-Span audience who did not realize that they were not watching live sessions of the House. When Speaker Tip O'Neill learned what was going on, he ordered C-Span to start panning its cameras across the empty chamber periodically, so the audience would realize these were out-of-session gatherings. A few days later O'Neill, who thought it critical that civility be maintained in politics, scolded Gingrich from the Speaker's chair high above the floor at the front of the chamber, shaking his finger, "You deliberately stood in that well before an empty House and challenged these people, and challenged their patriotism, and it's the lowest thing that I've ever seen in my thirty-two years in Congress."[5]

But things would only get worse. In 1987, after O'Neill retired, Gingrich began throwing bombs at the new Democratic Speaker of the House, Jim Wright.* "Gingrich's strategy called for not only questioning the ethics of individual Democrats but also for denigrating Congress as an institution," Critchlow wrote. For example, "[H]e pursued a scandal in which many members of the House, including Republicans, had kept large overdrafts at the House bank."⁶ The House banking affair was the kind of scandal the American people understood, and it tarnished the House badly, because it involved both Republicans and Democrats. (None of the members was stealing money, however. They had merely been slow to pay back the bank, and had therefore been effectively receiving interest-free loans. The practice was widespread, although it appears Republicans may have warned one another before the scandal blew up so as few of them as possible would be implicated.)

Gingrich, while claiming to be "a person of faith more than I go to church," in typical authoritarian fashion sought to define the scandals he created by portraying Republicans as godly and Democrats as antireligious liberals. And he knew how to do it. "Gingrich had come to believe that the politics of *perception* was everything," historian Dan Carter explained.** "It did not matter what really happened," only how it was defined for others to perceive. Accordingly, Gingrich distributed to fellow Republicans a list of key words to be used when describing Democrats: "*sick, traitors, corrupt, bizarre, cheat, steal, devour,*

---

*Gingrich brought his charges against Wright to the House Ethics Committee, which later issued a report suggesting Wright had arranged for bulk sales of his vanity book, *Reflections of a Public Man,* and had earned speaking fees in excess of the allowed maximum. In addition, Wright's wife, Betty, was given a job and perks that made it possible for him to skirt the limit on gifts. Rather than fight the charges, Wright resigned. Understandably, when Gingrich later accepted a $4.5 million advance for a book deal with Rupert Murdoch's publishing house, he was accused of hypocrisy and unethical behavior. Gingrich responded by returning the advance.

**Gingrich's tactics were developed through consultations with communications experts, and soon became standard operating procedure for Republicans. George W. Bush has taken "perception politics" to the extreme, packaging every-

self-serving, and *criminal rights.*"[7] *New Yorker* journalist David Remnick concluded, said Carter, that Gingrich was using "good" and "evil" rhetoric to make Republican challenges to Democrats' domestic policy "as severe and confrontational as the struggle with Soviet Communism at the height of the Cold War."[8] Gingrich would resign from the House in 1998 under a cloud. From the sidelines, and not long before Gingrich departed, Paul Weyrich had observed admiringly, "Newt Gingrich is the first conservative I have ever known who knows how to use power."[9] In fact, there was someone else Weyrich would come to know who used power even more aggressively and ruthlessly than Gingrich: Tom DeLay.

Tom DeLay's Tyranny of the Bare Majority

Tom DeLay's Double High authoritarian personality offers an almost textbook example of the four defining elements of a social dominator: the tendency to dominate; opposition to equality; desire for personal power; and amorality. His domination is apparent in his bare-knuckle Machiavellian management of the House. "DeLay has never been subtle about his uses of the power of Love and Fear," *Newsweek* reported. "In his majority whip's office on the Hill, he kept marble tablets of the Ten Commandments and a half-dozen bullwhips. Many politicians are conflict-adverse and avoid confrontation at all cost. Not DeLay." He was not nicknamed "the Hammer," "the Exterminator" (he once was in the pest control business), and the "Meanest Man in Congress" because of his compliant charm. DeLay, in a pattern followed by many Double High authoritarians, became a born-again Christian in 1984, when he was first elected to Congress.[10] He also quit drinking and became an outspoken moralist. He famously blamed high school

---

thing he does. This strategy appears to work for conservatives, in part because their right-wing authoritarian followers, as noted earlier, do not often question authority figures.

shootings, like those at Columbine, on the availability of birth control for teens and the teaching of evolution. DeLay's opposition to equality is less conspicuous, but it is certainly evident in the Texas redistricting plan he brokered (see pages 132–33). Not only did Republicans benefit under DeLay's plan at the expense of Democrats, but according to briefs filed with the Supreme Court, the plan was a disaster for blacks and Hispanics.[11] DeLay's drive to climb the House GOP leadership ladder is evidence of his desire for power. His own colleagues have described him as amoral. "If it wasn't illegal to do it, even if it was clearly wrong and unethical, [he did it]. And in some cases if it was illegal, I think [he] still did it. That's my view," said Representative Chris Shays (R-CT).[12] DeLay's Double High authoritarianism illustrates a host of the negative traits found in these extraordinary people.

Tom DeLay had not supported Gingrich's climb to the House GOP leadership ranks. In 1984, when Gingrich was lobbying for the job of minority leader, DeLay had only just arrived in Washington. DeLay's biographers say that he avoided Gingrich's "back bench bomb throwing" not because he was unwilling to adopt those methods, but because he had been warned off by others who doubted Gingrich's tactics would prevail. "DeLay goes with winners," his biographers wrote. "If he had been born in the Soviet Union and elected to the Duma in 1984, he would be a Marxist," they reported.[13] But in this case DeLay made a bad call, because Gingrich became minority leader in a very close vote (87 to 85), and he would not forget that DeLay had not backed him.

By early 1994 the GOP leadership believed that conditions were right for a possible takeover of the House. A large number of Democrats had retired in 1992, and more were doing so in 1994. In addition, President Clinton's national health care proposal had backfired, frightening both Republicans and Democrats. Clinton's protracted fight to permit gays in the military, along with his pro-choice stance, had rallied conservative Christians and started them marching double time. Republican House leaders had spent the previous decade successfully tearing down the House; Gingrich's campaign to denigrate Congress had largely succeeded. "The number of Americans expressing a great deal of confidence in Congress steadily declined from 1986 to 1994, after having risen in the years after Watergate," one scholar discovered.[14] Six weeks before the 1994 midterm election, Gingrich and the GOP leadership announced their "Contract with America," a promise that if Republicans were given control of Congress they would "dramatically change the way Washington does business, and change the business Washington does."[15] Trashing the Democratic Congress and then promising to clean it up was typical authoritarian-style manipulation, and authoritarian followers accordingly fell in line. Pat Robertson's Christian Coalition alone, which had replaced Jerry Falwell's Moral Majority, used churches to distribute thirty-three million voter guides (suggesting whom good Christians should vote for in their districts) in the two weeks preceding the election. Although churches risk losing their tax-exempt status by engaging in electoral politics, Christian conservatives have mastered the art of relaying political messages in the guise of "educational" materials that have a tremendous influence on voting.

Tom DeLay saw the 1994 election as an opportunity to gain his own place within the Republican leadership. DeLay played politics like bridge, always thinking several tricks ahead. Knowing he would not have Gingrich's support if the GOP took control of the House, and that Gingrich would be Speaker, DeLay figured out that the way to get his own place at the top of the pecking order was to win the position of majority whip by helping Republican candidates win the seats needed to take control of Congress. Gingrich was already running such a program, but after a decade in the House DeLay had one of the best fund-raising Rolodexes in Washington, and was more effective, providing both money and expertise to Republican candidates. "DeLay hired an experienced political consultant to direct his giving and advise the candidates he was backing. Mildred Webber was DeLay's handicapper and bag woman, picking races where he could get the most bangs for his bucks and delivering checks to candidates," his biographers report.[16] DeLay traveled to twenty-five states for fund-raisers, offering one-on-one guidance to fledgling campaigners. Many candidates were both pleased and startled by how much DeLay knew about them. DeLay's office became something of a concierge, and De-Lay a consigliere, for the new House Republicans. In the end, DeLay helped eighty candidates win their 1994 elections, so when it came time for this freshman class to select a majority whip, he had a lock on their hearts and minds. Even Gingrich was too wary of DeLay's well-known "mean streak" and "ruthlessness" to try to block him.[17] DeLay won the leadership post easily, defeating Gingrich's candidate. Gingrich ultimately figured out how to channel DeLay's ambition, and the men put personalities aside and got on about the business of running Congress their way.

Immediately, there was a new tone to House proceedings, as Gingrich and his lieutenants imposed authoritarian rule. It was not merely payback time for the Democrats, for Republicans wanted to build a permanent majority in America, and a one-party rule. In *The Cycles of American History* Arthur M. Schlesinger, Jr., observed that there is "a pattern of alternation in American history between negative and affirmative government—that is, between times when voters see private action as the best way of meeting our troubles and times in which voters call for a larger measure of public action."[18] Republicans were ready for negative government. One longtime and highly respected member of the House observed that the GOP rule resulted in a "decline in civility" with "bitter partisan exchanges and mean personal attacks." There was "antagonism, incivility, and the tendency to demonize opponents," making it "very difficult for members to come together to pass legislation for the good of the country."[19] Comity between the majority and minority all but disappeared, and members soon barely even knew one another, as the House held meetings only three days a week—Tuesday, Wednesday, and Thursday—with most members returning home for long weekends. C-Span, which had begun televising House proceedings in 1979, had made it less necessary for most members to be on the floor of the House, for they could follow the proceedings in their offices. Electronic voting also resulted in members' spending less time together. This suited the new authoritarian leadership's aim of tightly controlling the House, for knowing one's colleagues makes it more difficult to attack them, and authoritarian conservatism is constantly on the attack. They are not backslappers, but rather, backstabbers; they do not serve the public interest, but rather, their own.

Proponents of the Contract with America had claimed the "Democrats' ironhanded one-party rule of the House of Representatives over the last four decades led to arcane, arbitrary, and often secretive procedures that disenfranchised millions of Americans from representation in Congress," reported one congressional scholar.[20] Indeed, their long stint in power had given them a hubris, arrogance, and sense of invulnerability that had eroded the effective operation of the House. Republicans, in fact, had a valid complaint, and at the time they took control there was indeed a need for reform. But that is not what happened. If Democrats had run the House with an iron hand, Republicans were employing a iron fist at the behest of their leadership's autocratic rule.[21] Gingrich lorded over the House. Where power was once decentralized among committee chairmen who had earned their posts and fiefdoms through seniority, Gingrich eliminated the seniority system and had chairmen selected by the leadership, concentrating power in the Speaker's office.* But while Gingrich was autocratic (answering to no one else), he was not dictatorial (imposing his will on others). Dictatorship in the House would not occur until DeLay

---

*Not long after Gingrich's authoritarian approach became evident, a reporter for the *Independent* (London) observed that Gingrich was an avid reader of Frans de Waal, a Dutch ethnologist whose book *Chimpanzee Politics* was on the Speaker's list of twenty-five recommended books. In dead earnest the reporter noted striking parallels between Gingrich's rise to power and "apes striving to acquire the coveted status of 'alpha male,'" as de Waal's study described. John Carlinin, "How Newt Aped His Way to the Top," *Independent* (May 31, 1995), 13.

held full sway, which occurred with Gingrich's departure. By the time of the arrival of Bush and Cheney in 2001, House Republican leaders had imposed iron-clad controls on "the people's House," making it their own, with ambitions of assuming permanent authority.

Accordingly, "[m]ore radical changes, at the expense of democracy itself, have occurred since 2002 under Tom DeLay," explained the seasoned Washington observer Robert Kuttner, the cofounder and coeditor of *The American Prospect.*[22] Kuttner was one of the first to write about the authoritarian inclination of these conservatives (although he does not use the term) in a chilling analysis entitled "America as a One-Party State: Today's hard right seeks total dominion. It's packing the courts and rigging the rules. The target is not the Democrats but democracy itself." Kuttner focused on Congress, more specifically on the House of Representatives, and by 2002, he found, there was good reason to describe DeLay's operation as a "dictatorship." He also refuted the Republican claim that when the Democrats were in control they exercised the same leadership style, for what the Republicans have done to the House was beyond anything even imaginable by the Democrats. Kuttner focused on several means employed by the authoritarian conservatives to exercise control. Following I have quoted or paraphrased them, while adding a few thoughts of my own.

• **Extreme Centralization.** The legislative agenda of the House is (and always has been) controlled by the Speaker and the Committee on Rules.* Kuttner explained that, unlike their predecessors, Tom DeLay and House Speaker Dennis Hastert (whose chief of staff, Scott Palmer, he considered "as powerful as DeLay") practi-

---

*The Committee on Rules was created by the first Congress. Unlike in the Senate, where unlimited debate is permitted, legislation in the much larger House (currently at 435 members) proceeds to the floor pursuant to a rule issued by the Rules Committee. This committee lays out the procedures for legislation on the floor, governing the length of debate and the nature of any proposed amendments. Rules are voted on by the House, and it is well known that DeLay

cally write laws themselves. "Drastic revisions to bills approved by committee are characteristically added by the leadership, often late in the evening," Kuttner observed. "Under the House rules, 48 hours are supposed to elapse before floor action. But in 2003, the leadership, 57 percent of the time, wrote rules declaring bills to be 'emergency' measures, allowing them to be considered with as little as 30 minutes' notice. On several measures, members literally did not know what they were voting for."

• **No Amendments.** When the GOP took control of the House they promised they would do better than the Democrats, assuring all "that at least 70 percent of bills would come to the floor with rules permitting amendments." That did not happen; in fact, the opposite occurred. The "proportion of bills prohibiting amendments has steadily increased," from 56 percent the first year Republicans took control to 76 percent when Kuttner last examined them. Even these numbers understate the situation, Kuttner explained, since "all major bills now come to the floor with rules prohibiting amendments."

• **One-Party Conferences.** The Republican-controlled Senate has not yet stopped floor amendments, so when a Senate bill differs from a House bill, members are appointed by each body to confer and resolve the differences. Republicans, however, have cut both House and Senate Democrats out of the conferences. The Republicans meet, work out any differences, and then send a non-amendable bill back to each body for a quick up-or-down vote. Kuttner noted that members may be given a day to study bills exceeding a thousand pages, with "much of it written from scratch in conference." This is a practice that was once considered unacceptable by both parties.

---

considered votes on rules to be tests of party loyalty. Any House Republican who defied DeLay stood to suffer (e.g., lose his or her committee assignments and campaign funds, or face a DeLay-sponsored primary opponent in the next election).

- **No Legislative Hearings.** Obviously, when laws are written in conference committee meetings, they have not been discussed during hearings. Even when hearings are held at the committee level, however, Republicans frequently write laws without any input from Democrats, and they vote down any Democratic efforts to amend legislation in committee. Under Republicans, many laws are literally written by the special interests the laws seek to "regulate," an extraordinary outsourcing of the legislative process.
- **Appropriations Bill Abuses.** If annual appropriations bills are not enacted, the government runs out of money and must close down. When Newt Gingrich shut down the government in 1995, pressuring President Clinton in a game of political chicken that Gingrich lost, lawmakers were notified that the public would not tolerate such games. Appropriations bills must pass—a president dare not veto such legislation, regardless of what objectionable provisions it might contain. Accordingly, Republicans add to these bills an endless array of spending for pet pork-barrel projects. As one commentator noted, Republicans are spending "worse than drunken sailors."[23] Under GOP congressional leadership, "earmarked" (meaning pork) spending has soared. According to the *Wall Street Journal,* at the end of 2005 there were a staggering 13,998 earmarked expenses, costing $27.3 billion. When the Republicans took control in 1995 there were only 1,439 earmarked items. Needless to say, there is nothing conservative in these fiscal actions but there is much that is authoritarian about the wanton spending by these Republicans.

In early 2006, Norman Ornstein, a resident scholar at the American Enterprise Institute, and Thomas E. Mann, a senior fellow at The Brookings Institution, both men longtime experts on Congress and partisans for good government, also spoke out about the authoritarianism in the House, in an op-ed for the *New York Times:* "Over the past five years, the rules and norms that govern Congressional deliberation, debate and voting, have routinely been violated, especially in the House of Representatives, and in ways that mark a dramatic break from custom." Ornstein and Mann pointed out that House Republicans have far exceeded any overeaching by Democrats. "We saw similar abuses leading to similar patterns of corruption during the Democrats' majority reign," they said. "But they were neither as widespread nor as audacious as those we have seen in the past few years."[24]

Gingrich's departure from Congress in 1998 changed nothing, for his precedent became the base upon which Tom DeLay built his House, making the operation even more authoritarian. The removal of DeLay from leadership of Congress in a swirl of scandal in early 2006 likewise did not change the undemocratic and highly authoritarian nature of the House, notwithstanding promises by the new leadership to the contrary. The election of John Boehner of Ohio to DeLay's former majority leader post has changed nothing about the way House Republicans are conducting business. Boehner, like DeLay, has close ties to lobbyists; in fact, he once passed out money from the tobacco industry on the floor. Boehner has been part of the authoritarian power structure of the House for too long. All he offers is a fresh face and a more television-friendly manner.

Despite the increasingly flagrant erosion of once deliberative practices, Democrats have refused to complain. After writing *Worse Than Watergate* I asked a number of Democrats why they had not raised the issue during the 2004 campaign of Bush and Cheney's excessive secrecy. From those at the top of John Kerry's presidential campaign staff to several Democratic congressional candidates, I received the same answer: Secrecy is "process," which they are convinced interests no voters. Robert Kuttner also found Democrats reluctant to make an issue of these antidemocratic and authoritarian tactics. "Democrats are ambivalent about taking this issue to the country or to the press because many are convinced that nobody cares about 'process' issues,"

Kuttner reported. "The whole thing sounds like inside baseball, or worse, like losers whining." Yet in 1910, when Speaker Joe Cannon played similar games, Kuttner noted, "it was a very big deal indeed," and when the press investigated, public outrage toppled him.[25] I know several Republicans who are also troubled by their colleagues' activities, but as good right-wing authoritarian followers they have remained silent and compliant. And the processes of the House may well spread to the Senate, if Republicans maintain control, because more and more members of the House are being elected to the Senate.

Creating a Permanent Republican Majority

House Republicans have gone beyond raising money from well-heeled conservative sources as a means to better finance their candidates, and beyond rough campaign tactics, to hold their majority status. They have, in effect, literally rigged the system. Today House seats are amazingly secure, because Republicans have designed a strategy to give themselves safe congressional districts; once again Democrats remain silent because they do not want to be seen as whiners, or to raise process issues. When the *Congressional Quarterly* reported that in 2004, only 29 of 435 House races were truly competitive, and of those only 13 were "really close races," the *Economist* declared, "The sheer uncompetitiveness of most House races takes one's breath away. . . . In 2002, just four incumbents lost to challengers at the polls (another four lost in primaries). North Korea might be proud of this incumbent re-election rate: 99%." How did this happen? the *Economist* inquired. The answer is as old as the nation, but with the use of computers, the process has become much more refined: "By gerrymandering to cram Democrats into a smaller number of super-safe seats [primarily in urban areas] while spreading Republicans into a large number of 'designer districts' which they win by 55–60%," the investigators discovered. They pointed to the "particularly brutal" redistricting engineered by Tom

DeLay in Texas, which earned him an indictment for "money laundering," a serious felony charge under Texas law.[26]

The remarkable audacity DeLay exhibited in his Texas redistricting project—rigging, in effect, the entire state of Texas—enabled Republicans to pick up four additional seats in the House of Representatives. In 2001 DeLay, himself a former member of the Texas state legislature, began plotting a takeover of the Texas "Lege" by Republicans so they could redraw the state's congressional districts and send more Republicans to Washington. Lou Dubose wrote in the *Texas Monthly* that DeLay "meant to perpetuate, in one brash swipe, a conservative Republican majority and agenda in the U.S. House until the roosters quit crowing and the sun stayed down."[27] This was accomplished with the grease of elective politics: money. To win control of the Texas legislature DeLay set up a new political action committee, Texans for a Republican Majority (TRMPAC, known as "trim-pack"), and made himself the chairman of the honorary board. John Colyandro, a longtime associate of Karl Rove's who was well-known to DeLay, was appointed TRMPAC's executive director. Americans for a Republican Majority (ARMPAC), another DeLay organization (run by his top political aide, Jim Ellis) contributed $50,000 (or $75,000, according to a few reports) in seed money. Colyandro and Ellis, along with DeLay's daughter, began raising money from corporations throughout the country: $25,000 from Bacardi USA; $25,000 from Phillip Morris; $25,000 from Sears, Roebuck; and various amounts from countless others having absolutely no business with the Texas legislature but a lot of business with Tom DeLay in Washington. Even the Choctaw Indian tribe of Mississippi, which was represented in Washington by superlobbyist and DeLay friend Jack Abramoff, contributed $6,000. TRMPAC went on to raise $1.5 million during the 2002 campaign cycle, and spent almost all of it on winning control of the Texas legislature. DeLay's handpicked candidate, Tom Craddick, became Speaker of the Texas House, and in this position would help DeLay redraw the political map of the state. The misstep that returned to haunt this undertaking was that Texas law prohibits corporations from contributing to Texas election campaigns.*

Texas Republicans, once in control of the Lege, pushed to enact their redistricting plan, while Democrats employed numerous tactical and procedural moves to try to prevent this. At one point, Democratic legislators left the state in droves to prevent Republicans from obtaining the quorum necessary for enacting gerrymandered districts into law. Tom DeLay called the Federal Aviation Administration and demanded they send airplanes out to locate the missing Democratic legislators, dubbed the "Killer D's" by the media.** The Killer D's could stall only so long, however, and in 2003 the Texas legislature enacted a new redistricting plan. This action was unprecedented; throughout the twentieth century such redistricting had been undertaken only in response to the decennial U.S. Census's update of population figures. Much of the negotiation took place behind closed doors, in conference committee, with DeLay brokering the deal and insisting the plan meet his approval. DeLay, who personally carried drafts of the new law back and forth between the Texas House and Senate, resisted any and all attempts to make the plan fair, so determined was he to secure every possible advantage for Republicans.[28]

"By drawing districts that snaked hundreds of miles across various counties," the NAACP reported, "Republicans drained African American and Latino voters from integrated Democratic districts and

---

*Tom DeLay, Jim Ellis, and John Colyandro were indicted by Travis County, Texas, district attorney Ronnie Earle for money laundering. More specifically, they were accused of sending some $190,000 of the $1.5 million they had collected from corporations nationally to the Republican National Committee in Washington, which then issued new checks, worth a total of $190,000, to candidates running for the Texas legislature.

**This use of his position would later result in a mild reprimand from the mostly moribund House Ethics Committee.

replaced them with enough white Republican voters to outnumber remaining white Democratic voters. As a result, DeLay converted a 32-member Texas Congressional delegation that had been evenly divided between the parties into one in which Republicans enjoyed a 10-seat advantage after the 2004 election."[29] Under the federal Voting Rights Act, Texas was required to submit any changes in its voting laws to the federal government for approval by the Department of Justice. After it sent its 2003 redistricting plan to Washington, five lawyers and two analysts in the department's Civil Rights Division rejected it in a seventy-three-page memorandum highlighting its flaws. But Bush appointees at the Justice Department rejected the findings of their own experts and approved the highly partisan plan.[30] When opponents of the scheme took it to federal court, they ran aground because of the uncertainty of the law under existing U.S. Supreme Court rulings. It was not until late 2005 that the Supreme Court agreed to hear their objections, which makes it unlikely the issue will be resolved before the 2006 congressional elections. In the past, the conservative majority of the Supreme Court has tried to stay out of such political issues, so it remains uncertain whether the high Court will make a ruling in the case. But everyone should hope that the justices opt to clean up this mess, for its ramifications are national.

Indeed, the actions of DeLay and his allies in the Texas legislature have already encouraged similar activity (so far unsuccessful) in other states controlled by Republicans, namely Georgia and Colorado. In turn, a few Democrats, relying on the adage that "you can't play touch football when the other guy is playing tackle," have proposed that states they now control, such as Illinois, New Mexico, and Louisiana, pursue their own partisan redistricting plans. But so far Democrats have chosen to talk, not to play this game. DeLay's actions in Texas provided less than a handful of additional votes, but Republicans have shown that with their authoritarian style they can and will govern the

House, and the nation, with only the slightest majority.* They have maintained control of the House by mastering "the one-vote victory" strategy, which DeLay has made into an art form.

Although he is not particularly close to Bush II, since he had been openly critical of his father (claiming that moderate Republicans like Bush I were moral compromisers), DeLay is a team player and recognizes the power of the White House, so he has been more than willing to push Bush administration programs. As majority leader, he knew how to count votes and how to twist arms to enact laws with almost no majority support. "Time and again," the *Washington Post* reported, "on high-profile bills involving Medicare, education and other programs, [the GOP leaders] have calibrated the likely yeas and neas to the thinnest margin possible, enabling them to push legislation as much to their liking as they can in a narrowly divided and bitterly partisan House."[31] For example, the *Post* reported, the 2003 vote on Medicare was 216–215, the Head Start vote was 217–216, and those in favor of providing vouchers for children in the District of Columbia public schools prevailed with a 209–208 vote. By picking up four more votes from Texas in 2004, Republicans gained even greater control. DeLay—and no doubt his successor, John Boehner—held Republican members of the House in line through threats and money and, by playing hardball, demanded and obtained votes when he needed them. But the leaders are not foolish and understand that some moderate members cannot vote for every hard-right measure and survive in office. So the GOP leadership rotates among the moderates in the ranks, not forcing all of them to comply with every vote, but using them one at a time when one vote is needed for victory, as well as when voting on rules. The system is blatantly imperious, completely undemocratic, and conspicuously authoritarian. Massachusetts

---

*Bush lost the popular vote in 2000 but immediately commenced pushing the nation to the right as if he had a mandate; Electoral College votes are not really a popular mandate, since a simple majority in any given state will result— in most states—in the winner's getting all the electoral votes.

Democrat Barney Frank, with two decades of service in the House, correctly stated that the "House of Representatives is no longer a deliberative body."[32]

The K Street Project:
Jack Abramoff and His Friends

DeLay, his later successor John Boehner, and key authoritarian cronies have also assembled what may prove the most corrupt lobbying operation in Washington since the "Ohio Gang" was run out of their infamous "little green house" at 1625 K Street in 1923.[33] K Street, a wide boulevard lined with office buildings in downtown Washington, D.C., is the corridor where many powerful lobbying firms base their operations. When Republicans took control of Congress in 1995, one of their first moves was to seize control of the lobbying sector.* When he became Speaker of the House, Newt Gingrich deputized then majority whip Tom DeLay to make sure House Republicans were getting their share of campaign dollars from K Street, and to inform the lobbying firms and trade associations that if they wanted access to GOP leaders, they should hire Republicans to lobby.[34] This undertaking soon became known as the K Street Project. DeLay was assisted by Pennsylvania Republican Senator Richard Santorum, who regularly approved the names of people to be hired by the K Street firms, and John Boehner "formed his alliances on K Street when he served as chairman of the GOP conference from 1995 to 1998."[35] To make cer-

---

*Recently, the *American Conservative* addressed the shameful growth of lobbying in Republican-controlled Washington, revealing its staggering growth: "The Cato Institute's David Boaz reports that the number of registered lobbying firms jumped from 1701 to 2060 in the last six years; over the same period, lobbyist spending went up 50 percent, and the number of companies with lobbyists rose 58 percent. The number of lobbyists in the nation's capital approaches 35,000, doubling the number in 2000." Doug Bandow, "Republic for Sale," *American Conservative* (February 13, 2006), 7.

tain lobbying firms were, in fact, hiring conservative Republicans, Grover Norquist, head of Americans for Tax Reform and the project's coarchitect, also constantly monitored the operation.* "We don't want non-ideological people on K Street, we want conservative Republicans on K Street," Norquist stated.[36]

But the K Street Project was about more than just finding jobs for Republicans; it was about money—the big money needed to maintain a Republican majority. "Washington conservatives and the Republican leadership in Congress," wrote informed political observer John Judis, were pursuing "a strategy for retaining Republican control of Congress and for winning the White House." That strategy, Judis reported, was to turn K Street, and the business interests it represents, "into loyal soldiers in the new Republican revolution. In exchange for legislative favors, Gingrich, DeLay, and other congressional leaders expected that the businesses would provide funds to keep them in office."[37] When lobbying firms or special interest groups hired someone to the Republican leadership's disliking, they were punished. For example, in 1998, when the Electronic Industries Alliance (EIA) hired former Democratic representative Dave McCurdy of Oklahoma to head its Washington office, DeLay effectively vetoed the hire. "First, DeLay put out the word that McCurdy would not be welcome in Re-

---

*Norquist's Americans for Tax Reform was formed in 1985 with a mission to "oppose any effort to increase the taxes on individuals and business." To accomplish this goal, it circulates petitions to elected officials at the local, state, and national levels, asking them to promise that they will oppose all taxes. Norquist's Web site boasts that "President George W. Bush, 222 House members, and 46 Senators have taken the pledge. On the state level, 6 governors and 1,247 state legislators have taken the pledge." See http://www.atr.org/index.html. Norquist once famously stated, "My goal is to cut government in half in twenty-five years, to get it down to the size where we can drown it in the bathtub." Norquist also operates a Web site that reports on openings at lobbying firms and on new hires. It notes that while the Democrats once employed "graft," the K Street Project represents good government, where like-thinking people can implement their common values. See http://www.kstreetproject.com/index.php.

publican leadership offices," reported Lou Dubose and Jan Reid, which would clearly make McCurdy an ineffective lobbyist. When EIA refused to fire McCurdy, DeLay upped the stakes by pulling from the House calendar consideration of the Digital Millennium Copyright Act, an essential piece of legislation for protecting intellectual property on the Internet that a coalition of industry people, including EIA, had worked on for two years. When an end run through the Senate was attempted, DeLay again blocked the bill when it came to the House. "When DeLay used his position as majority whip to block its final passage in the House, he sent K Street a loud, crude message," Dubose and Reid observed. "He also probably broke the law."[38] Extortion is not something that registers easily with a Double High authoritarian who is busy manipulating the world.

With impunity DeLay "regularly engage[d] in pay-to-play lawmaking and flagrant abuses of power," one reporter noted.[39] DeLay was taking names and making lists, not only of who was being hired to lobby, but of how much money was being contributed to Republicans. Rumor in Washington was that DeLay had "a little black book" he kept on his desk, which he opened whenever a lobbyist came to see him to determine whether he was pleased with the latest contribution made by the organization the lobbyist represented. If DeLay was not happy, he would not be particularly helpful to the lobbyist. When he was satisfied, though, he let it be known through favorable action. *Newsweek* columnist Jonathan Alter did not believe the gossip, so he asked DeLay about it. "DeLay not only confirmed the story," Alter later wrote, "he showed me the book." DeLay claimed his time was limited, explained Alter. "Why should he open his door to people who were not on his team?"[40]

As a result of the embarrassing indictment of Tom DeLay and the guilty plea of the man with whom he had worked most closely on K Street, Jack Abramoff, Republicans were forced to take a few pre-emptive measures. Those campaigning for his job as majority leader—Representatives Roy Blunt (R-MO), John Boehner (R-OH), and John

Shadegg (R-AZ)—all pledged to lighten up on the K Street Project's extortion racket. Yet *Roll Call* reported that all of them were, at the same time, relying on their K Street contacts to help them win.[41] Even friendly observers acknowledged that Republicans were doing little to change their ways. "The truth is that none of this will truly reduce corruption any more than the previous lobbying reform did," according to the editors of the *Wall Street Journal*. "If the Members were serious about reform," the *Journal* advised, "they'd put in place rules that restrict *themselves.* They could insist, for example, that at least three days pass after final legislation is drafted, so they could actually read the bills before they vote on them. Or they could eliminate 'earmarks,' which have proliferated under GOP rule and are now a preferred way that members pay off lobbyists."[42]

Once Boehner became majority leader, even the proposed cosmetic changes were dropped, and it was back to business as usual. Republicans have, for all practical purposes, effectively imposed one-party rule on Washington. "It is breathtaking," said Thomas Mann, a senior scholar at the Brookings Institution. "It's the most hard-nosed effort I've seen to use one's current majority to enlarge and maintain that majority."[43] Republicans have accomplished one-party rule by "patronage, cronyism and corruption," observed Paul Krugman of the *New York Times*,[44] who might well have been describing Jack Abramoff's mantra.

Abramoff, who contributed mightily toward one-party dominance, is another poster boy for Double High authoritarian conservatism, a disposition that has been evident from the outset of his career. He entered Republican politics at a relatively high level, through the College Republicans. In 1980, while an undergraduate at Brandeis, he met Grover Norquist, who was then an MBA student at Harvard. The two teamed up, with Abramoff taking the more visible role as head of the Massachusetts Federation of College Republican Clubs, and produced over ten thousand youth votes for Reagan. This turned out to be a significant contribution, because although Reagan carried Massachusetts, it was by only three thousand votes.[45] After graduation, Abramoff and Norquist headed for Reagan's Washington, and in 1981, Abramoff sought the chairmanship of the College Republican National Committee (CRNC), spending ten thousand dollars of his personal funds to campaign for a job that did not pay much more. To win the chairmanship, Franklin Foer of the *New Republic* reported, "Abramoff and his campaign manager, Norquist, promised their leading competitor, Amy Moritz, the job of CRNC executive director if she dropped out of the race. Moritz took the bait, but it turned out that Abramoff had made the promise with his fingers crossed. Norquist took the executive director job."[46] The jobs brought prestige to two young conservatives on the make and plugged them into the Republican Party power network. At that time, heavy-hitting conservative millionaires, like beermeister Joseph Coors and Nixon's former treasury secretary, William Simon, were providing increasingly large sums of money to attract young people to conservatism. Abramoff would serve as CRNC's chairman from 1981 to 1985, one of the longest terms since the founding of the organization in 1892.[47]

"The [College Republican National] Committee is the place were Republican strategists learn their craft and acquire their knack for making their Democratic opponents look like disorganized children," Foer wrote of his firsthand look at the "importuning, backstabbing and horse trading" of the 2005 contest for its chairmanship. "Walking through the halls of the [2005] convention," Foer reported, "it was easy to see the genesis of tactics deployed in the [2000] Florida recount and by the Swift Boat Veterans for Truth [in 2004]. Republicans learn how to fight hard against Democrats by practicing on one another first." Grover Norquist advised 2005 conventioneers, "There are no rules in a knife fight."*[48]

---

*This is typical Norquist, who views politics as war, and invokes chilling language whenever discussing political matters. In another political contest, for example, he explained, "Our goal is to inflict as much pain as possible. It is not

Abramoff's dominating personality was likewise apparent early in his career. As chairman of the College Republicans while a student at Georgetown University Law Center,* he played the political game by any means, fair or foul. For example, in 1983, Abramoff launched an attack on Ralph Nader's efforts to get college campuses to undertake public interest research projects, and to devote part of their activities fee to such purposes. Abramoff sent out materials accusing such public interest groups of promoting leftist political ideals, and of being "instrumental in leading anti-Reagan and anti-free market forces on campuses." He described these student groups as "a major threat to democracy on American campuses" and as "unethical, undemocratic and unconstitutional." Nader called Abramoff's material what it was, "a total smear."[49] The same year Abramoff formed the purportedly non-partisan, tax-exempt USA Foundation, obtained funding from leading Republican donors, and then proceeded to violate the law prohibiting such groups from participating in political campaigns. The *Washington Post* reported that just as the 1984 Reagan reelection campaign was entering its final phase, Abramoff arranged, through his foundation, "more than 100 campus rallies and a possible Rose Garden ceremony on the first anniversary of the U.S. invasion of Grenada." Abramoff's letter promoting these events, almost ludicrous because it is so blatantly deceptive, put a facade of legitimacy on what he dubbed "Student Liberation Day." "I am confident that an impartial study of the contrasts between the Carter/Mondale failure in Iran and the Reagan victory in Grenada will be most enlightening to voters 12 days before the general election," Abramoff wrote.[50] Earlier that year, Abramoff

---

good enough to win; it has to be a painful and devastating defeat. We're sending a message here. It is like when the king would take his opponent's head and stick it on a spike for everyone to see." John Maggs, "Grover at the Gate," *National Journal* (October 11, 2003), 31. (These are words that could have been spoken by Joseph de Maistre himself.)

*Abramoff's résumé indicates he received his JD from Georgetown University Law Center in 1986, but he was not licensed to practice law.

had "invited his counterpart at the College Democrats, Steve Gersky, to tour the country to debate the issues of the 1984 presidential campaign." Gersky cordially accepted, and the Republicans even paid for the tour. (One can only imagine where Abramoff found the funds.) But Abramoff chose campuses where he knew he would get a friendly reception, and did not tell Gersky where the debates would be held. When Abramoff spoke, canned applause was piped in. Bill Belk, the outgoing president of the Young Democrats, later mournfully explained Gersky's failure to win any of these debates: "They set him up."[51]

Double High authoritarians are, of course, amoral, and Abramoff has consistently displayed this characteristic. For example, in 1985 he served as the executive director of the Citizens for America, a conservative organization headed by drugstore magnate Lewis Lehrman, who had challenged New York governor Mario Cuomo in a close race in 1982 and still had political ambitions. Lehrman, upon returning from a trip out of the country, discovered he was "boxed out of the bookkeeping" of Citizens for America, notwithstanding being head of the organization. He had his personal lawyer investigate, and later reported, "It was one big party," as Abramoff and those he had hired "had gone hog wild." According to the *Washington Post,* Abramoff was charged with mismanaging funds, and he and his staff—including "field director" Grover Norquist, who was off in South Africa—were all fired.[52] Nonetheless, a decade later, Abramoff cited his work with Citizens for America prominently in his résumé.[53]

"His greatest strength was his audacity," remarked Jeff Bell, who has known Abramoff since his days at Citizens for America.[54] But this characterization vastly understates Abramoff, as the two indictments to which he pleaded guilty in 2005 attest. Abramoff's scam to purchase a fleet of SunCruz Casinos ships by faking a wire transfer of $23 million to close the $147.5 million transaction was more stupid than audacious, for it was inevitable that his cash contribution would be discovered missing. That scam alone resulted in a five-count indictment for fraud, with one count of conspiracy; Abramoff pleaded guilty to everything except conspiracy. Abramoff's fleecing of his Native American clients also transcended audaciousness. When the Senate Indian Affairs Committee discovered his scheme, its members were at something of a loss to describe it. Senator John McCain observed that people had been stealing from American Indians since the sale of Manhattan Island, but "what set [Abramoff's] tale apart, what makes it extraordinary, is the extent and degree of the apparent exploitation and deceit." Straining to find words to describe Abramoff's activities, Senator Byron Dorgan (D-ND) said that they were representative of "a cesspool of greed, a disgusting pattern, certainly, of moral corruption . . . a pathetic, disgusting example of greed run amok."[55]

Abramoff began his relationship with the tribes by getting himself hired as their Washington lobbyist. (His arrangement with each tribe was a little different, but the pattern was the same.) Abramoff handled only tribes that had casinos, because they were making enormous amounts of money. Once the tribes hired him, he told them they also had to retain Michael Scanlon, Tom DeLay's former press secretary. Scanlon, who was not registered as a lobbyist (and thus not required to report to Congress) but a political and communications consultant, would help tribal members win elections to their tribal councils, and once friendly members ran those councils, both Abramoff and Scanlon began billing them extravagantly for an array of activities. What Abramoff failed to mention to his clients was that he also received 50/50 kickbacks from Scanlon. The *New York Times* reported that "Abramoff and his sidekick not only bilked Indian tribes of up to $66 million; they also mocked them as 'monkeys' and 'morons.'"* But there is nothing kind-hearted about authoritarians, particularly when they are busy manipulating.

Newt Gingrich, Tom DeLay, Jack Abramoff, and their cohorts are

---

*The Senate Indian Affairs Committee subpoenaed the e-mails from Abramoff's two employers. They can be viewed at www.indian.senate.gov. Time after time they show Abramoff shamelessly manipulating his clients.

all conservatives and are all authoritarians. One of the more remarkable traits of such individuals is their ability to get away with so much before they are called to task, which can partially be explained by authoritarian followers' being attracted to such personalities and ready to be led by them with no questions asked. But sooner or later, the Double High authoritarian personality, in particular, seems to more or less self-destruct as a result of endless aggression and a lack of conscience. While possession of an authoritarian personality does not necessarily lead to their downfall, if past is prologue, their insatiable desire for power, combined with remarkable self-righteousness, enables them to easily cross the lines of propriety, and the law.

Authoritarian Conservatism in the U.S. Senate

While most of Abramoff's relationships were with members of the House, he also worked with senators, but the Senate, so far, is not an authoritarian body, so the problems he created for the House are not likely to be as serious for the Senate. This is not to say that there is no authoritarianism in the Senate, for it is growing there as well, as Republicans, who would like to extend their power in the Senate in a fashion similar to what they have in the House, are oblivious to the fact that by doing so they would make the Senate into a mini–House of Representatives, thereby fundamentally changing the interaction between the inherently cautious Senate and the more impulsive House. Under the Constitution, each house of Congress makes its own rules. With each new Congress, the House reconstitutes itself, adopting new rules with a majority vote. The Senate, however, considers itself a continuing body, because each senator serves for six years and only a third of the Senate stands for election at any given time. A two-thirds vote, or the approval of sixty-seven senators, is therefore required to change its rules.

Because of its smaller size, with only two senators representing each state, the Senate has always allowed for more open and extended debate than the House of Representatives, which serves to protect minority views or, in effect, to prevent a tyranny of the majority. The first recorded occasion when a minority senator used extended debate to defeat a proposal was in 1790; the senator was arguing against moving the location of Congress from New York City to Philadelphia. Between 1820 and 1860, lengthy debate in the Senate became something of a common procedure for protecting the views of the minority party, and by 1856, it became a right when it was formalized in the Senate's rules.[56]

In 1917, during the presidency of Woodrow Wilson, the Senate adopted a rule permitting a "cloture vote," which provided that a vote of two thirds of the body could end a filibuster. A two-thirds vote on a matter before the Senate typically represents close to a national consensus, and by placing this rule on the books, it was assured that a small minority could not defeat the overwhelming will of the American people. Nonetheless, the Senate did not invoke the provision even once from 1927 until the early 1960s. Senators were reluctant to vote for cloture because they wanted to keep the right for themselves, and did not wish to incur the wrath of a colleague by imposing a cloture vote on another senator or group of senators who felt so strongly about a matter that they were willing to mount a filibuster. Jimmy Stewart's 1939 portrayal of a heroic use of the filibuster in *Mr. Smith Goes to Washington*—in which Stewart's character, Jefferson Smith, takes on corruption in the establishment but is ultimately silenced by cloture—influenced the public's support of the filibuster and opposition to cloture votes. In the mid-1950s and early 1960s, however, it became problematic when Southern senators used it to block the passage of civil rights legislation addressing basic rights for African Americans to education, voting, housing, and public facilities. When the landmark 1964 Civil Rights Act was tied up for seventy-four days, newspaper and television coverage of this bigoted Southern intransigence outraged Americans, and public opinion insisted that it be broken and the act passed. After that episode, the Senate changed its rules. Senate majority leader Mike Mansfield, a mild-mannered Montana Democrat, developed a system to preserve the Senate's tradition of unlimited debate without tying the Senate into procedural gridlock. Mansfield in effect introduced the modern filibuster.

For decades before the advent of Mansfield's system, in order to conduct a filibuster a senator had to be recognized by the presiding officer and then had to maintain the floor by talking. Because one man (or woman) can talk for only so long without sitting, eating, sleeping, or addressing other human necessities, the senator running it was permitted to yield to a colleague to continue it, thus operating like a tag team. Groups of senators would agree in advance to relieve one another to prevent loss of the floor and to make it possible to continue round-the-clock. They would sleep on sofas in the Senate cloakroom; some even wore a device known to long-distance bus drivers as a motorman's pal, enabling them to relieve themselves without leaving the Senate floor. Thus, whenever there was a filibuster, all other Senate business came to a halt until they either got the unwanted proposal removed from the Senate's agenda or a cloture vote ended it.

Mansfield's proposal changed all this. The Senate, by long tradition a highly collegial body, does most all of its business, of necessity, by unanimous consent. Under Mansfield's "two-track" system, the Senate agreed, by unanimous consent, to spend its mornings on the matter being filibustered, and afternoons on other business. Professors Catherine Fisk and Erwin Chemerinsky pointed out in a study that this system worked for everyone. On the one hand, the two-track system strengthened the ability of the majority to withstand a filibuster by enabling it to conduct other business. On the other hand, it made it easier for the minority, which no longer had to hold the floor continuously to prevent something less than a supermajority from cutting it off. In time, the mere prospect of a filibuster became enough to block consideration of a given matter. Based on successive changes of the Senate rules, the supermajority needed for a cloture vote was re-duced to a vote by sixty senators. Thus, when a senator informs the leadership of plans to filibuster—and the leadership knows that he or she has the support of at least sixty senators and, therefore, the ability to invoke cloture and override the threatened filibuster—the matter will not even go to the floor for a vote. The modern filibuster has therefore become silent, since its mere threat results in stopping a de-bate in its tracks.

Because the filibuster is a negative procedure, and one that frus-trates the will of a simple majority, those trying to force something through the Senate with something like a "one-vote victory" will often complain about how the minority is tying up the Senate. While such opposition has given it a bad reputation, the minority party must be able to rely on it to prevent the tyranny of a bare majority. In its pres-ent form it is, in essence, a minority veto. To overcome it requires a supermajority—a supermajority the Republicans do not currently com-mand. Accordingly, authoritarian conservatives in the Republican ranks of the Senate, many of whom once served in the House, where a sim-ple majority always prevails, want to change the rules. But because they do not have the two-thirds support necessary for doing so, Re-publicans are prepared to rely on a parliamentary gimmick that would drastically change the nature of the Senate, by eliminating the Senate's unlimited debate for judicial nominees, which could then be extended across-the-board. It is so radical, and with such potentially devastating consequences for this traditionally highly cooperative and collegial body, that it is viewed as certain to create the equivalent of a "nuclear winter," and for that reason it is called the "nuclear option."

The possible use of the nuclear option first arose when the Demo-crats lost control of the Senate following the 2002 election, and Pres-ident Bush started sending it increasingly hard-right nominees for federal judgeships. Democrats decided that their best option was to do what Republicans had done when Democrats controlled both Congress and the White House. During the 1968 presidential campaign, President Lyndon Johnson nominated two liberal justices for Supreme Court seats, proposing to move Abe Fortas from associate justice to chief justice and then to place Homer Thornberry in Fortas's seat. Senate Republicans filibustered the Fortas nomination, which gave the next president, Richard Nixon, the opportunity to appoint a new chief justice. But when Democrats adopted that strategy and started filibustering Bush's lower-court nominees to prevent him from packing the federal judiciary with right-wing judges and justices, conservatives became furious. Republicans refused to treat this as fair play, even though during the Clinton presidency, Senate Republicans had blocked votes on judicial nominations by simply refusing to process them, which meant some sixty Clinton nominees never even had a hearing before the Senate Judiciary Committee. But when Democrats sought to block Bush's nominees, Republicans refused to treat this as fair play.

Here is how the nuclear option would work, as explained by *The Hill,* the newspaper that covers Congress. Rather than seek a vote to change the rules of the Senate, which they would lose since they do not have a two-thirds majority, Republicans would seek a ruling from the presiding officer of the Senate—most likely Vice President Dick Cheney, who is the president of the Senate—that Rule XXII, the cloture vote rule, does not apply to so-called executive matters such as judicial nominations submitted to the Senate by the president, but only to legislative business. Republican senators would likely argue that filibustering the president's business, which consists of matters on the "executive calendar" such as nominations and treaties, would be a violation of the separation of powers. Needless to say, such a procedural ruling would be contrary to long practice, but Cheney would almost certainly give the GOP members exactly what they want, and Democrats would have little recourse. It takes only a simple majority to override a ruling of the presiding officer, but the Democrats do not have one. Nor could the Democrats follow the Killer D's example in

Texas by simply walking out, for the fifty-one Senate Republicans could run the Senate in their absence with more than enough senators for a quorum.

To date, the nuclear option has not been exercised, although Senate majority leader William Frist was ready to pull the trigger before a group of seven moderate Republican senators joined with seven Democrats to prevent the authoritarian conservatives from imploding the Senate.* The Gang of Fourteen (sometimes called the "Mod Squad" because they are all moderates) reached an agreement, which they executed in writing, that eliminated the use of the nuclear option—at least temporarily.[57] The gist of their understanding was that the seven Democrats would not vote with their party on filibustering judicial nominations except in "extraordinary circumstances," and the Republicans in turn agreed not to vote with their party and the Republican leadership for the exercise of the nuclear option. (By subtracting seven votes from either side, the moderates, in essence, took control.) It was basically a good-faith effort, since only a few details were worked out, including that the Democrats would prevent further filibustering of three of Bush's nominees. It was a perfect example of the way the Senate should work, using the give-and-take of compromise. The Gang of Fourteen has continued to meet, but their agreement is binding only for the 109th Congress, which will end in January 2007. Authoritarian conservatives in the Senate will likely try the nuclear option again if Republicans control the Senate in 2007, should Democrats try to use the filibuster on judicial nominees. Needless to say, there is nothing conservative about destroying Senate precedent and tradition, but

---

*The Republicans were led by Senator John McCain (AZ), who was joined by Senators Lindsey Graham (SC), John Warner (VA), Olympia Snowe (ME), Susan Collins (ME), Michael DeWine (OH), and Lincoln Chafee (RI). The Democrats were led by Senator Ben Nelson (NE), and he was joined by Senators Joe Lieberman (CT), Robert Byrd (WV), Mary Landrieu (LA), Daniel Inouye (HI), Mark Pryor (AR), and Ken Salazar (CO).

then, authoritarians are not troubled with conscience, even if they call themselves conservatives.

The Authoritarianism of the Senate Leader Who Wants to Be President

It was Senate majority leader William Frist who led the Senate to the brink of nuclear catastrophe. Frist had been a well-known heart transplant surgeon at Vanderbilt University's hospital in Nashville, Tennessee, before he was elected to the Senate in 1994. Before becoming majority leader he had made almost no serious news whatsoever since arriving in Washington, although he was occasionally featured in human interest stories. He provided emergency care for the man who shot a Capitol Police guard, and, in turn, was shot by the guard; and after the anthrax attacks in the Senate, his explanation of how the deadly poison worked was enlightening.

A December 31, 2001, profile in *Newsweek* described him as "brainy and intense, confident to the point of arrogance," "a daredevil by nature," "ambitious, eager to be noticed, [but not] a team player at heart—and White House strategists know it." His seemingly iconoclastic independence was appealing, and many welcomed his selection by his Senate peers to replace Senator Trent Lott (R-MS) as majority leader. After being told by an insider that if Vice President Dick Cheney's health took a serious turn for the worse, Bill Frist was at the top of Bush's list to replace him, I decided to read the hagiography by Charles Martin, *Healing America: The Life of Senate Majority Leader William H. Frist, M.D.,* which revealed that Frist has been slated to be president of the United States since he was only a few days old.

It is a novel story. It seems that when Bill Frist was busy campaigning for the Senate in 1994, his associate, Dr. Karl VanDevender, was responsible for running the Frist Clinic, which recently had admitted a longtime Frist family employee, the trusted yardman, housekeep, and handyman, whom they affectionately called "Mr. John."

On election night Karl VanDevender was monitoring Mr. John, who was fading fast of kidney failure. At one point in the evening, as VanDevender kept an eye on the television and reported the returns, Mr. John whispered his last words. "Dr. Karl," he said, "since the day this happened, more than forty-four years ago, I've only told two people—my pastor and my wife." VanDevender brought a chair to Mr. John's bedside and leaned in close to get every word of Mr. John's astonishing story.

Soon after Bill Frist's mother brought him home from the hospital, she appeared on the front porch carrying a baby basket with Bill sound asleep in it. He was only a few days old. Bill's mother said she wanted to go down the street to her sister's house, and she asked Mr. John to wait with baby Bill until she returned. "I'll be back in five minutes," she promised, and off she went. "So I sat down on the porch next to the boy," Mr. John continued, "and no sooner had she left than a bright light came down from heaven. An angel wrapped his golden wings around the baby and said, 'John, don't worry about this baby. He's going to be fine.'" Mr. John caught his breath and finished reporting the angel's words. "'One day, he's going to be president of the United States.'" With this, Mr. John took another deep breath, and added, "That Senate race? That ain't nothing. He's got that in the bag." Mr. John died that night, shortly after learning Bill Frist had defeated an eighteen-year incumbent, Democratic senator Jim Sasser.[58]

With his laserlike mind, Frist makes Bush and Cheney look like filament bulbs near burnout, and their authoritarianism was troubling enough. Frist is Richard Nixon with Bill Clinton's brains, and Nixon was no mental slouch. Frist is without question a social dominator, and dominators, obviously, cannot hide their tendency to dominate. No one describes Bill Frist's dominating personality better than Frist himself in his first book, *Transplant: A Heart Surgeon's Account of the Life-and-Death Dramas of the New Medicine.* The memoir opens with Frist at the top of his game as a cardiac surgeon, and it is clear that in the operating room, he is the man in charge. He called himself a good quarterback, a position he played at a private high school. It is immediately clear that Bill Frist has always been a driven individual—a born dominator and seeker of power. As the "youngest of five children," he wrote, he could "hardly help but be a demanding little tyrant." Frist says of his kindergarten years, "I ruled not just over my family but over my friends—or should I say subjects—who always opted to come to my house."[59] In the lower grades, "I longed to be first in everything, to be king of the hill, the grammar school *capo di capi*. I imagine I was quite insufferable. I hated—and often too quickly abandoned—anything at which I did not excel. I sought out whatever made me feel useful, different, and in control. I felt most comfortable with slightly younger boys who could look up to me, admire me. . . . I resented anyone my age who was more popular, bigger, faster, or smarter. I was jealous of them. I feared them. They might take over." In high school, he acknowledged he "became a deadly serious overachiever," with his "raging hormones of adolescence" spawning "an urge to excel and a desire to lead." He was class president for three of four years, yearbook editor, quarterback of the football team, and voted most likely to succeed during his senior year.[60]

Frist was in a serious motorcycle accident during his high school years. While he said this brush with death punctured some of his "sense of self-importance," the accident also somewhat strangely resulted in "a romantic patina to an aloofness that had been growing in me since earliest childhood." He was building what he calls a "Great Wall" between himself and his peers, "emotional brick by emotional brick." His Great Wall runs throughout his narrative, and he explained that only later did he "come to believe that every man who wants to lead builds such a wall, though few of them talk about it." Frist reported that by the time he headed to Princeton for his undergraduate studies, his "wall was almost complete. Few of my early acquaintances dared or cared to scale it, and I languished behind it without many close friends."[61]

As is often the case with authoritarians, politics caught Frist's attention during his college years; he would graduate from Princeton in 1974. He spent the summer of 1972 in Washington as an intern in the office of Democratic congressman Joe Evins, the senior member of the Tennessee delegation. Evins advised Frist that if he planned to go into politics he should start with a career outside of the political world. Frist even cast his romantic life in terms of dominance. "Imagining myself a leader," and a Ulysses no less, he wrote that when heading off to Harvard Medical School, "I possibly wanted a Penelope back home waiting for me." He found her, proposed, and dumped her just days before the wedding.

At medical school Frist had his Great Wall fully erected and was determined to outdo himself: "I realized that instead of molding doctors, medical school was in the business of stripping human beings of everything but the raw, almost insane, ambition you must have to simply get through." This, he confessed, is when an infamous incident occurred that Frist explained was the result of his temporarily losing sight of the big picture. What he described, however, is actually typical of a dominator playing the game his way and then justifying his own conduct. Frist had taken time off from his regular coursework to study cardiac physiology through laboratory work. He spent "days and nights on end in the lab, taking hearts out of cats, dissecting each heart," and studying and recording the effects of various medicines on the hearts. With six weeks to go to complete his project, Frist ran out of cats. "Desperate, obsessed with my work, I visited the various animal shelters in the Boston suburbs, collecting cats, taking them home, treating them as pets for a few days, then carting them off to the lab to die in the interest of science. . . . It was, of course, a heinous and dishonest thing to do, and I was totally schizoid about the entire matter. . . . I was going a little crazy."[62]

Frist was likely not going crazy; rather, he was manipulating to succeed. Lying to people who run animal shelters—not to mention misleading the poor animals, who, as Ron Rosenbaum wrote in the

New York Observer, had just come off "mean-street" unaware that they were headed for execution—was cruel. Rosenbaum checked the General Laws of Massachusetts, and clearly Frist, a serial cat killer, could have been prosecuted for cruelty to animals.[63] No doubt Frist committed fraud in obtaining the animals as well. This issue arose during the 1994 Senate campaign, and one of Frist's professional campaign consultants conceded that the revelation was a bullet they had dodged. "Thank God he wasn't experimenting with dogs," the consultant observed, because "that would have killed him in coon-hunting Tennessee."[64]

When Bill Frist was first elected he promised Tennessee voters that he would limit himself to two terms. With his second term ending in 2006, and having made it clear that he would not run for the Senate again, it appears Frist may be ready to attempt to fulfill the promise of Mr. John's angel. But he faces a serious problem, for like many social dominators in the political arena, he was tempted to overreach and was caught. Frist owns stock in the Hospital Corporation of America (HCA), a corporation his father founded and his brother built. When Frist arrived in the Senate he placed his shares in a blind trust, meaning he theoretically did not know how the trustee was handling his investment, thereby insulating himself from any conflict of interest in voting as a senator. Publicly, Frist has told conflicting stories about whether he tracked the status of this trust.[65] It is clear he did, however, because on June 13, 2005, a month before the company issued its second-quarter earnings—which would fail to meet the estimates of Wall Street analysts—Frist sold his shares in the company. At the time Frist unloaded his holdings they were selling at their highest value in years, between $57.21 and $58.60. When the earnings report was issued, the stock's price dropped almost $5.00.[66] Anyone who had a major holding in the company, as Frist did, would have made a great deal of money by selling the shares before the bad news was made public—millions of dollars. (Martha Stewart, meanwhile, went to jail for her deception about receiving insider information that made her a few thousand.) Frist claims he did nothing wrong, but both the Securities and Exchange Commission and the United States Attorney for the Southern District of New York are investigating to determine whether he acted on inside information about the company on which his brother Tom now serves as a member of the board of directors and of which Tom was once chairman.[67] But as threatening as this investigation might be to Frist's bid for the presidency, even more troublesome will be his record as Senate majority leader, where his leadership skills have been tested.

"Most Capitol Hill observers now regard Frist as 'the weakest majority leader in perhaps 50 years,'" said Charles Cook, the editor of a nonpartisan political report, in an interview with Bloomberg News. Cook, who has one of the best records for predicting political contests, said he did not think that Frist "has a snowball's chance in hell" of getting the GOP nomination. If Frist's standing with his peers suffered, he also damaged his image as a clear-thinking man of medicine when he pandered to the religious right during the debate over Terri Schiavo, the severely brain-damaged woman being kept alive by a feeding tube in a Florida hospital. After viewing videos prepared by a group supporting federal intervention to halt the withdrawal of life-support measures, Frist reported—as Dr. Frist—that Terri Schiavo was "not somebody in a persistent vegetative state." Both the House and Senate passed a law granting a federal court jurisdiction in the case, and President Bush flew back to Washington to sign the emergency measure. The federal judge, however, agreed with the state judges who had reviewed, and rereviewed, all the expert testimony, and had refused to intervene. The court battle to keep Schiavo on life support eventually ended with her death, and an autopsy showed that she had been blind and that her brain had atrophied severely. Dr. Frist's behavior in the incident was quite remarkable, given the simple message he had delivered to the Senate in his maiden speech on January 11, 1995, when he first came to Washington. "As a recently elected citizen-legislator, I carry a very distinct advantage: closeness to the people," Frist explained. He had listened to people's thoughts and concerns, and he shared them with his colleagues: "Get the federal government off our backs. . . . The arrogance of Washington is stifling us, and we are capable of making our own decisions."[68]

The Authoritarian Vice Presidency: Evil Is Not Excluded

Dick Cheney is the most powerful vice president in American history. His power comes from his knowledge of how Washington really works, and it far exceeds that of the man he ostensibly works for. Unlike Bush, Cheney relishes the minutiae of government policy and process, and he has surrounded himself with a staff that is stronger and far more competent than the president's personal staff. Unlike prior vice presidents, Cheney and his people have often taken the lead on issues, with the White House staff falling in line. Cheney has long been a behind-the-scenes operator, for he was badly burned by the news media during his tenure as White House chief of staff. His ego does not need the spotlight, and his dark view of the world and life is, in any case, better suited to working behind closed doors.

Notwithstanding Cheney's claims that the powers of the presidency are insufficient to fight terrorism, the office has enormous inherent powers. And when it does not, the president traditionally goes to Congress to petition for whatever additional power is needed; no Congress is going to deny any president essential powers to protect the nation. Cheney, it seems, had been traumatized as Ford's chief of staff when the Congress began dismantling Nixon's imperial presidency. "In the aftermath of Vietnam and Watergate," Cheney told the *Wall Street Journal*, "there was a concerted effort to place limits and restrictions on presidential authority . . . the decisions that were aimed at the time at trying to avoid a repeat of things like Vietnam or . . . Watergate." For most people adopting such measures would be considered good government; Cheney believes otherwise. "I thought they were misguided then, and have believed that given the world that we live in, that the president needs to have unimpaired executive authority."[69] He has repeated that line time after time, without ever explaining exactly why the post-Watergate measures were misguided, or why efforts by Congress to prevent another Vietnam, which took some fifty thousand American lives for no good purpose, were faulty. Since Cheney has been vice president he has never been interviewed by a reporter inclined (or permitted) to ask the hard questions, so Cheney has never had to explain himself. The man he works for looks only at the politics of any given matter, and does not have the depth of knowledge to challenge his vice president. Cheney's relationships with his staff and his informal advisers in and out of government are ones in which the vice president poses the questions, and he is never required to give answers. When Cheney speaks publicly—which is not often—he pontificates, or dictates.

It is true that Dick Cheney has served at both ends of Pennsylvania Avenue. He held positions in both the Nixon (and got out before Watergate) and Ford White Houses. He spent over a decade on Capitol Hill, first as a congressional aide, and later as a congressman from Wyoming who worked his way up the House GOP leadership ladder, before being named to a cabinet post, as Secretary of Defense (under Bush I). It is an exceptional government career. Cheney did not become the youngest White House chief of staff by accident; he did not become the number-two leader of the House Republicans because of his mild manner; and he did not serve as both chairman of the board and chief operating officer of the Halliburton Corporation because of his good looks. Cheney is an authoritarian dominator. He studies the landscape, and then figures out how to get the ground he wants for himself. He has demonstrated remarkable ability in making it to the top, most recently by selecting himself as vice president of the United

States. What is always overlooked with Dick Cheney is how he performs when he arrives in his various jobs. The answer is, in truth, not very well. Cheney is surely proof of the "Peter Principle" (that people in a hierarchy eventually rise to their level of incompetence).

Josh Marshall,* writing in the *Washington Monthly*, was the first journalist to observe this fact about Cheney; the piece was titled "Vice Grip: Dick Cheney is a man of principles. Disastrous Principles."[70] Marshall had discovered that Cheney has made one serious mistake after another as vice president, although "in the Washington collective mind," he has the reputation of a "sober, reliable, skilled inside player." Marshall found that the facts belie Cheney's reputation, and he has made a consistent string of "mistakes—on energy policy, homeland security, corporate reform." Since Marshall wrote his piece this list of serious errors has only grown. Marshall attributed Cheney's ineptness to a career that has largely isolated him from the real world. As Marshall described it, Cheney is part of the "hierarchical, old economy style of management [that] couldn't be more different from the loose, nonhierarchical style of, say, high-tech corporations or the Clinton White House, with all their open debate, concern with the interests of 'stake-holders,' manic focus on pleasing customers (or voters), and constant reassessment of plans and principles. The latter style, while often sloppy and seemingly juvenile, tends to produce pretty smart policy. The former style, while appearing so adult and competent, often produces stupid policy." Marshall is also describing the distinction between a nonauthoritarian White House and an authoritarian operation.

An examination of Cheney's career reveals that it is marked by upward mobility and downward performance. For example, the best

---

*Josh Marshall, as anyone who follows the better blogs knows, today runs the growing and always insightful (regardless of one's political point of view) Talking Points Memo and TPM Café blogs at htttp://www.talkingpointsmemo. com/.

thing Cheney did for Halliburton as chairman and CEO was to step down and help them get no-bid contracts to rebuild Iraq and federal help with their asbestos claims liability; Cheney's attempt to run for president failed at the conception stage; he was undistinguished as Secretary of Defense, and many believe he was actually disappointed when the cold war ended on his watch, and not by his doing; his years in Congress have left a voting record that any fair-minded person would be ashamed of; and he was way over his head as Ford's chief of staff, which resulted in the remaining Nixon staff's appreciating how good Haldeman had been in the job; and, of course, he helped Ford lose his bid to become an elected president in the race against Jimmy Carter.

Bad judgment is Dick Cheney's trademark. It was not George Bush who came up with the idea of imposing blanket secrecy on the executive branch when he and Cheney took over. It was not George Bush who conceived of the horrible—and in some cases actually evil—policies that typify this authoritarian presidency, such as detaining "enemy combatants" with no due process and contrary to international law. It was not George Bush who had the idea of using torture during interrogations, and removing restraints on the National Security Agency from collecting intelligence on Americans. These were policies developed by Cheney and his staff, and sold to the president, and then imposed on many who subsequently objected to this authoritarian lawlessness. It was Cheney and his mentor, Secretary of Defense Donald Rumsfeld, who convinced Bush to go to war in Iraq, which is proving to be a protracted calamity. As Colin Powell's former top aide, Laurence Wilkinson, rather bluntly puts it: In 2002 Cheney must have believed that Iraq was a spawning ground for terrorists, "otherwise I have to declare him a moron, an idiot or a nefarious bastard."[71] Colonel Wilkinson, it appears, has a rather solid take on the vice president's thinking, for there is no evidence that Cheney believed—or had any basis for such a belief—that Iraq was a spawning ground for terrorism—before we made it into one.

The issue of Dick Cheney's judgment must be raised because he is the catalyst, architect, and chief proponent of Bush's authoritarian policies. In fact, Cheney's authoritarian vice presidency has simply swallowed the president, and Cheney sought to take the office way beyond even Nixon's imperial presidency, which they had accomplished by the end of the first term.* Insidiously, Cheney and his staff are proceeding with strategic moves, largely out of sight, that are undertaken regularly to accomplish his goal, and often at the political expense of the president, which creates periodic, but growing, rifts between the men. These include things like ramming through the White House a presidential signing statement regarding a new law. Rather than vetoing legislation when it arrives at the White House, the White House (read: Cheney and his staff) issues a brief statement giving its interpretation of the new law as it relates to presidential powers. These statements are consistently different from the clear intent of Congress, so Bush and Cheney have, in effect, told Congress to go to hell on the few occasions when the Republican Congress has stood up to the White House. Typical was its response when Senator John McCain (R-AZ) sought to end the use of torture by Americans when interrogating putative terrorists.

George Bush has repeatedly insisted, "We do not torture." Secretary of State Condoleezza Rice has repeatedly claimed that the United States does not engage in "cruel, inhuman, or degrading treatment." And CIA director Porter Goss affirms that his agency "does not do torture. Torture does not work." But no one believes the Bush administration on this issue, and for good reason. When the so-called torture

*As I suggested in *Worse Than Watergate* (page 40) I have never been certain that Cheney will not go the distance of a full second term. When the *Washington Times's Insight* magazine runs stories heralding this potential it has some basis. See Anonymous, "Cheney seen retiring after midterm elections," *Insight on the News* (February 27–March 5, 2006) at http://www.insightmag.com/Media/MediaManager/cheney3.htm.

memos prepared by the Department of Justice were leaked—after the photos of torture at Abu Ghraib had surfaced—they revealed that the White House had managed to get the Justice Department to virtually define away torture. As the *Economist* commented, the words of the Bush administration officials on torture count "for little when the administration has argued, first, that during time of war, the president can make just about anything legal, and, second, that the UN Convention Against Torture does not apply to interrogations of foreign terrorist suspects outside the United States." Similarly, Senator John McCain, who was tortured as a POW in Vietnam and took pride in the belief that his country would never resort to using such measures, did not believe the Bush administration. In 2004 Congress passed a bipartisan amendment to the defense authorization bill, reaffirming that detainees in U.S. custody could not be subject to torture or cruel treatment as those terms have been previously defined by the U.S. government. "But since last year's DOD bill," Senator McCain informed his colleagues, "a strange legal determination was made that the prohibition in the Convention Against Torture against cruel, inhuman, or degrading treatment does not legally apply to foreigners held outside the United States." Or, as the senator put it more bluntly, "They can apparently be treated inhumanely." The Bush/Cheney administration's reading of the law was pure expediency. Judge Abe Sofaer, who negotiated the torture convention, wrote an op-ed explaining that there was never any intention to limit the torture agreement to American soil. McCain had a powerful case for why his amendments were needed.

In October and November of 2005, Senator McCain offered his amendments to the Defense Department's authorization bill and its appropriations bill to prohibit the United States from engaging in torture. This was legislation that could not be vetoed without halting the war in Iraq. The first McCain-sponsored amendment was titled "Uniform Standards for the Interrogation of Persons Under the Detention of the Department of Defense." It simply stated that persons "in the custody or under the effective control of the Department of Defense" can only be interrogated pursuant to the United States Army Field Manual on Intelligence Interrogation (which prohibits torture). The second McCain-sponsored amendment was titled "Prohibition On Cruel, Inhuman, or Degrading Treatment or Punishment of Persons Under Custody or Control of the United States Government." This provision required that individuals in the custody of, or under the physical control of, the United States government, regardless of nationality or physical location, not be subjected "to cruel, inhuman, or degrading treatment or punishment."

Amazingly, when Cheney learned of these amendments, he tried to block them. Who could conceive of an American vice president demanding that Congress give the president the authority to torture anyone, under any circumstances? Yet that is exactly what Cheney wanted. Fortunately, Congress—finally—showed some institutional pride and told Cheney that it would not countenance torture, under any circumstances. It was also remarkable that Senate majority leader Bill Frist set aside his Hippocratic Oath and unsuccessfully attempted to use procedures to prevent Senator McCain from offering the amendments. Finally, the White House threatened that President Bush, who had not vetoed a single piece of legislation since assuming office, would do so for any bill that contained McCain's amendments, even if it meant shutting off funds for the Department of Defense (a move that would have posed no small threat to national security). This threat announced, in effect, that the authorization to torture was more important than the well-being of the nation.

The administration's public explanation for its opposition to McCain's amendments, as made by those few willing to promote these actions, bordered on pathetic. Senator Ted Stevens (R-AK) claimed during the Senate debate on the amendments that they would have a reverse impact, resulting in more torture. Stevens reached this conclusion by claiming that the international teams that pursue terrorists, being aware of restrictions on Americans, would not give the United States custody of terrorists that they found. This contention is so full of holes that it is barely necessary to refute it. Not all groups that search for terrorists are international, and in fact, that is the exception to the rule. And typically, Americans command these undertakings, so the contention that prisoners accused of terrorism would somehow be taken away from America and tortured—against America's will—by other nations is absurd. In fact, the current practice is exactly the opposite: Through what is called "rendition," America now allows its own suspects to be turned over to countries that torture with impunity, and that do not honor the kinds of rights the U.S. Constitution guarantees. This practice is also contrary to international law.

Reports indicated that Dick Cheney's favorite argument—the one he made in trip after trip to closed-door meetings on Capitol Hill to get authority, at minimum, for the CIA to be able to torture—is the old "ticking bomb" gambit. So frequently has this specious argument been employed to justify torture that it deserves to be shot down with more than a passing reference. The argument runs like this: A nuclear bomb has been planted in the heart of a major American city, and authorities have in custody a person who knows where it is located. To save possibly millions of lives, would it not be justified to torture this individual to get the necessary information to stop it? Absolutely. Is not this lesser evil justified? Of course it is. And this argument is a wonderful means to comfort those who have moral problems with torture. Its beauty is that once you concede there are circumstances in which torture might be justified, morally and legally (through what criminal law calls the defense of necessity: that an act is justified to save lives), you are on the other side of the line. You've joined the torture crowd. To paraphrase Bush, you have joined the evildoers.

A number of great minds and moral authorities rely on this logic, so Cheney is not alone. Nonetheless, it is a bogus argument, a rhetorical device. It is seductively simple, and compellingly logical. But it is also pure fantasy. The conditions of ticking bomb scenarios are in the same remote category as a meteor or asteroid hitting earth. No one has more effectively probed the fallacies of this line of thinking than Georgetown University School of Law professor David Luban. Writing in the *Washington Post,* Luban explains why, while it makes good television melodrama, this scenario does not produce critical thinking.[72] Luban surgically dissects this argument at greater length in the October 2005 *Virginia Law Review* in his essay "Liberalism, Torture, and the Ticking Bomb." Citing moral philosopher Bernard Williams, Luban wrote that "there are certain situations so monstrous that the idea that the processes of moral rationality could yield an answer in them is insane," and "to spend time thinking what one would decide if one were in such a situation is also insane, if not merely frivolous." As Professor Luban noted, "McCain has said that ultimately the debate is over who we are. We will never figure that out until we stop talking about ticking bombs, and stop playing games with words."[73]

Senator McCain, joined by former military judge and current senator Lindsey Graham (R-SC), called the bluff of the White House, and pushed forward with his amendments. The U.S. Senate approved them overwhelmingly with a vote of 90 to 9 in favor.* (Senator Corzine [D-NJ], who was running for governor, was absent.) Not surprisingly, the House of Representatives, as far as the Republican leadership was concerned, was not willing to accept the McCain amendments. A year earlier Speaker of the House Dennis Hastert had tried to slip a provision into a law authorizing the CIA to torture. But he was caught, and

---

*The nine senators who voted against McCain's amendment—and *for* torture—deserve special recognition, for they are true authoritarians: Senators Wayne Allard (R-CO), Christopher Bond (R-MO), Tom Coburn (R-OK), Thad Cochran (R-MS), John Cornyn (R-TX), James Inhofe (R-OK), Pat Roberts (R-KS), Jeff Sessions (R-AL), and Ted Stevens (R-AK).

the effort died. Senator McCain was negotiating with the House, and with the White House, when Congressman John P. Murtha (D-PA) forced the issue to the House floor, calling for a motion to instruct the House conferees to accept the language of the McCain amendments. "No circumstance whatsoever justifies torture. No emergencies, no state of war, no level of political instability," Murtha, a heavily decorated and much respected veteran, said. Only one lonely voice dared to speak against Murtha's motion: Congressman C. W. Bill Young of Florida opposed the McCain amendments because he did not believe terrorists should have the protection of our Constitution. That argument was absurd; terrorists already have that protection, and McCain's amendments do not change the existing law. Young's contention went nowhere, and the subsequent vote sent a clear message to Bush and Cheney: The motion carried by 308 yeas and a remarkable 122 nays (all authoritarian).

Bush later invited McCain to the White House and at a photo-opportunity session in the Oval Office appeared to concede and back down. Cheney was not to be seen, for he was no doubt busy making sure the signing statement Bush would issue would make clear that the White House did not believe the Congress could tell the president (read: Cheney) whether he could or could not use torture. The artfully worded statement said, "The executive branch shall construe [the McCain amendment law] in a manner consistent with the constitutional authority of the President . . . as Commander in Chief," adding, that by doing so it "will assist in achieving the shared objective of the Congress and the President . . . of protecting the American people from further attacks." As the *Boston Globe* reported, a number of legal scholars read this, as I did, as Bush and Cheney saying, We will do whatever we want, notwithstanding the law prohibiting torture.[74]

Cheney sent a clear signal of his plans for the ongoing efforts to further enhance presidential powers by elevating David Addington, his former counsel, to replace his indicted former chief of staff, Scooter Libby. Addington is a low-profile, high-powered, table-pounding, sarcastic when-not-shouting-in-your-face attorney.[75] Addington is a paradigm authoritarian, instrumental in gathering the team of lawyers who prepared legal opinions for the Department of Justice authorizing American interrogators to engage in torture. Addington teamed up with John Yoo, a law professor who clerked for the most far-right members of the federal judiciary—first Judge Laurence Silberman of the D.C. Circuit Court of Appeals, and then U.S. Supreme Court Justice Clarence Thomas—and who had never met a presidential power that Article II of the Constitution excluded. Together they worked on figuring out how to get around criminal laws that prohibit torture and electronic surveillances of Americans. In doing so they have offered highly specious arguments that start with the end result they seek and twist the law to fit the conclusion they want to reach. Not surprisingly, they have horrified the intellectually honest legal minds of other conservative Bush lawyers, like former deputy attorney general James Comey, who got out of the Justice Department, it appears, as quickly as he could. And former assistant attorney general Jack Goldsmith left Justice when he had had enough of Addington's power tantrums.[76]

Addington, who was in his early teens during Vietnam and Watergate, reportedly shares the view of his boss that "the executive branch was pitifully weakened by the backlash" to these events.[77] One has to wonder about Cheney and Addington's motives in seeking to restore the presidency to what they believe to be its pre–Vietnam and Watergate backlash days. Are these men unaware of why Congress clamped down on presidents' spying on Americans? Have they not read the transcripts of Richard Nixon pounding on his desk to demand a break-in at the Brookings Institution because he wanted documents he believed to be in their vault? Could they be unaware of the record of J. Edgar Hoover's FBI when it had unfettered powers? Why, if the powers of the presidency are wanting, do they not go to Congress and lay out what they need, rather than violating the law to see if they can get away with it? Do they not realize they are calling for— and are busy implementing—an authoritarian presidency, unchecked by the Congress or the courts? Have they forgotten that the underlying ideal of our democracy is the rule of law—not rule by presidential whim? It is still not clear how far these men want to take their authoritarianism, but I cannot find any examples of authoritarians leading any government where the governed wanted to go.

Legitimizing Authoritarian Conservatism: The Ugly Politics of Fear

If George Bush had not selected Dick Cheney as his running mate in 2000, and if the terrorist attacks on New York and Washington had not occurred in 2001, authoritarian conservatism could not have surfaced in the executive branch with its current ferocious sense of purpose. When a president embraces a concept, though, it gains legitimacy throughout the federal establishment, as political appointees—those several thousand men and women who serve at the pleasure of the president, head up various departments and agencies, or work on the White House staff—follow their leader. Depending on the president (or, in the case of the current administration, the vice president), varying degrees of dissent are tolerated in the decision-making process, but once policy is set, political appointees are expected to carry it out or leave. This is what happens within an authoritarian government. For example, when Jack Goldsmith (now on the faculty of Harvard Law School) disagreed with the authoritarian policies being issued by the White House—policies calling for the use of torture and directing the National Security Agency to violate the Foreign Intelligence Surveillance Act by not seeking warrants for electronic surveillance of Americans—he became a marked man. Goldsmith left the Justice Department, as have other high-level attorneys who wanted no part of the administration's disregard for the rule of law.[78]

As Bush proceeds with his second term, we have had some six years to observe him. It is abundantly clear that he is a mental lightweight with a strong right-wing authoritarian personality, with some social dominance tendencies as well. Bush's leading authorities are "his gut," his God, and his vice president. Cheney, it appears, knows how to manipulate the president like a puppet, and handles his oversized ego by making him believe ideas or decisions are his own when, in fact, they are Cheney's. While Bush does not appear to be a Double High, the vice president is a classic Double High, including—among other things—by his "go fuck yourself" dismissal of those with whom he disagrees.[79] Cheney is the mind of this presidency, with Bush its salesman. Bush simply does not have the mental facility or inclination for serious critical analysis of the policies he is being pushed to adopt.

Bush and Cheney saw 9/11 as an excuse to indulge their natural authoritarian and conservative instincts. In so doing, they have brought out the worst in conservatism: They have justified and rationalized their increasing use of authoritarian tactics in the name of fighting terrorism. Without terrorism, George W. Bush would have likely been a one-term president; with terrorism as a raison d'être, Bush and Cheney's authoritarianism has not been questioned seriously enough.

Many of the activities carried out as a result of Bush and Cheney's authoritarianism have been labeled "radical."* A partial list of synonyms for "radical" includes "extremist," "fanatical," "far-out," "immoderate," "intransigent," "militant," "nihilistic," "revolutionary," "uncompromising," and even "lawless."[80] Radicals are those "favoring or effecting extreme or revolutionary changes"; those "favoring drastic political, economic, or social reforms"; persons "who hold or follow strong convictions or extreme principles; extremists"; and persons "who advocate

---

*Bill Safire reported in his political dictionary that when campaigning for his first term as president, Franklin Roosevelt offered a good description of a radical: "[S]ay that civilization is a tree which, as it grows, continually produces rot and dead wood," FDR said. "The radical says: 'Cut it down.' The conservative says: 'Don't touch it.' The liberal compromises: 'Let's prune, so that we lose neither the old trunk nor the new branches.'" William Safire, *Safire's New Political Dictionary: The Definitive Guide to the New Language of Politics* (New York: Random House, 1993), 407.

fundamental political, economic, and social reforms by direct and often uncompromising methods."[81] The mainstream foreign press was the first to take note of the fact that the Bush administration was not in the least following a conservative agenda. For example, the *Australian* (November 2, 2004) observed that American "conservatives have become radicals"; the *Financial Times* of London (November 22, 2004) referred to "Republican radicals" being eager for more tax cuts; and the *Guardian* (January 23, 2005) described the Bush and Cheney administration as "one of the most radical Republican governments in recent American history." American newspapers soon took the same viewpoint. A *Boston Globe* editorial (May 21, 2005) called Utah's senator Orrin Hatch "a well-known Republican radical," and the *San Francisco Chronicle* (May 20, 2005) referred to "radical Republicans." There have been many such descriptions of today's Republicans, but the source of their radicalism has been ignored. All of the terms used to define radicalism also accurately describe the actions of authoritarians. Just as the mainstream American news media was slow to attach the term "radical" to describe the current Republican administration and Congress, the media seems disinclined to describe the conduct underlying this radicalism as authoritarian.

However, journalist-turned-blogger Joshua Marshall has a remarkable ability to be among the first to spot developments in Washington, as he did in identifying the authoritarianism of the Bush administration. In analyzing a speech by Al Gore on January 16, 2006,[82] addressing the Bush administration's remarkable abuses of power, Marshall wrote, "The point Gore makes in his speech that I think is most key is the connection between authoritarianism, official secrecy and incompetence. The president's critics are always accusing him of law-breaking or unconstitutional acts and then also berating the incompetence of his governance. And it's often treated as, well . . . he's power-hungry and incompetent to boot! Imagine that! The point though is that they are *directly connected.* Authoritarianism and secrecy breed incompetence; the two feed on each other. It's a vicious cycle.

Governments with authoritarian tendencies point to what is in fact their own incompetence as the rationale for giving them yet more power"[83] (italics Marshall's).

Among the most troubling of the authoritarian and radical tactics being employed by Bush and Cheney are their politics of fear. A favorite gambit of Latin American dictators who run sham democracies, fear-mongering has generally been frowned upon in American politics.* Think of the modern presidents who have governed our nation—Roosevelt, Truman, Eisenhower, Kennedy, Johnson, Ford, Carter, Reagan, Bush I, and Clinton—and the various crises they confronted—the Great Depression, World War II, the Korean war, the cold war, the Cuban missile crisis, the war in Vietnam, Iran's taking of American hostages, the danger to American students in Grenada, Saddam's invasion of Kuwait, the terrorist bombings at the World Trade Center in 1993, and Timothy McVeigh's 1995 bombing of the federal building in Oklahoma. None of these presidents resorted to fear in dealing with these situations. None of these presidents made the use of fear a standard procedure or a means of governing (or pursuing office or political goals). To the contrary, all of these presidents sought to *avoid* preying on the fears of Americans. (It will be noted that Nixon is not

---

*For example, President Alberto Fujimori manipulated the people of Peru for electoral gains and to justify authoritarian practices in 2000 by using the threat of terror. "Elitists and dictators have used fear tactics to control their constituencies since the beginning of time," noted scholar R. D. Davis in "Debunking the Big Lie," in *National Minority Politics* (November 30, 1995), 37. Chris Ney and Kelly Creedon, authors with expertise on Latin American politics, wrote that "fear won the election" in El Salvador in 2004, noting, "The rhetoric and tactics mirror those employed by other Latin American right-wing parties, including that of former Chilean dictator Augusto Pinochet." They conclude with an observation remarkably applicable to American democracy: "The targeted use of fear is a powerful motivator, especially for people who have been traumatized by war, state terrorism, or economic insecurity. The implications for democratic government—whether newly formed or well-established—are deeply disturbing." Chris Ney and Kelly Creedon, "Preemptive Intervention in El Salvador," *Peacework* (May 2004), 15.

included in this list because he did use fear in both his 1968 and 1972 presidential campaigns, and he continued to use this tactic once in office.)

Frightening Americans, nonetheless, has become a standard ploy for Bush, Cheney, and their surrogates. They add a fear factor to every course of action they pursue, whether it is their radical foreign policy of preemptive war, their call for tax cuts, their desire to privatize social security, or their implementation of a radical new health care scheme. This fearmongering began with the administration's political exploitation of the 9/11 tragedy, when it made the fight against terrorists the centerpiece of its presidency. Bush and Cheney launched America's first preemptive war by claiming it necessary to the fight against terrorism. Yet it is almost universally agreed that the war has actually created an incubator in Iraq for a new generation of terrorists who will seek to harm the United States far into the future. Even well-informed friends of the Bush administration have adopted this view. Senator John McCain, in a 2004 speech to the Council on Foreign Relations, expressed his concern that we had "energized the extremists and created a breeding ground for terrorists, dooming the Arab world" in Iraq,[84] and former National Security Adviser (to Bush I) Brent Scowcroft bluntly said of the war in Iraq, "This was said to be part of the war on terror, but Iraq feeds terrorism."[85]

Among the few who have spoken out against the politics of fear, no one has done so more forcefully, and with less notice in the mainstream news media, than former vice president Al Gore, who was the keynote speaker at a conference in February 2004 titled "Fear: Its Political Uses and Abuses." Gore analyzed the administration's continuous use of fear since 9/11 and expressed grave concern that no one was correcting the misinformation being fed to Americans by Bush and Cheney. "Fear drives out reason. Fear suppresses the politics of discourse and opens the door to the politics of destruction," Gore observed. "President Dwight Eisenhower said this: 'Any who act as if freedom's defenses are to be found in suppression and suspicion and fear confess a doctrine that is alien to America.' But only fifteen years later," Gore continued, "when Eisenhower's vice president, Richard Nixon, became president, we saw the beginning of a major change in America's politics. Nixon, in a sense, embodied that spirit of suppression and suspicion and fear that Eisenhower had denounced." Getting right to the point, Gore continued, "In many ways, George W. Bush reminds me of Nixon more than any other president. . . . Like Bush, Nixon understood the political uses and misuses of fear." While much of the press has ignored Bush's and Cheney's fearmongering, letters to the editor occasionally surface to address it, like the letter from Steve Mavros to the *New York Times* saying he was "sick and tired of living in fear," yet "President Bush and Vice President Dick Cheney want us to fear everything. Fear the terrorists, fear Muslims, fear gays."[86]

By and large Bush, Cheney, and their White House media operation have churned out fear with very few challenges from the media. Cheney regularly tells Americans that we are "up against an adversary who, with a relatively small number of people, could come together and mount a devastating attack against the United States," adding, "The ultimate threat now would be a group of al Qaeda in the middle of one of our cities with a nuclear weapon."[87] Did the interviewer ask how likely that might be? Or what the government was doing to prevent it or to minimize its impact? No such questions were raised. The Bush White House understands that the media will treat their fearmongering as news, because fear sells news; it keeps people reading, watching, and waiting for updates. There is more fear to come, for the Bush White House is relying on it in their campaign for the 2006 midterm congressional elections. This, in turn, will set the stage for the 2008 presidential election, where authoritarians will make certain fear is a prominent part of the platform.

Bush's top political strategist, Karl Rove, gave the word to the political troops at a meeting of the Republican National Committee in early 2006. "America is at war—and so our national security is at the forefront of the minds of Americans," Rove said, as he rattled the White House saber. "The United States faces a ruthless enemy—and we need a commander-in-chief and a Congress who understand the nature of the threat and the gravity of this moment. President Bush and the Republican Party do. Unfortunately, the same cannot be said for many Democrats."[88] I have said little about Rove, principally because this is not a book about the Bush White House. But Karl Rove has all the credentials of a right-wing authoritarian, and if he has a conscience, it has hardly been in evidence during the five years in which he has been in the public eye. He is conspicuously submissive to authority, exceedingly aggressive in pursuing and defending the policies and practices he embraces (namely, whatever George W. Bush believes, or that which is politically expedient), and he is highly conventional. As a political strategist, Rove appreciates the value of fear, so it is not surprising that he proclaimed that the 2006 midterm elections would be won or lost based on how frightened Americans are about terrorism.

A writer for *Harper's* magazine recently collected facts that illustrate the 9/11 terror attack from a "detached perspective," leaving out hot hyperbole by making a cold comparison of hard numbers regarding causes of death in the United States:

> In 2001, terrorists killed 2,978 people in the United States, including the five killed by anthrax. In that same year, according to the Centers for Disease Control, heart disease killed 700,142 Americans and cancer 553,768; various accidents claimed 101,537 lives, suicide 30,622, and homicide, not including the [terror] attacks, another 17,330. As President Bush pointed out in January [2004], no one has been killed by terrorists on American soil since then. Neither, according to the FBI, was anyone killed here by terrorists in 2000. In 1999, the number was one. In 1998, it was three. In 1997, zero.* Even using 2001 as a baseline, the ac-

*The total number of fatalities resulting from the 1995 bombing of the Alfred P. Murrah Federal Building in Oklahoma City, Oklahoma, was 168.

tuarial tables would suggest that our concern about terror mortality ought to be on the order of our concern about fatal workplace injuries (5,431 deaths) or drowning (3,247). To recognize this is not to dishonor the loss to the families of those people killed by terrorists, but neither should their anguish eclipse that of the families of children who died in their infancy that year (27,801). Every death has its horrors.[89]

On a broad base, Jim Harper, the director of Information Policy Studies at the Cato Institute, has observed, "We can compare the risk of terrorist attack to other dangers our country has historically faced: During the height of the Cold War, we drew within a few figurative minutes of midnight—the moment that the Soviet Union and United States would hurl their world-ending arsenals at one another." Harper further noted that "we didn't throw out the rulebook during the Cold War. The executive branch did not make extravagant claims to power," as are Bush and Cheney.[90]

Despite such realities, the Bush administration continually presents the public with a worst-case scenario. Clearly, the most serious threat from terrorists is that they obtain a weapon of mass destruction (WMD). But we face another very serious threat: namely, that our own government terrorizes us so much that we are willing to give up the ideals of democracy in exchange for reducing our fear. This threat to democracy seems well understood by Osama bin Laden and his troops. I have noted in the past, and I believe even more strongly today, that "the real danger posed by terrorism for our democracy is not that they can defeat us with physical or military force," rather "terrorism presents its real threat in provoking democratic regimes to embrace and employ authoritarian measures that (1) weaken the fabric of democracy; (2) discredit the government domestically as well as internationally; (3) alienate segments of the population from their government, thereby pushing more people to support (passively, if not outright actively) the terrorist organizations and their causes; and (4) undermine the government's claim to the moral high ground in the battle against the terrorists, while gaining legitimacy for the latter.'"[91] This is precisely what is happening in America today, as Bush and Cheney are being sucker punched by Osama bin Laden. Authoritarianism is everywhere in the federal government, not because Bush and Cheney do not realize what they doing, but because they are authoritarians, and they are doing what authoritarians do. In the process they have weakened the fabric of democracy, discredited the American government as never before in the eyes of the world, caused people to wonder if terrorists have a legitimate complaint, and taken the United States far from the moral high ground in refusing to abide by basic international law.

In citing the worst-case potential of the next terror attack in the United States—a nuclear weapon, a "dirty bomb," or a chemical or biological weapon that could kill or injure millions of Americans—the Bush administration is not making a baseless argument. Such things could happen. But there is much that can be done to reduce the potential, as well as the impact, of a WMD terror attack. It would, therefore, seem logical—if the Bush administration is truly concerned about such a catastrophic terror strike in the United States—for it to focus its efforts on such measures, rather than simply frightening people.

How serious is the Bush administration about addressing the possibility of another major terror attack in the United States? Remarkably, not very. Notwithstanding the level of importance the administration purportedly places on fighting terrorism, according to the 9/11 Commission's 2005 year-end "report card" Bush and Company were given five Fs, twelve Ds, and two incompletes in categories that included airline passenger screening and improvement of first responders' communication systems. The bipartisan members of the 9/11 Commission found that "there has been little progress in forcing federal agencies to share intelligence and terrorism information and sharply criticized government efforts to secure weapons of mass destruction," according to the *Washington Post*.* "We believe that the terrorists will strike again," 9/11 Commission chairman Thomas H. Kean told reporters. "If they do, and these reforms that might have prevented such an attack have not been implemented, what will our excuses be?"[92] When the president and his cohort continue to raise the threat of terrorism but refuse to implement even the minimum measures recommended by the commission, it is clear they are playing the politics of fear. No one knows when, if ever, terrorists will use a weapon of mass destruction in the United States, but using the issue to frighten people while not addressing the 9/11 Commission's concerns is worse than irresponsible; it is cruel.

It appears that most Republicans are content to allow the Bush White House to engage in fearmongering if that is what is needed to win elections. Many contend that terrorism, after all, is a real threat, and they feel safer with Republicans in charge, because they believe Republicans will deal with the issue more effectively than Democrats. Of course, demagoguery is not new; there have always been and always will be politicians who appeal to emotions rather than reason, because it works.

There are, in fact, relatively few people who are truly intimidated by the possibility of terrorist attacks.** Those few who are genuinely frightened, however, help Bush and Cheney. Dr. Jost and his collaborators, in the study reported in Chapter 1, found that fear of terrorism

*For a copy of the full report, which also contains grades for some forty different recommendations previously made by the commission, see http://www.9-11pdp.org/press/2005-12-05_report.pdf.

**Polls both in the United States and Western Europe show only a relatively small number of people are so concerned about terrorism that it has an impact on their lives. For example, a Harris Poll (February 4, 2004) in both the United States and Britain found that "[m]ost people in both countries do not worry a lot about a possible attack. People in Great Britain are slightly more worried

is a useful recruiting tool for Republicans. When the Bush administration reminds people of terrorism, it clearly works to their political benefit. Jamie Arndt, a psychology professor at the University of Missouri, reported, "Reminders of death create anxiety that causes people to cling to cultural and societal touchstones." Because the president is such a touchstone, "he may benefit from keeping [terrorism] in people's mind," Arndt said.[93] This finding is corroborated by public opinion polls. While political exploitation of terror does not make a tremendous difference in voting behavior, it has been sufficient to keep Bush in the White House. At the outset of the 2004 presidential campaign, President Bush was more trusted than Senator Kerry to do a good job protecting the country from terrorists by a substantial margin of 53 percent to 37 percent.[94] A CNN exit poll taken at the end of the race, after Bush had repeatedly raised the issue of terrorism, showed that people voted for Bush over Kerry on this issue by a similar—but better for Bush—58 percent to 40 percent margin.[95]

Fearmongering has serious political consequences. Timothy Naftali, a diplomatic historian at the University of Virginia who worked as a consultant to the 9/11 Commission, is troubled by the ramifications of Bush, Cheney, et al.'s use of fear and their politicizing of policies needed to deal with terrorism. A reviewer for *Foreign Affairs* noted that in Naftali's view, "the Bush administration's reliance on a 'politics of fear' has stymied a mature national conversation about counterterrorism. He urges the government to keep terrorism at the forefront of its concerns and pursue a pragmatic foreign policy while helping the public put the threat in perspective and evaluate the difficult tradeoffs between national security and civil liberties."[96] Al Gore, in his keynote

than Americans about the possibility of a terrorist attack somewhere in the country, but the difference is very small. Twelve percent (12%) of the British, compared to 9% of Americans, worry 'often,' while 59% of the British worry 'occasionally' or 'often,' compared to 55% in the United States." See http://www.harrisinteractive.com/harris_poll/index.asp?PID=437.

address at the 2004 conference on fear, also noted the consequences of Bush's preying on American fears. "Fear was activated on September 11 in all of us to a greater or lesser degree," Gore observed. "And because it was difficult to modulate or to change in particular specifics, it was exploitable for a variety of purposes unrelated to the initial cause of the fear. When the president of the United States stood before the people of this nation—in the same speech in which he used the forged document—he asked the nation to 'imagine' how fearful it would feel if Saddam Hussein gave a nuclear weapon to terrorists who then exploded it in our country. Because our nation had been subjected to the fearful, tragic, cruel attack of 9/11, when our president asked us to imagine with him a new fear, it was easy enough to bypass the reasoning process, and short-circuit the normal discourse that takes place in a healthy democracy with a give-and-take among people who could say, Wait a minute, Mr. President. Where's your evidence? There is no connection between Osama bin Laden and Saddam Hussein.' At one point, President Bush actually said, 'You can't distinguish between Saddam Hussein and Osama bin Laden.' He actually said that," Gore added, and with disappointment explained how even he had trusted Bush to do the right thing, but that Bush had abused the trust people had in him.[97]

In short, fear takes reasoning out of the decision-making process, which our history has shown us often enough can have dangerous and long-lasting consequences. If Americans cannot engage in analytical thinking as a result of Republicans' using fear for their own political purposes, we are all in serious trouble. I am sure I am not alone in worrying about the road that we are now on, and where the current authoritarianism is taking the country. I only wish more people would talk about it.

What's Wrong with Authoritarianism?

The study of authoritarianism began during the Holocaust, as scientists could not understand why people in Germany and Italy were tolerating, if not supporting, Hitler and Mussolini. They wanted to know if that sort of blind allegiance could develop in the United States. Accordingly, they set about the task of finding out what types of people were susceptible to authoritarian leadership. After a half century, they have found answers, which I have outlined in this book.

I have discussed, in broad terms, the growing authoritarianism that conservatives are making part of American government and politics. Needless to say, I find this trend troubling. I am struck by how an understanding of authoritarianism explains the patterns of behavior that I have seen time and again during my years of observing government and politics. It answered questions about why people who call themselves conservatives act or respond as they do. I have only touched on the subject. Authoritarian behavior is often described as "protofascists," which led me to read deeply and widely about fascism. For example, Professor Robert O. Paxton recently observed that a "fascism of the future—an emergency response to some still unimagined crisis— need not resemble classical fascism perfectly in its outward signs and symbols. . . . An authentically popular American fascism would be pious, antiblack, and, since September 11, 2001, anti-Islamic as well."[98] Are we on the road to fascism? Clearly we are not on that road yet. But it would not take much more misguided authoritarian leadership, or thoughtless following of such leaders, to find ourselves there. I am not sure which is more frightening: another major terror attack or the response of authoritarian conservatives to that attack. Both are alarming prospects.

Like Dick Cheney's, my memory is seared by Vietnam and Watergate, and so it appears is Bob Altemeyer's. His work initially caught my attention because he noticed that as Watergate unfolded, the public was very slow to react. For example, the Watergate burglars from the Nixon reelection committee were arrested inside the offices of the Democratic National Committee on June 17, 1972. Polls conducted shortly before the 1972 elections showed that some 62 percent of the voters dismissed the Watergate break-in and resulting investigation as "mostly politics."[99] Notwithstanding the growing and hard evidence of the president's deep involvement, public opinion was slow to change or turn against Nixon. Americans want to believe in their president, and for that matter, their own representatives or senators—although they may hold Congress and politicians in general in low esteem. Altemeyer understood what few did: It was not public opinion that forced Nixon from office. He correctly noted that Nixon resigned "because [Nixon's] attorney had forced the disclosure of evidence so damaging that it seemed certain he would be convicted of high crimes by the Senate." This is true, but there is more to the story.

In fact, Nixon had many defenses that he could have mounted had he gone to trial in the Senate, many of which Bush and Cheney are promoting today under the rubric of national security and the inherent power of the presidency. The reason Nixon did not go to trial was not his loss of support on Capitol Hill, which he might have rebuilt, but rather because he lost the support of his defenders, principally on the White House staff. Other than White House counsel Fred Buzzhardt, and possibly chief of staff Al Haig (with whom Buzzhardt had roomed at West Point), no one was aware that Nixon was lying about what he knew and when he knew it once the cover-up had initially fallen apart. Nixon provided the lawyer he had hired to defend him in the House's impeachment inquiry, James St. Clair, with false information, and St. Clair—as it happened—was a man of integrity and not a right-wing authoritarian follower. When he found out that his client had lied to him he had two choices: to resign or to join the new cover-up. He was, as it happened, interested in participating in the latter. Nixon at one point considered defying the Supreme

Court ruling that he turn over his incriminating tapes (evidence that revealed that his defense was a sham) on the very grounds that Bush and Cheney argue: They have authority under the Constitution to read it and comply with it as they see fit. Once it was apparent that Richard Nixon had broken the law, he made the most significant decision of his presidency: the decision to honor the rule of law and resign.

What does this have to do with authoritarianism? Everything, for there is little doubt in my mind that Bush and Cheney, in the same situation, would not budge; rather, they would spin the facts as they always have, and move forward with their agenda. The president and vice president, it appears, believe the lesson of Watergate was not to stay within the law, but rather not to get caught. And if you do get caught, claim that the president can do whatever he thinks necessary in the name of national security. Bush and Cheney have also insulated and isolated themselves so that when they break the law—which they have done repeatedly—they have already built their defense. To protect themselves, they have structured their White House as La Cosa Nostra might have recommended, and surrounded themselves with men who owe their careers to their bosses. All of the key staff people close to Bush and Cheney have very long relationships with them. These have been mutually beneficial relationships. Stated differently, Bush and Cheney are protected by staff who will take a bullet for them. That, I believe, is precisely what Scooter Libby is doing for Dick Cheney regarding the Valerie Plame leak, and if he goes down, he knows that Cheney will take care of him, unlike Haldeman and Ehrlichman, who were on their own when Nixon cut them loose (and they turned on Nixon). Scooter Libby is now gainfully employed by the Hudson Institute, a conservative think tank, and according to the *Washington Post*, "[H]is salary is on par with the going rate for the deep thinkers—presumably at least as much as his $160,000 White House gig—and that, if he wants, he'll probably still have time to do some consulting or work on a second novel."[100]

Bush and Cheney are protected as well by loyal supporters (ranks of right-wing authoritarian followers). When those few individuals out in the departments and agencies who have been distressed by the White House policy on torture or electronic surveillance of Americans have leaked information about such activities, the political damage has been minimal. The White House takes the hit, and then claims, "Hell, yes, we're protecting Americans from terrorists." Many of Nixon's abuses of power were motivated by a similar desire to "protect Americans from communists." Nixon, for all his faults, had more of a conscience than Bush and Cheney. They cannot think of a mistake they have made since coming into office, and in doing so display self-righteousness far beyond Nixon's. Bush and Cheney are Double High authoritarians, far above Nixon's league.

What has driven this book is the realization that our government has become largely authoritarian. It is run by an array of authoritarian personalities, leaders who display all those traits I have listed—dominating, opposed to equality, desirous of personal power, amoral, intimidating, and bullying; some are hedonistic, most are vengeful, pitiless, exploitive, manipulative, dishonest, cheaters, prejudiced, mean-spirited, militant, nationalistic, and two-faced. Because of our system of government, these dominators are still confronted with any number of obstacles, fortunately. Yet authoritarians seek to remove those complications whenever they can. They are able to do so because the growth of contemporary conservatism has generated countless millions of authoritarian followers, people who will not question such actions. How, then, can authoritarianism be checked?

Not easily. Bob Altemeyer's work reveals that only a few right-wing authoritarians who become aware of their conduct deal with it. They stop trusting those who are not to be trusted; they put away their prejudice; they drop their mean-spirited, narrow-minded intolerance; and stop trying to bully people. They realize their inconsistencies and contradictory beliefs, and start thinking critically; they learn to deal with the fear that has driven them to find comfort in authority figures that never really deliver, who would rather keep them fearful. They find true conservatism, which respects the rule of law. They find their consciences. Unfortunately, this is a very small number of individuals; they are the exception and not the rule.

"Probably about 20 to 25 percent of the adult American population is so right-wing authoritarian, so scared, so self-righteous, so ill-informed, and so dogmatic that nothing you can say or do will change their minds," Altemeyer told me. He added, "They would march America into a dictatorship and probably feel that things had improved as a result. The problem is that these authoritarian followers are much more active than the rest of the country. They have the mentality of 'old-time religion' on a crusade, and they generously give money, time and effort to the cause. They proselytize; they lick stamps; they put pressure on loved ones; and they revel in being loyal to a cohesive group of like thinkers. And they are so submissive to their leaders that they will believe and do virtually anything they are told. They are not going to let up and they are not going to go away."

Research, however, reveals there is a solid majority of Americans who are not right-wing authoritarians, that there are countless millions of liberals, moderates, and conservatives with consciences, people who shudder at the prospect of giving away our hard-earned democratic principles, and who cherish our liberties. These are individuals who question their leaders and their policies, and that is as it should be. Democracy is not a spectator sport that can be simply observed. To the contrary, it is difficult and demanding, and its very survival depends on active participation. Take it for granted, and the authoritarians, who have already taken control, will take American democracy where no freedom-loving person would want it to go. But time has run out, and the next two or three national election cycles will define America in the twenty-first century, for better or worse.

ACKNOWLEDGMENTS

Acknowledgments are always a pleasure to write, not because they are done at the end of the project; rather, because they provide an opportunity to call attention to those whose assistance has, in an author's view, significantly added to the undertaking. This work began with my trusted and able agent, Lydia Wills, who placed it in the good hands of Rick Kot at Viking, whose experience and professionalism are found on every page. Thus, that which works and reads well, credit Rick; that which does not, please blame me. In addition, others at Viking who deserve credit for their contributions include: Alessandra Lusardi (assistant editor), Sharon Gonzalez (production editor), Francesca Belanger (designer), Grace Veras (production manager), Paul Buckley (art director), Hal Fessenden (foreign rights), and Viking publisher Clare Ferraro.

A special thanks to Sarah Shoenfeld, who did some early research for me at the National Archives and, when my hard drive crashed at the end of my writing, provided her sharp eyes and pencil to help me tidy up the manuscript. And to political scientists Jerry Goldman and Ken Janda of Northwestern University, whose graphic view of conservatism I have borrowed from their seminal textbook, *The Challenge of Democracy,* along with polling data that Ken Janda provided me. Also thanks to my readers Stanley Kutler and David Dorsen, friends who permit me to impose on their valuable time and who will tell me of errors they might spot, but who are not responsible for those I have not found.

Researching this book provided something of an epiphany. I am not trained in the social sciences, but I realized when reading studies relating to conservatism and authoritarianism undertaken by social scientists that I had found important information which was unknown to the general public. Professor John Jost of New York University helped me grasp the work he and his colleagues have undertaken in their massive study of conservatism, and he kindly provided me additional reading material to better follow the work of social and political psychology. John Jost's work led me to the studies of Bob Altemeyer, who, in turn, went beyond the call of duty to assist me in realizing the relationship of contemporary conservatism and authoritarianism.

The attention that I have given Bob Altemeyer's work in these pages is directly related to its importance, for it is not possible to fully address contemporary conservatism without dealing with the increased role of authoritarianism—they are, in fact, inseparable. If this book accomplishes anything, it is my hope that it will raise awareness of this fact and lead to further analysis and information for the general reader. Given Bob Altemeyer's fine mind, quick wit, and vast knowledge, not to mention his skill as a writer, I have encouraged him to do a book about authoritarians for the general reader. I truly hope he does so. His professional peers already know and respect his prodigious work, and they are aware of the implications of the growing authoritarianism in government. His findings are too important to not be widely understood by all involved with the political process. No less than the future of democratic government might be at stake.

Finally, I must acknowledge the man who first encouraged this project: Senator Barry M. Goldwater. I have no way of knowing how he would feel about what I have found and reported but I thank him for starting me off. I do know, however, that conservatives could surely use his conscience today.

APPENDICES

James Burnham's Analysis of Conservatism

The following table summarizes James Burnham's analysis of conservatism as he found it in the late 1950s, at the outset of the modern conservative movement. It paraphrases and quotes Burnham's material, adding necessary explanations from his more complete descriptions as appropriate. (While I have no question that Burnham can speak for the founders of modern conservatism regarding conservative thinking, liberals may find his analysis of their point of view less than complete.) My summary is based on Burnham's *Congress and the American Tradition*, pages 3–123, and principally drawing from pages 28–29, 61, 90, and 122–23.

The Conservative Syndrome	The Liberal Syndrome
1. Conservatives believe that government involves a non-rational factor. Without allowance for magic, luck, or divine favor, there is no convincing explanation for why one government works better than another. There is no rational explanation for why one person should submit to the rule of another's absent habit, tradition, or faith. But without	**1.** Liberals have a general confidence in the ability of the human mind to comprehend through rational science problems of government and society, and they often trust in a particular ideology as a key to a successful government.

such submission, government
dissolves or relies on force,
which is nonrational. The
conservative distrusts abstract
political ideology as a principle
or formula for political life.

2. Conservatives believe that
human nature is essentially
corrupt, or evil, and is limited
in its potential; therefore,
conservatives do not believe
in utopian or ultimate solutions
to major social problems.

2. Liberals believe that most
human weaknesses and errors
are the result of weak social
structure or inadequate
education, for human potential,
if not infinite, has no discernible
a priori limitations; therefore, it
is not unrealistic for humans
to work toward an ideal society
in which problems such as
war, poverty, and suffering
do not exist.

3. Conservatives respect tradition,
established institutions, and
conventional modes of conduct.
They are reluctant to initiate
quick or deep changes in
traditional ways, and seek to
restrict or slow the pace of
changes that have become
unavoidable or morally
imperative.

3. Liberals do not believe tradition
alone justifies favoring an
institution or mode of conduct;
and they are willing to accept
quick, drastic, and extensive
social changes based on rational
and utilitarian grounds.

4. Conservatives believe in a diffusion of "sovereignty" (used by Burnham to mean "governmental power") and a still wider diffusion of power, thus honoring the "separation of powers" and "checks and balances" envisioned by the Constitution.

4. Liberals think that diffusion of power may be useful against "reactionary forces" but are not much troubled by most power's being in the hands of beneficial social entities (the common man, the people, workers, and farmers) and will waive concerns about power altogether for certain ideological goals (full employment, racial equality, social welfare, or peace).

5. Conservatives reject unrestricted plebiscitary (direct election by all the people) democracy in favor of representative government in which a number of indirect institutions mediate between the people and those in charge.

5. Liberals tend to approve of plebiscitary democracy, seeking forms of government that express the will of the majority as directly and intimately as possible (e.g., direct popular elections for president, direct primaries, initiative and recall, popular referendums, election of judges, extension of suffrage, and the like).

6. Conservatives believe in "states' rights," or the retention by each state of an effective share of the federal government's sovereignty, because this diffuses power.

6. Liberals see "states' rights" as either unimportant (an anachronism) or inefficient, for it leads to reactionary policies like pro-segregation, anti-labor, and anti-internationalist measures.

7. Conservatives believe in the autonomy of the various branches of the federal government, and oppose encroachment or usurpation by any of them upon the other branches.

8. Conservatives believe the public should support limiting government powers.

9. Conservatives feel that the American constitutional system embodies principles of clear and permanent value.

10. Conservatives want decentralization and localization of government.

11. Conservatives believe private, profit-making enterprises are the most just and effective means for economic operation and development.

7. Liberals think that strict separation of the branches of government hinders government's ability to solve major problems.

8. Liberals think the public should support greater government power to accomplish progressive goals.

9. Liberals hold that the Constitution is a living document, with its meaning dependent on time and circumstances.

10. Liberals think that decentralization and localization can hinder solutions to modern problems.

11. Liberals are critical of private economic enterprise, and believe in government control of private activities, if not some measure of government ownership. They find private enterprises are frequently opposed to the interests of the people and the nation, and that, in many cases, the government can do a better job than private enterprise.

12. Conservatives hold that the private life of the individual, as opposed to the destiny of the nation or of society, should be the focus of metaphysical, moral, and practical interest.

12. Liberals feel that an expanding sphere of government involvement—in social and cultural life as well as in the economy—results in the best mode of life for people. Thus, expansion of government activity aids in attainment of a good life.

13. Conservatives favor Congress over the executive branch of government.

13. Liberals favor the executive branch, with its administrative bureaucracy, over Congress.

While the majority of the "syndromes" set forth by Burnham have remained constant during the past half century, in a surprising number of instances conservatives and liberals have changed places (the positions described in numbers 7, 8, 12, and 13), and in others their differences are not as significant as when Burnham catalogued them (the positions described in numbers 1, 3, 4, and 5).

Right-Wing Authoritarian Survey
The Right-Wing Authoritarianism Scale*

Note: In including this scale with Bob Altemeyer's permission, I agreed not to include the full procedure for scoring. In one of our exchanges he told me that "because people tend to believe their own psychological test scores far, far more than they should, my profession discourages letting people know what they have scored on a test." He also noted that "when people know they are answering an authoritarianism measure, that can affect how they respond—which is another reason for treating individual scores with a grain of salt." Nonetheless, a reader can get a good sense of where he or she might fall in the world of RWAs from a review of the following questions. This scale is one of several developed by Altemeyer. His current scale has just twenty questions, and he has found it as effective as this thirty-two-question scale.

1. The established authorities generally turn out to be right about things, while the radicals and protesters are usually just "loud-mouths" showing off their ignorance.
2. Women should have to promise to obey their husbands when they get married.

*With permission of Bob Altemeyer, University of Manitoba, Winnipeg, Manitoba, Canada.

3. Our country desperately needs a mighty leader who will do what has to be done to destroy the radical new ways and sinfulness that are ruining us.

4. Gays and lesbians are just as healthy and moral as anybody else.

5. It is always better to trust the judgment of the proper authorities in government and religion than to listen to the noisy rabble-rousers in our society, who are trying to create doubt in people's minds.

6. Atheists and others who have rebelled against the established religions are no doubt every bit as good and virtuous as those who attend church regularly.

7. The only way our country can get through the crisis ahead is to get back to our traditional values, put some tough leaders in power, and silence the troublemakers spreading bad ideas.

8. There is absolutely nothing wrong with nudist camps.

9. Our country *needs* free thinkers who will have the courage to defy traditional ways, even if this upsets many people.

10. Our country will be destroyed someday if we do not smash the perversions eating away at our moral fiber and traditional beliefs.

11. Everyone should have their own lifestyle, religious beliefs, and sexual preferences, even if it makes them different from everyone else.

12. The "old-fashioned ways'" and "old-fashioned values" still show the best way to live.

13. You have to admire those who challenged the law and the majority's view by protesting for women's abortion rights, for animal rights, or to abolish school prayer.

14. What our country really needs is a strong, determined leader who will crush evil and take us back to our true path.

15. Some of the best people in our country are those who are challenging our government, criticizing religion, and ignoring the "normal way things are supposed to be done."

16. God's laws about abortion, pornography, and marriage must be strictly followed before it is too late, and those who break them must be strongly punished.

17. It would be best for everyone if the proper authorities censored magazines so that people could not get their hands on trashy and disgusting material.

18. There is nothing wrong with premarital sexual intercourse.

19. Our country will be great if we honor the ways of our forefathers, do what the authorities tell us to do, and get rid of the "rotten apples" who are ruining everything.

20. There is no "ONE right way" to live life; everybody has to create their own way.

21. Homosexuals and feminists should be praised for being brave enough to defy "traditional family values."

22. This country would work a lot better if certain groups of troublemakers would just shut up and accept their group's traditional place in society.

23. There are many radical, immoral people in our country today who are trying to ruin it for their own godless purposes, whom the authorities should put out of action.

24. People should pay less attention to the Bible and the other old forms of religious guidance, and instead develop their own personal standards of what is moral and immoral.

25. What our country needs *most* is discipline, with everyone following our leaders in unity.

26. It's better to have trashy magazines and radical pamphlets in our communities than to let the government have the power to censor them.

27. The facts on crime, sexual immorality, and the recent public disorders all show we have to crack down harder on deviant groups and troublemakers if we are going to save our moral standards and preserve law and order.

28. A lot of our rules regarding modesty and sexual behavior are just customs that are not necessarily any better or holier than those that other people follow.

29. The situation in our country is getting so serious, the strongest methods would be justified if they eliminated the troublemakers and got us back to our true path.

30. A "woman's place" should be wherever she wants to be. The days when women are submissive to their husbands and social conventions belong strictly in the past.

31. It is wonderful that young people today have greater freedom to protest against things they don't like and to make their own "rules" to govern their behavior.

32. Once our government leaders give us the "go ahead," it will be the duty of every patriotic citizen to help stomp out the rot that is poisoning our country from within.

Social Dominance Orientation Survey*

Note: This scale testing social dominance orientation does not include its scoring. Those interested in further information should consult F. Pratto, J. Sidanius, L. M. Stallworth, and B. F. Malle, "Social Dominance Orientation: A Personality Variable Predicting Social and Political Attitudes," *Journal of Personality & Social Psychology* (1994), 741–763, at file:///H|/website/pubs/PrattoSidanius1994.pdf.

1. Some groups of people are simply not the equals of others.
2. Some people are just more worthy than others.
3. This country would be better off if we cared less about how equal all people were.
4. Some people are just more deserving than others.
5. It is not a problem if some people have more of a chance in life than others.
6. Some people are just inferior to others.
7. To get ahead in life, it is sometimes necessary to step on others.
8. Increased economic equality.
9. Increased social equality.
10. Equality.
11. If other people were treated more equally we would have fewer problems in this country.
12. In an ideal world, all nations would be equal.
13. We should try to treat one another as equals as much as possible. (All humans should be treated as equals.)
14. It is important that we treat other countries as equals.

*With permission of Jim Sidanius, University of California, Los Angeles.

NOTES

Preface

1. Georgie Anne Geyer, "Impolite Society: How ideological zeal and social distance silenced a disputatious capital," *American Conservative* (January 16, 2006), 25.
2. Eric Nordon, "Interview of G. Gordon Liddy," *Playboy* (October 1980) from *Playboy* CD collection of interviews.
3. See Watergate Special Prosecution Force, January 9, 1974, Memorandum to Bill Merrill from Phil Bakes, Subject: "Charles Colson—Synopsis of Areas where Colson may be Perjuring Himself or Have Some Involvement." This memorandum sets forth nine areas of interest to the prosecutors, which I have summarized: (1) Colson's testimony that he had no knowledge regarding the recruitment of homosexuals to support McGovern, and the fact that his top aide Bill Rhatican contradicts this. (2) Colson's claim that he never instructed Jack Caulfield to firebomb the Brookings Institution; rather, he claimed that Ehrlichman instructed him to have Caulfield obtain the Brookings documents. Ehrlichman denied giving Colson such an instruction. Caulfield and this author testified that not only did Colson give such instructions, but I had to fly to California to turn them off. (3) Colson denied discussing phony State Department cables with Howard Hunt, or having knowledge that Hunt had prepared such, that would have shown an involvement of the Kennedy administration in the assassination of South Vietnam leader Diem. Hunt contracted Colson's denials, as did secretaries. (4) Colson's own memorandum, obtained by the prosecutors, contradicted his testimony about whether Dan Ellsberg should be criminally prosecuted. (5) Evidence of Colson's role in the break-in of the office of Dr. Fielding, Ellsberg's psychiatrist, for which Colson would later be indicted. (6) Colson's contradictory testimony about when he learned of the Ellsberg break-in. (7) Colson's possible destruction of evidence, since he walked out of the White House with his files, returning only some of them after he left, with the omissions being conspicuous. The prosecutors believed "Colson may

have sanitized his files." (8) Evidence that Colson orchestrated a physical assault on Dan Ellsberg and others when they were demonstrating in May 1972. (9) The suspicion of the prosecutors that Colson had suborned perjury of several people.

4. This $14 million figure was given in open court by an attorney for one of the insurance companies involved. We believe it is a conservative number, and, in fact, the actual amount may have exceeded $18 million. Not long after we filed our lawsuit, and had defeated the early motions to get the case dismissed, St. Martin's general counsel, David Kaye, boasted to a group of attorneys at a bar association meeting that they were going to employ a scorched-earth spending policy—endless motions, depositions, etc.—that would make us regret having filed the suit, and force us to drop it. It is a very small world, for Kaye's remarks got back to me within days of his making them. While we could not outspend an insurance company, we simply planned accordingly, husbanding and marshaling our resources, and making our own preemptive moves. One day I will write about this lawsuit, for I believe public figures—who find defamation law stacked against them—should hold others responsible for false and harmful statements.

5. My Los Angeles attorneys (Doug Larson and John Garrick of Iverson, Yoakum, Papiano & Hatch) had cleared their calendars for a trial against Liddy back in Washington, and, in fact, we were packing up files and making plans to return to Washington, when the federal judge handling the case, U.S. District Court Judge Emmett Sullivan, forced a settlement with Liddy. That was fine by me, because it was not really fair to our lawyers, given that Liddy's assets were hidden in his wife's name; it would take years to unwind his affairs, and we wished his wife, Frances, no ill. More important, my Washington-based attorney, David Dorsen, was very interested in keeping Liddy busy for a few more years. David told me that he had offered to represent Maxie Wells (whose telephone had been wiretapped in 1972) in a lawsuit against Liddy, for Liddy was also defaming her based on Phillip Bailley's fantasies, and she was ready to file an action. I told David we would assist in any way we could. But Liddy got lucky when Maxie sued him. The case landed with a federal judge in Maryland, where Liddy resided, who could not have been friendlier to him. The judge threw the case out, claiming Ms. Wells was a public figure, and that she could not meet the high standard of proof required. Dorsen got the case reversed by the U.S. Court of Appeals for the Fourth Circuit, but the reversal meant that when the case went to trial, he had less than a friendly judge. Indeed, the judge refused to permit Mo or me to testify, yet permitted Liddy's lawyers to put on a parade of witnesses who claimed they all believed *Silent Coup*. With a hostile trial judge, Maxie did not have a chance. Yet the undertaking was quite satisfying for me—someone had to pay some hefty legal bills (maybe seven

figures) for Liddy's defense, because St. Martin's had cut him off with our settlement. I suspect that Liddy's wife and financial keeper was not terribly satisfied with this outcome; shortly thereafter, I was told, they separated.

6. For example, in 1994 New York's Republican senator, Alfonse D'Amato, said of Whitewater, "This is worse than Watergate" (*Dallas News,* November 7, 1996); in 1996 House Speaker Newt Gingrich, even though he engaged in similar practices, called Clinton's White House fund-raising activities "worse than the Watergate scandal" (ABC News, *World News Tonight,* March 6, 1997); and according to Monica Crowley, Richard Nixon said Whitewater was "worse" because "in Watergate, we didn't have profiteering, and we didn't have a body" (referring to the suicide of Vince Foster). Monica Crowley, *Nixon in Winter* (New York: Random House, 1998), 312.

7. Peter Baker, *The Breach: Inside the Impeachment and Trail of William Jefferson Clinton* (New York: Scribner, 2000), 19.

8. *Watergate: Chronology of a Crisis* (Washington: Congressional Quarterly, 1975), 170.

9. See *Goldwater v. Ginsberg,* 414 F.2d 324 (1969).

10. Notes, telephone conversation with Senator Barry M. Goldwater, November 1994.

11. Correspondence with Senator Goldwater about our project is among his papers at the Arizona Historical Foundation.

12. Robert G. Vaughan, "Transparency—The Mechanisms: Open Government and Accountability," *Issues of Democracy* (electronic journal of the U.S. Department of State, vol. 5, no. 2, August 2000) at http://usinfo.state.gov/journals/itdhr/0800/ijde/vaughn.htm.

Chapter One: How Conservatives Think

1. Ramesh Ponnuru, "Getting to the bottom of this 'neo' nonsense: Before you talk about conservatives, know what you're doing," *National Review* (June 16, 2003).

2. Russell Kirk, *The Conservative Mind: From Burke to Eliot* (Washington: Regnery, 2001), 8.

3. George H. Nash, *The Conservative Intellectual Movement in America* (Wilmington, DE: Intercollegiate Studies Institute, 1998), xiii–xv.

4. Jonah Goldberg, "What Is 'Conservative'? We're Comfortable with Contradiction," *National Review* Online (May 11, 2005) at http://nationalreview.com/goldberg/goldberg200505111449.asp.

5. Michael K. Deaver (ed.), *Why I Am a Reagan Conservative* (New York: Morrow, 2005), xv.

6. Frank S. Meyer, *In Defense of Freedom and Related Essays* (Indianapolis: Liberty Fund, 1996), 155.

7. Kirk, *The Conservative Mind: From Burke to Eliot,* 89.

8. Franklin Foer, "Ur-Conservative," *Washington Monthly* (October 2004), 54.

9. Anonymous, "Santorum: 'Conservatism Is Common Sense,'" *Human Events* (August 1, 2005), 3.

10. A less than exhaustive search of these conservative publications revealed a number of references to conservatism as an ideology. For example, the December 11, 1995, *National Review* discusses "making conservatism the ideology of Western revival"; a December 31, 1999, *Human Events* refers to Reagan's "ideological conservatism"; the August/September 2003 *American Spectator* states "America is moving rapidly toward conservatism as its prevailing ideology and the Republican Party as its governing party"; a December 20, 2004, issue of the *Weekly Standard* refers to "the elasticity of conservative ideology"; and the January 13, 2003, *American Conservative* asked how conservatism turned into an ideology (the cold war, they respond). Suffice it to say there is no rigid conservative ideology on whether or not conservatism is an ideology.

11. Nash, *The Conservative Intellectual Movement in America,* 198.

12. James Burnham, *Congress and the American Tradition* (New Brunswick, NJ: Transaction Publishers, 2003), 128–29. (This is a republication of the 1959 original edition.)

13. George F. Will, "Why Didn't He Ask Congress?" *Washington Post* (December 20, 2005), A-31

14. George F. Will, "National Review Hits 40," *National Review* (December 11, 1995), 102.

15. Burnham, *Congress and the American Tradition,* 298.

16. Ibid., 128–29.

17. Ibid., 122.

18. There are a number of works (probably three dozen or more) in which this story is told. These include Dan T. Carter, *From George Wallace to Newt Gingrich: Race in the Conservative Counterrevolution: 1963–1994* (Baton Rouge: Louisiana State University Press, 1996); John B. Judis, *The Paradox of American Democracy: Elites, Special Interests, and the Betrayal of Public Trust* (New York: Pantheon Books, 2000); and Stephan Lesher, *George Wallace: American Populist* (Reading, PA: Addison-Wesley Publishing, 1994).

19. Among the better historical accounts that have been written are (listed chronologically): Godfrey Hodgson, *The World Turned Right Side Up: A History of the Conservative Ascendancy in America* (Boston: Houghton Mifflin Co., 1996); Lee Edwards, *The Conservative Revolution: The Movement That Remade America* (New York: Free Press, 1999); Jonathan M. Schoenwald, *A Time for Choosing: The Rise of Modern American Conservatism* (New

York: Oxford University Press, 2001); and Gregory L. Schneider (ed.), *Conservatism in America Since 1930: A Reader* (New York: New York University Press, 2003).

20. Lewis L. Gould, *Grand Old Party: A History of the Republicans* (New York: Random House, 2003), 488.

21. See Joseph Scotchie, *The Paleoconservatives: New Voices of the Old Right* (New Brunswick, NJ: Transaction, 1999).

22. William Rusher, "Toward a History of the Conservative Movement," *Journal of Policy History,* vol. 14, no. 3 (2002). See also Kirk, *The Conservative Mind,* 476.

23. Historian Jennifer Burns has called this "a rare work of history that remains the authoritative treatment of its subject nearly thirty years after publication." Rarer still, she explained, is the fact that it appeared in prepublication form as a forty-seven-page insert in the *National Review* (December 5, 1975). Ms. Burns noted that this "work exerts a deep influence on our common understanding of conservatism in America." While George Nash's politics are difficult to discern from his work, Ms. Burns reports that he is a conservative. See Jennifer Burns, "In Retrospect: George Nash's *The Conservative Intellectual Movement in America Since 1945*," *Reviews in American History,* vol. 32 (2004), 447–62. (I have relied heavily on Nash's work because of the near universal esteem with which it is held by conservatives among all the factions.)

24. Nash, *The Conservative Intellectual Movement in America,* xv.

25. Because conservatives do not view the Declaration of Independence as based on liberalism, I had to scratch my head for an authority that was clearly neither liberal nor conservative yet stated the obvious fact of its classic liberalism. The Wikipedia online encyclopedia has its weaknesses (for example, its entry for yours truly has clearly been distorted by my detractors, but I have never bothered to correct it to see if the entry is self-correcting), yet I thought this a good source to make my point, for clearly conservatives have been quite active in getting their point of view into the Wikipedia. Of the Declaration, and the Constitution, Wikipedia states that "the United States Constitution and the United States Declaration of Independence are both documents that embody many principles of classic liberalism." See "classic liberalism" at http://en.wikipedia.org/wiki/Classical_liberalism.

26. Unfortunately, Nash happened to mangle his material and its source regarding this significant point. Nash stated: "On one occasion, Jeffrey Hart of Dartmouth College in effect conceded the Declaration to the liberals. He then insisted that its doctrine was not theory of the Constitution, whose Preamble had conspicuously failed to list 'rights' or 'equality' among the purposes of the new government of 1788. There were, in fact, two theories of government present in the Revolutionary War period, and liberals could

claim only one of them." Nash cited John Hallowell, *American Political Science Review*, vol. 58 (September 1964), 687. However, the Hallowell book review to which Nash refers makes no mention of Jeffrey Hart, who had a very interesting read on the Declaration. He said, "I regard the Declaration of Independence as just that, a declaration of independence from England, written by Englishmen in the Colonies to establish their position on a foundation that would be accepted in England. In that context, the phrase 'all men are created equal' means that Americans are equal to Englishmen in their capacity for self-government. When we go beyond the Prologue to the list of particulars in the indictment of George III, we have that passage about him inflicting the 'savage Indian tribes' upon our frontier settlements, the Indians slaughtering Americans without regard to age or sex. This, I think, 'de-universalizes' the 'all men are created equal' in capacity for self-government. The Indians were a stone-age people who had not invented the wheel and had no written language." (E-mail exchange with author.)

27. Nash, *The Conservative Intellectual Movement in America,* 194–95.

28. Ibid., 207–8.

29. Ibid. Nash reported "the ever-argumentative" Frank Meyer's reaction to Jaffa's position, chiding his fixation with Lincoln's interpretation of the founding documents. He did not refute Jaffa's assertion, however.

30. Ibid., 194.

31. See Louis Hartz, *The Liberal Tradition in America: An Interpretation of American Political Thought Since the Revolution* (New York: Harcourt Brace, 1955), 308. The progenitors of American conservatism apparently felt compelled to push credulity, because unlike the English and Europeans, Americans did not have to revolt against the feudalism of an ancien régime to gain their freedom; rather, they only had to remove the economic shackles of monarchy. Accordingly, conservatives have simply denigrated America's founding generation to rid them of their "liberal tradition." They trivialize the oppressive demands that the distant monarchy placed on the nation's forebearers, a situation that forced men (and women) who wished to be loyal to the Crown to undertake actions that were anything but conservative by breaking ties with their motherland and fighting a bitter and protracted war of liberation. This is not to say that there was nothing conservative whatsoever about this revolution. One can find strains of conservatism in even the most liberal, radical, or reactionary of actions. While no one would call Joseph Stalin a conservative, his actions in seeking to maintain his power, and that of the Communist Party in Russia, were conservative actions. In the early 1960s, legendary American historian Samuel Eliot Morison wrote, "the principles of the American Revolution were essentially conservative; the leaders were thinking of preserving and securing the freedom they already enjoyed rather than, like the Russians, building some-

thing new and different." Samuel Eliot Morison, *The Oxford History of the American People, Vol. One: Prehistory to 1789* (New York: Meridian, 1994), 355. Morison's argument is not unlike saying that Stalin was a conservative in seeking to "preserve and secure" communism. While such conservative principles may have been subscribed to by the elite, it is difficult to find them in Tom Paine's *Common Sense,* which stirred both colonial leaders and followers, or in Paine's *Crisis,* which rallied many during the war. Early conservative scholars like Morison claimed a conservative tradition for America based on the slimmest of philosophical and historical reeds. It is ironic that conservatives honor tradition, but when that tradition is not quite what they wish, they just rewrite it.

32. David McCullough, *1776* (New York: Simon & Schuster, 2005), 294.

33. *Federalist Paper No. 14* at http://press-pubs.uchicago.edu/founders/documents /v1ch4s22.html.

34. Nash, *The Conservative Intellectual Movement in America,* 195.

35. Ibid.

36. Clinton Rossiter, *Conservatism in America,* 2nd ed. (New York: Knopf, 1962), 69, 262. Neoconservatives have claimed Rossiter as one of their own. See Norman Podhoretz, "Neoconservatism: A eulogy," *Commentary* (March 1996), 19.

37. This column provided a vehicle for the senator to sharpen his own thinking on the subject. Given his duties in the Senate and his active schedule as a Republican spokesperson, giving talks throughout the country, he enlisted his former campaign manager, Stephen Shadegg—who he knew shared his thinking—to write many of the columns, with the senator suggesting topics and then editing the copy. For his definition of conservatism and conservatives, see Barry Goldwater, "How Do You Stand, Sir?" *Los Angeles Times,* September 27, 1960.

38. Barry Goldwater, *The Conscience of a Majority* (Englewood Cliffs, NJ: Prentice-Hall, 1970), xii.

39. Barry M. Goldwater with Jack Casserly, *Goldwater* (New York: Doubleday, 1988), 121.

40. Barry Goldwater, *Conscience of a Conservative* (Shepherdsville, KY: Victor Publishing, 1960), 13.

41. Notes, telephone conversation with Senator Barry M. Goldwater, March 1995.

42. Goldwater, *Conscience of a Conservative,* 14.

43. Philip Gold, *Take Back the Right: How the Neocons and the Religious Right Have Betrayed the Conservative Movement* (New York: Carroll & Graf Publishers, 2004), 65.

44. William Safire, "Inside a Republican Brain," *New York Times* (July 21, 2004), A-19.

45. They included the original "triad of *Human Events* for the activists, *Modern Age* for the academics and *National Review* for everybody," plus "the *American Spectator, Policy Review, Commentary*, the *Weekly Standard, Public Interest, First Things* and *Chronicles*. They also cite religiously oriented journals, *Crisis*, a Catholic monthly, and *World*, an evangelical weekly." David Wagner, "Who's Who in America's Conservative Revolution?" *Insight* (December 23, 1996), 18.

46. Ibid.

47. For example, here is a list of the most commonly recurring labels conservatives used to describe themselves (or each other) that I have noted in my research: "traditional conservatives," "paleoconservatives," "old right," "classic liberal conservatives," "social conservatives," "cultural conservatives," "traditional conservatives," "Christian conservatives," "fiscal conservatives," "economic conservatives," "compassionate conservatives," "neoconservatives," and "libertarians."

48. Poll numbers were not easy to come by, but after posting an inquiry on Josh Marshall's TPM Café, thanks to a blog reader identified only as "uc," I located what appears to be the most recently published breakdown in, of all places, the *Mortgage News* (February, 17, 2005). See http://www.tpmcafe.com/author/J%20Dean.

49. William A. Galston and Elaine C. Kamarck, "The Politics of Polarization," *The Third Way Middle Class Project* (October 2005), Table 15, "Ideological self-identification of the U.S. electorate, 1976–2004," 42. Political scientist Kenneth Janda, who examined the left-right placement responses to the 2004 National Election Survey—widely considered by academics as being among the most reliable numbers gathered—provided me with a general overview of the nation's political leanings after the 2004 election. Here I have focused only on the postelection numbers (which are very similar to the preelection responses) of the 1,006 (randomly selected) people who responded to the following question: "We hear a lot of talk these days about liberals and conservatives. Here is a seven-point scale on which the political views that people might hold are arranged from extremely liberal to extremely conservative. Where would you place YOURSELF on this scale, or haven't you thought much about this?" The responses were:

Extremely liberal	20 people	(3 percent)
Liberal	103 people	(10 percent)
Slightly liberal	125 people	(10 percent)
Total on the left	*248 people*	*(23 percent)*
Moderate or middle-of-the-road	279 people	(26 percent)
Total in the middle	*279 people*	*(26 percent)*

Slightly conservative	143 people	(13 percent)
Conservative	166 people	(16 percent)
Extremely conservative	31 people	(3 percent)
Total on the right	***340 people***	***(32 percent)***
Had not thought about	187 people	
or did not know, or	10 people	
refused to answer	2 people	
Total without a position	***199 people***	***(19 percent)***

50. Brian Mitchell, "Bush Spending Yet to Alienate the Hard Core," *Mortgage News* (February 17, 2004) at http://www.home-equity-loans-center.com/Mortgage2_14__04/News6.htm.
51. This conclusion is justified by extrapolation from other polling data, and none of these conservative subgroups appear to exceed 10 percent. For example, the Pew Research Center for the People and the Press has polled different types of political attitudes, and has divided Republicans into three groups: "Enterprisers," who are extremely partisan and deep believers in the free-enterprise system, whose social values reflect a conservative agenda (presumably businesspeople or those closely associated with them); they constitute 9 percent of the adult population of the United States; "Social Conservatives," who are conservative on issues ranging from abortion to gay marriage and express some "skepticism" about the world of business; they constitute 11 percent of the adult population; and "Pro-Government Conservatives," who by definition support the government and stand out for their strong religious faith and conservative views on moral issues; they make up 9 percent of the population. The Pew Research Center for the People and the Press, "The 2005 Political Typology" (May 10, 2005), 53–55.
52. Sidney Blumenthal, *The Rise of the Counter-Establishment: From Conservative Ideology to Political Power* (New York: Perennial Library, 1988), 6.
53. John W. Dean, "What Is Conservatism?," *FindLaw's Writ* (December 17, 2004) at http://writ.news.findlaw.com/scripts/printer_friendly.pl?page=/dean/20041217.html. This column was based on analysis of all the key conservative think-tank Web sites.
54. While it is a crude test of the bipolar world of conservative journals, an electronic search of two leading conservative journals for the occurrences of key terms confirms what I have long recognized as a reader of these publications—there is conservatism and liberalism, with occasional sprinklings of "communism" and "socialism," neither of which exists in any viable form in the United States. For example, a search of the *National Review* (from

January 22, 1988, to September 21, 2005) showed: 3,560 documents found for (conservative or conservatives or conservatism); 403 documents found for (libertarian or libertarians or libertarianism); 3,207 documents found for (liberal or liberalism); 475 documents found for (progressive or progressives or progressivism); and 26 documents found for (communitarian or communitarians or communitarianism). And a search of *Human* Events from January 1998 to September 21, 2005, showed: 4,546 documents found for (conservative or conservatives or conservatism); 207 documents found for (libertarian or libertarians or libertarianism); 3,387 documents found for (liberal or liberalism); 225 documents found for (progressive or progressives or progressivism); 155 documents found for moderate republican; and 2 documents found for (communitarian or communitarians or communitarianism).

55. See, for example, Eric Alterman, "Fact Checking Ann Coulter" at http://www.whatliberalmedia.com/apndx_1.htm; "NY Times Praises Coulter's Footnotes. It Should Have Looked a Few Up," *Daily Howler* at http://www.dailyhowler.com/dh072202.shtml; a Google search of "ann coulter fact check" produced thirty-two thousand hits!

56. See http://www.harrisinteractive.com/harris_poll/index.asp?PID=548.

57. Henri Tajfel and John C. Turner, "The Social Identity Theory of Intergroup Behavior," in John T. Jost and Jim Sidanius, eds. *Political Psychology* (New York: Psychology Press, 2004), 276–91.

58. John C. Eastman, "The End of Federalism," *Claremont Institute* (October 24, 2005) at http://www.claremont.org/writings/051024eastman.html?FORMAT=print.

59. Ibid.

60. See, for example, the books: *Men in Black: How the Supreme Court Is Destroying America* (Washington, D.C.: Regnery Publishing, 2005) by Mark R. Levin; *Courting Disaster: How the Supreme Court Is Usurping the Power of Congress and the People* (Brentwood, TN: Integrity Publishers, 2004) by Pat Robertson; and *The Supremacists: The Tyranny of Judges and How to Stop It* (Dallas, TX: Spencer Publishing Co., 2004) by Phyllis Schlafly. Blogs and essays: Bobby Eberle, "Conservative Base Should Rally Around Alito," GOPUSA at http://www.gopusa.com/cgi-bin/ib3/ikonboard.pl?act=ST;f=37;t=25034; James Dobson's Focus on the Family Supreme Court Resource Center at http://www.family.org/cforum/feature/a0037317.cfm; and the Cato Supreme Court Review at http://www.cato.org/pubs/scr/index.html.

61. For example, Ms. Miers's nomination caused howls of unhappiness from high-profile conservatives like Boalt law professor John Yoo, neoconservatives David Frum (a former Bush speech writer) and Bill Kristol (editor of *The Weekly Standard*), as well as columnists Charles Krauthammer and George Will. No less than the icon of conservatism's perfect Supreme Court

justice Robert Bork himself (who was rejected by the Senate when President Reagan named him for the high court) came out against Harriet Miers.

62. John Derbyshire, "The Corner: Hallmark Harriet," *National Review* Online at http://corner.nationalreview.com/05_10_23_corner-archive.asp#080857.

63. Bernard Chapman, "Highest Common Denominator: An Interview with John Derbyshire," at http://www.enterstageright.com/archive/articles/0503/0503derbyshire.htm.

64. John T. Jost, Jack Glaser, Arie W. Kruglanski, and Frank J. Sulloway, "Political Conservatism as Motivated Social Cognition," *Psychological Bulletin*, vol. 129, no. 3 (2003), 339–75. To offer an opposing view, the same issue of *Psychological Bulletin* published Jeff Greenberg and Eva Jonas's "Psychological Motives and Political Orientation—The Left, the Right, and the Rigid: Comment on Jost, et al. (2003)," 376–82. Copies of the study (along with a response and a rebuttal) can be found at http://www.wam.umd.edu/~hannahk/bulletin.pdf; a response to the study is at http://www.wam.umd.edu/~hannahk/gjonas.pdf; and the authors' reply to the response is at http://www.wam.umd.edu/~hannahk/reply.pdf.

65. John Jost, "Media FAQ's: Answers by John Jost." (Provided to the author by Dr. Jost.)

66. Kathleen Maclay, "A Look at the Psychology of Conservatism," *Garlic & Grass: A Grassroots Journal of America's Political Soul* (July 23, 2003). One self-identified "Burkean conservative," J. J. Ray, a social scientist based in Australia, offered a few substantive comments, but none of his American peers (conservative, moderate, or liberal) thought he should be taken seriously. Ray wrote a response to the study for David Horowitz's FrontPageMagazine.com, taking a surprising low road for a purported academic, in calling the Jost et al. study the work of "Academic Fakers." (See J. J. Ray, "Academic Fakers," FrontPageMagazine.com (August 27, 2003) at http://www. frontpagemag.com/Articles/ReadArticle.asp?ID=9544.)

67. Jost, Glaser, Kruglanski, and Sulloway, "Political Conservatism as Motivated Social Cognition."

68. Ibid., 342–44.

69. Jost, "Media FAQ's: Answers by John Jost."

70. Jonah Goldberg, "They Blinded Me with Science," *National Review* Online (July 24, 2003) at http://www.nationalreview.com/goldberg/goldberg072403.asp.

71. Ann Coulter, "Closure on Nuance" (July 31, 2003) at http://www. townhall.com/columnists/anncoulter/ac20030731.shtml. When attacking the Jost study Rush Limbaugh based his comments not on the study, but on a press release written by Kathleen Maclay, who works as a publicist for the University of California, Berkeley. Limbaugh called the study "shockingly

tolerant of anti-Semitism," but there is nothing in the Maclay press release or in the study that is, in any fashion, directly or indirectly anti-Semitic. When Limbaugh posted this program on his Web site, he hyperlinked his reference to "anti-Semitism" to a *Wall Street Journal* column from a year earlier that has nothing whatsoever to do with conservatism or the study. See Collin Levey, "Anti-Semitism Goes PC: The Latest Campus Cause: Solidarity with Arab Terrorists," WJS.com *Opinion Journal* (April 11, 2002). Had Limbaugh read the study he would have learned that the authors made a special effort to seek out and incorporate results obtained in twelve different countries, including Israel. They found with Israeli university students that intolerance of ambiguity scores were indeed significantly higher among moderate and extreme right-wing students compared with moderate and extreme left-wing students. How Limbaugh can read tolerance of anti-Semitism into the Jost study defies comprehension.

72. Arie W. Kruglanski and John T. Jost, in collaboration with Jack Glaser and Frank J. Sulloway, "Political Opinion, Not Pathology," *Washington Post* (August 28, 2003), A-27.

73. Ibid. Kruglanski and Jost wrote: "It's wrong to conclude that our results provide *only bad news for conservatives*" (emphasis added). In short, they acknowledge their news was bad for conservatives, but they had bad news for liberals as well; namely, that the 9/11 terrorist attacks had increased threat and death anxiety, which gets conservative juices flowing. In times of high uncertainty, the unambiguous good versus evil message of a conservative leader plays well.

74. Jack Block and Jeanne H. Block, "Nursery School Personality and Political Orientation Two Decades Later," *Journal of Research in Personality* (2005).

75. Ibid.

76. Austin Bramwell, "Defining Conservatism Down," *American Conservative,* vol. 4, no. 16 (August 29, 2005), 7.

77. Society Desk, "Weddings: Sarah Maserati, Austin Bramwell," *New York Times* (September 7, 2003), 9-17. (They were married on September 6, 2003.)

78. See David D. Kirkpatrick, "Young Right Tries to Define Post-Buckley Future," *New York Times* (July 17, 2004), and http://www.townhall.com/phillysoc/Gala40th.htm.

79. Sarah Bramwell, May 1, 2004, speech to the Philadelphia Society, at http://www.townhall.com/phillysoc/bramwellchicago.htm.

80. Perry Bacon, "Yale panelists spar over speech and sexuality," *Yale Daily News* (November 17, 1999).

81. Austin Bramwell, "Pleading the Fourteenth," *American Conservative* (January 31, 2005) at http://www.amconmag.com/2005_01_31/article2.html.

NOTES213

82. A University of Oregon history professor, Peggy Pascoe, pointed out that the "arguments white supremacists used to justify anti-miscegenation laws—that interracial marriages were contrary to God's will or somehow unnatural—are echoed today by the most conservative opponents of same-sex marriage. And supporters of same-sex marriage base their case on the Equal Protection clause of the Fourteenth Amendment, echoing the position the U.S. Supreme Court took when it declared anti-miscegenation laws unconstitutional in the case of *Loving v. Virginia*." Peggy Pascoe, "Why the Ugly Rhetoric Against Gay Marriage Is Familiar to This Historian of Miscegenation," *History News Network* (April 19, 2004) at http://hnn.us/articles/4708.html.

83. Bramwell, "Defining Conservatism Down," 7.

84. David Horowitz, *Radical Son: A Generational Odyssey* (New York: Touchstone, 1998), 396.

85. David Horowitz, "A Conservative Hope" (undated, but according to the new footnotes, post-1996) at http://www.discoverthenetwork.org/guideDesc.asp?catid=156&type=issue.

86. David Nather and Seth Stern, "Classic Conservative Creed Supplanted," *Congressional Quarterly* (March 28, 2005), 778.

Chapter Two: Conservatives Without Conscience

1. Stanley Milgram, *Obedience to Authority: An Experimental View* (New York: Harper Perennial, 1969), 1.

2. Ibid., 205. (When reviewing his experiments, Milgram did not identify any particular types of temperaments as corresponding with obedience or disobedience, for science at that time had not progressed sufficiently. Milgram, however, offered social psychologists one major lesson based on his study: "[O]ften, it is not so much the kind of person a man is as the kind of situation in which he finds himself that determines how he will act.")

3. As requested by Dr. Milgram, I discussed my work at the White House, including how I had taken direction from superiors, but protested and foiled Colson's plan to "firebomb the Brookings Institution." When I had learned of Liddy's illegal intelligence plans, I objected to my superior and did my best to foil those plans as well, but they were approved without my knowledge. Out of loyalty I went along with the initial Watergate cover-up, but when I realized that the illegality of the cover-up was becoming more serious than the matters being covered up, I tried from within to end it. When that failed I broke rank, after telling all my White House colleagues, including a key member of the White House staff, exactly what I was going to do. These are subjects I have addressed at length in testimony and in two

books. See U.S. Senate, "Presidential Campaign Activities of 1972: Senate Resolution 60," Hearings Before the Senate Committee on Presidential Campaign Activities, U.S. Senate, 93rd Cong., 1st Sess., Books 3 and 4 (June 25–29, 1973); John W. Dean, *Blind Ambition* (New York: Simon & Schuster, 1976) and John W. Dean, *Lost Honor* (Los Angeles: Stratford Press, 1982).

I knew long before Milgram's conference that I am not one who is easily inclined to simply go along with others. My notes from this conference show that I discussed two specific incidents that were probably revealing of my nature. One related to a favorite prank of the cadets at prep school, a collective act of defiance designed purely to annoy faculty members on duty as proctor during evening study hours. It was known as a "door slam." At dinner, or before the study period commenced, the word was passed in hushed whispers throughout the dormitory that at a given time every person in the dorm would open his door and then slam it shut. I thought these drills senseless and juvenile, and disruptive of study time, so I refused to participate despite great peer pressure. In fact, I repeatedly told organizers of door slams that if asked, I would not protect them.

Until that conference I had forgotten about what had occurred when I was pledging a college fraternity. One evening I witnessed one of the upperclassmen, a little fellow who was drunk, taking great joy out of paddling a pledge brother twice his size until his bottom was bloody. The next day, when the upperclassman was sober, I told him that if I witnessed such senseless hazing again, I would leave the pledge class and try to take the entire pledge class with me. When he threatened to paddle me for my insolence, I told him to grow up, for this was just between us. He quickly backed down, but a few days later he was at it again, beating one pledge after another for invented infractions of impossible pledge rules (like failure to recite the Greek alphabet both forward and backward, flawlessly). After this incident I told the president of the fraternity that it was either the upperclassman or us, for by then I had the entire pledge class ready to walk. To cut to the end of the story, the hazing rules were changed.

4. Milgram, *Obedience to Authority,* 5.
5. Stanley L. Kutler, *Abuse of Power: The New Nixon Tapes* (New York: Free Press, 1997), 3, 6, 8, 10, 13, 17. (Repeatedly in the remarkable conversations Nixon demands a break-in at the Brookings Institution.)
6. G. Gordon Liddy, *Will* (New York: St. Martin's Press, 1980), 77 (regarding black-bag jobs), 157–69 (Liddy describes how he concocted the plan to break into Ellsberg's psychiatrist's office, noting that he "was forbidden to participate directly in the mission," but despite his orders, he did so, claiming he "was the only game in town"), 255. Liddy explains that, contrary to his orders and his promise to his superiors that his activities would not be

linked to him or anyone with whom he was associated, he used the head of
security for the Nixon reelection campaign, James McCord, as part of his
burglary team at the Watergate, because "McCord was the only game in
town."

7. George Lakoff and John Jost radio interviews, "The Science of Conservatism," WBAI-FM (November 12, 2005). See also George Lakoff, *Moral
Politics: How Liberals and Conservatives Think* (Chicago: University of
Chicago Press, 2002), 33. (Lakoff's work is fascinating, and his credentials
are strong, but his book really provides no documentation. He does provide
a laundry list of references at the back of the book, but it is impossible to tell
where his material comes from. It appears he speaks largely ex cathedra.
Since there was no way to examine his sources, I found I could not use his
material. I was unsuccessful in my efforts to contact him, with my e-mail resulting only in my being added to the mailing list of his foundation.)

8. T. W. Adorno, Else Frenkel-Bruswik, Daniel J. Levinson, R. Nevitt Sand-
ford, in collaboration with Betty Aron, Maria Hertz Levinson, and William
Morrow, *The Authoritarian Personality* (New York: Harper & Row, 1950), v.

9. Ibid., ix.

10. Alan Wolfe, "'The Authoritarian Personality' Revisited," *Chronicle of Higher
Education,* vol. 52 (October 7, 2005), B-12.

11. Ibid.

12. Bob Altemeyer, *The Authoritarian Specter* (Cambridge, MA: Harvard University Press, 1996), 8.

13. Bob Altemeyer is an American scholar who went to Canada to teach psychology at the University of Manitoba, where for several decades he has
been a relentless researcher. An article written for *Political Psychology* described Altemeyer's work since the 1970s as "convincing [other] scholars (in
Canada and beyond) of the fruitfulness of [his] endeavors," for he has undertaken literally "hundreds of experiments in the past three decades,"
achieving "admirable robustness in terms of [his work's] reliability and va-
lidity." Paul Nesbitt-Larking, "Political Psychology in Canada," *Political
Psychology,* vol. 25, no. 1 (2004), 97, 106–7. The *Oxford Handbook of Political Psychology* reported that Altemeyer's work "powerfully predicts a wide
range of political, social, ideological, and intergroup phenomena." David
O. Sears, Leonie Huddy, and Robert Jervis (eds.), *Oxford Handbook of Political Psychology* (New York: Oxford University Press, 2003). Because Altemeyer's work is critically insightful to understanding contemporary conservatism, it is regrettable that the principal audience for his extensive writing is
composed of other psychologists and social scientists. In an effort to translate his findings, I asked him many questions over an extended period that
he was kind enough to answer. Any mistakes in presenting his work are
mine, not his.

14. A person being tested is typically asked to indicate the extent to which he or she agrees or disagrees with each statement by being given the following options: very strongly disagree (−4), strongly disagree (−3), moderately disagree (−2), and slightly disagree (−1), and corresponding positive values for agreement (ranging from +1 to +4). If the respondent feels neutral about a statement, he or she can give an answer that has no value—a zero. If he or she strongly agrees with part of a statement (+3), but slightly disagrees with another part of the statement (−1), the respondent would be in moderate agreement (+2) after doing the math.

15. Stanley Feldman, "Enforcing Social Conformity: A Theory of Authoritarianism," *Political Psychology*, vol. 24, no. 1 (2003), 41, 44.

16. "In a detailed review of the research . . . [it has been] shown that authoritarianism is consistently associated with right-wing but not left-wing ideology." Feldman, "Enforcing Social Conformity: A Theory of Authoritarianism," 42.

17. "A large array of studies . . . document high correlations between Authoritarianism and Conservatism." Gerard Saucier, "Isms and the Structure of Social Attitudes," *Journal of Personality and Social Psychology*, vol. 78, no. 2 (2000), 366–67.

18. Bob Altemeyer, *The Authoritarian Specter*, 296.

19. Markus Kemmelmeier, "Authoritarianism and Candidate Support in the U.S. Presidential Elections of 1996 and 2000," *Journal of Social Psychology* (April 2004), 218.

20. Bob Altemeyer, "The Other 'Authoritarian Personality.'" In John T. Jost and Jim Sidanius, *Political Psychology* (New York: Psychology Press, 2004), 88.

21. Sears et al., eds. *Oxford Handbook*, 577.

22. Ibid., 579.

23. Bob Altemeyer, "Highly Dominating, Highly Authoritarian Personalities," *Journal of Social Psychology*, vol. 144, no. 4 (2004), 422–25.

24. Ibid.

25. Ibid.

26. Marc Stewart Wilson, "Social Dominance and Ethical Ideology: The End Justifies the Means?," *Journal of Social Psychology*, vol. 143, no. 5 (2003), 549 (citing Sidanius et al.).

27. Ibid.

28. Bob Altemeyer, "What Happens When Authoritarians Inherit the Earth? A Simulation," *Analyses of Social Issues and Public Policy*, vol. 3, no. 1 (December 2003), 161.

29. Ibid. See also Bob Altemeyer, "Highly Dominating, Highly Authoritarian Personalities," 431–35.

30. Ibid., 439.

31. Ibid.

32. Bob Altemeyer, "What Happens When Authoritarians Inherit the Earth?,"
161.

33. Altemeyer, "Highly Dominating, Highly Authoritarian Personalities," 445.

34. In Altemeyer's formulation, "Our conscience is the part of our minds that
makes us feel guilty: (1) we can feel guilty because we did not do the right
thing (but instead did nothing), and (2) (more commonly) we can feel
guilty because we did something wrong. Conscience, or (perhaps more use-
fully) the strength of someone's conscience, is a very tricky thing to measure. It is a very private experience, and no one can know exactly how
someone's guilt feels to him. And guilt usually means feeling shame, and for
some reason people don't like to reveal how ashamed they are of themselves."

35. There are some indirect ways to make measurements, for example, "by using anonymous surveys in good testing circumstances with the 'Hidden
Observer' technique"—a metaphorical concept based on the suggestion
that such an observer exists within each of us—Altemeyer made some in-
triguing findings. He asked a group of high-scoring right-wing authoritarians he had tested earlier—who almost across-the-board had strongly agreed
with a statement about the existence of "an Almighty God who will judge
each person after death"—whether the "Hidden Observer" in them agreed
with this statement. He got surprising answers. About a fifth said they had
some doubts about God's existence, which they had shared with someone
else, and about a third conceded that they had secret doubts about God's
existence that they had shared with no one. Altemeyer said he felt this to be
one of the most amazing things right-wing authoritarians have ever admitted in his surveys.

36. Bob Altemeyer, *Enemies of Freedom* (San Francisco: Jossey-Bass Publishers,
1988), 147–51.

37. Ronald J. Sider, *The Scandal of the Evangelical Conscience* (Grand Rapids,
MI: Baker Books, 2005), 17.

38. Altemeyer, *The Authoritarian Specter,* chapter 5.

39. Lance Morrow, "The Brawlers," *National Review* (October 25, 1999), 20.

40. Charles Lane and Jennifer Bradley, "Daddy's Boy," *The New Republic* (January 22, 1996), 15.

41. U.S. Senate, "Presidential Campaign Activities of 1972," Hearings Before
the Select Committee on Presidential Campaign Activities, Book 10 (Washington: Government Printing Office, 1973), 3922–24.

42. Ibid.

43. See Fred I. Greenstein, "Can Personality and Politics Be Studied Systemati-
cally." In John T. Jost and Jim Sidanius, eds., *Political Psychology: Key Read-
ings* (New York: Psychology Press, 2004), 108, 118.

Chapter Three: Authoritarian Conservatism

1. Jay M. Shafritz, *American Government & Politics* (New York: Harper Perennial, 1993), 418.
2. Charles W. Dunn and J. David Woodard, *The Conservative Tradition in America* (Lanham, MD: Rowman & Littlefield, 1996), 88–89.
3. Bill Schardt, "Joseph de Maistre (1753–1821): A Great and Virtuous Man?," *Newcastle Philosophy Society* at http://www.newphilsoc.org.uk/Freedom/berlinday/a_great_and_virtuous_man.htm.
4. A brief biography of Joseph de Maistre and a Maistre home page administered by Richard Lebrun at St. Paul's College, University of Manitoba, is located at http://www.umanitoba.ca/faculties/arts/history/links/maistre/maistre.html. Lebrun has written a full biography of this early conservative, *Joseph de Maistre: An Intellectual Militant* (McGill-Queen's University Press, 1988). This work is described by the publisher as follows: "The Joseph de Maistre revealed here is a more complex figure than either the bloody-minded apologist for conservatism portrayed by his liberal critics or the steadfast Church Father of his traditional Catholic admirers. Maistre was a scholarly magistrate in the tradition of Montesquieu, a man who had been open to the trends of his time but was profoundly shaken by the violence of the French Revolution. Appalled by the prospect of chaos, he used his rhetorical skills as a lawyer to defend monarchical institutions and traditional Catholicism. Lebrun argues that only with the opening of the family archives and the discoveries in recent studies are we able to appreciate Maistre's struggles to understand the upheavals of his time, his doubts and hesitations, and his reasons for taking the public positions he chose."
5. Peter Viereck, *Conservatism: From John Adams to Churchill* (Princeton, NJ: Van Nostrand, 1956), 11.
6. Nash's *The Conservative Intellectual Movement in America* (Wilmington, DE: Intercollegiate Studies Institute, 1998) makes only two passing references to de Maistre; similarly, Russell Kirk makes two fleeting references to de Maistre in *The Conservative Mind: From Burke to Eliot* (Washington, DC: Regnery, 2001), and the way in which he first comes into the narrative, with no introduction whatsoever, gives one the feeling that he was edited out.
7. Dunn and Woodard, *The Conservative Tradition in America*, 89–90.
8. Ibid., 100.
9. John W. Dean, *Worse Than Watergate: The Secret Presidency of George W. Bush* (New York: Little Brown, 2004), 132–36. This book spells out the unprecedented nature of the aggressive policies of the Bush/Cheney administration.
10. John Lyman, "Who Is Scooter Libby? The Guy Behind the Guy Behind the

Guy," Center for American Progress Web site (October 28, 2005) at http://www.americanprogress.org/sit/p.aspz?c=biJRJ8OVF&b=109719& printmode=1.

11. Michael C. Desch, "George 'Wilson' Bush: How the dark side of America's Liberal Tradition drives us to global crusades in democracy's name," *American Conservative* (November 21, 2005), 24–25. Michael C. Desch is a Professor at the George Bush School of Government and Public Service at Texas A&M University.

12. Melanie Scarborough, "The Security Pretext: An Examination of the Growth of Federal Police Agencies," Cato Institute Briefing Paper No. 94 (June 29, 2005) at http://www.cato.org/pub_display.php?pub_id=3828.

13. Norman Ornstein, "Checks and Balances? The President Has Few, if Any," *Roll Call* (December 21, 2005) at http://www.aei.org/publications/ pubID.23607/pub_detail.asp.

14. See Abraham H. Maslow, *Maslow on Management* (New York: John Wiley & Sons, 1998), 292. Maslow wrote in this classic, "The more grown people are, the worse authoritarian management will work, the less well people will function in the authoritarian situation, and the more they will hate it. What this means is that people who have experienced freedom can never really be content again with slavery, even though they made no protest about the slavery before they had the experience of freedom."

15. See, e.g., Patrick J. Buchanan, "America's Next War," Creators Syndicate (August 23, 2004); Max Boot, "Q & A: Neocon power examined," *Christian Science Monitor* at http://www.csmonitor.com/specials/neocon/boothtml; and Jay Solomon and Neil King, Jr., "As 'Neocons' Leave, Bush Foreign Policy Takes Softer Line," *Wall Street Journal* (February 6, 2006).

16. In a December 18, 2005, speech, President Bush all but conceded the point that America is provoking terror. He stated, "If you think the terrorist would become peaceful if only America would stop provoking them, then it might make sense to leave them alone." George W. Bush, "Bush Says Iraqis See Democracy as Their Future," U.S. Department of State, at http:// usinfo.state.gov/mena/Archive/2005/Dec/19-15664.html. Writing in the *Yale Law Journal*, Jeffery Manns discusses the reality that American foreign policy's provocation of terrorism requires the government to help with insurance coverage of terrorist activity. Jeffery Manns, "Insuring Against Terror?" *Yale Law Journal*, vol. 112:8 (2003). Philip C. Wilcox, president of the Foundation for Middle East Peace, asserted, "The administration has focused on the destruction of terrorists and terrorist groups as the solution to terrorism. Certainly, we must do this, but terrorism is a symptom of deeper conflicts. If destroying terrorists is all we do, it's only a palliative. Unless we understand, try to eliminate or at least contain the problems that breed terrorism, we're going to fail, and the virus of terrorism will continue to grow

and spread. Some have called this approach appeasement, but it's not. It's common sense. Iraq is emerging to surprise the administration, as a new breeding ground for terrorism that didn't exist previously." Philip C. Wilcox, Jr., "Imperial Dreams: Can the Middle East Be Transformed?," *Middle East Policy,* vol. 10 (Winter 2003), 1.

17. Athan G. Theoharis and John Stuart Cox, *The Boss: J. Edgar Hoover and the Great American Inquisition* (Philadelphia: Temple University Press, 1988), 102.

18. See, e.g., Curt Gentry, *J. Edgar Hoover: The Man and the Secrets* (New York: W. W. Norton, 1991); Athan Theoharis, *The FBI & American Democracy: A Brief Critical History* (Lawrence: University Press of Kansas, 2004); William C. Sullivan with Bill Brown, *The Bureau: My Thirty Years in Hoover's FBI* (New York: W. W. Norton, 1979); and Anthony Summers, *Official and Confidential: The Secret Life of J. Edgar Hoover* (New York: G. P. Putnam's Sons, 1993).

19. Sullivan with Brown, *The Bureau,* 136–37.

20. Summers, *Official and Confidential,* 434.

21. Paul Johnson, *A History of the American People* (New York: HarperCollins, 1997), 837.

22. Jonathan M. Schoenwald, *A Time for Choosing: The Rise of Modern American Conservatism* (New York: Oxford University Press, 2001), 48.

23. Sullivan with Brown, *The Bureau,* 49. Sullivan documented the Kennedy situation. I have personal knowledge of the Nixon situation.

24. Congressman Dan Burton, a conservative Republican from Indiana, introduced legislation on July 25, 2002 (HR 5213) to rename the FBI headquarters building and remove the name of J. Edgar Hoover from the building. Burton was joined by bipartisan cosponsors: Steven LaTourette (R-OH), Christopher Shays (R-CT), William Delahunt (D-MA), John Lewis (D-GA), and John Tierney (D-MA). Even the *Wall Street Journal's* editorial pages has called for "stripping J. Edgar Hoover's name from FBI headquarters." Anonymous, "A Real Surveillance Scandal," *Wall Street Journal* (January 10, 2006), A-14.

25. In a conversation I had with Vice President Agnew in December 1970, he told me of his admiration for Hoover at a time when others in the Nixon White House were trying to get Hoover to resign.

26. Richard Nixon, *RN: The Memoirs of Richard Nixon* (New York: Grosset & Dunlap, 1978), 411–12.

27. *Facts on File Yearbook 1970* (New York: Facts on File, Inc., 1971), 698.

28. Terri Bimes, "Reagan: The Soft-Sell Populist," in W. Elliot Brownlee and Hugh David Graham, eds., *The Reagan Presidency: Pragmatic Conservatism & Its Legacies* (Lawrence: University Press of Kansas, 2003), 61.

29. Richard Reeves, *President Nixon: Alone in the White House* (New York: Simon & Schuster, 2001), 159–60.

30. This material is drawn largely from Phyllis Schlafly's Web site at http://www.phyllisschlafly.com/.
31. Elizabeth Kolbert, "Firebrand: Phyllis Schlafly and the Conservative Revolution," *The New Yorker* (November 7, 2005) at http://www.newyorker.com/printables/critics/051107crbo_books.
32. The source of this material is in part the National Women's Party Web site on the ERA at http://www.equalrightsamendment.org/, and in part Ruth Murray Brown's book *For a "Christian America"—A History of the Religious Right* (Amherst, NY: Prometheus Books, 2002), 15–62.
33. Phyllis Schlafly, "Is the Era of Big Government Coming Back?" *The Phyllis Schlafly Report,* vol. 35, no. 7 (February 2002) at http://www.eagleforum.org/psr/202/feb02/psrfeb02.shtml.
34. John Micklethwait and Adrian Wooldridge, *The Right Nation: Conservative Power in America* (New York: Penguin Press, 2004), 81.
35. I can remember Richard Nixon grousing, in 1971, that Republicans had but one small think tank, the American Enterprise Institute, which today is also an affluent great-granddaddy. In recent years there has been a proliferation of right-wing think tanks. For example, the Heritage Foundation Web site refers to some 564 experts or organizations espousing conservative views, including the Nixon Center for Peace and Freedom in Washington, D.C. (See the Heritage Foundation, "Policy Experts," at http://policyexperts.org/organizations/organizations_results.cfm.) Do think tanks matter? Do all their books, position papers, seminars, and briefings influence policy? No definitive answer is possible, for there is no way to measure accurately. Donald E. Abelson, *Do Think Tanks Matter? Assessing the Impact of Public Policy Institutes* (Montreal: McGill–Queen's University Press, 2002). But clearly they have influence. Former conservative activist and writer David Brock (who had his own eye-opening experiences with conservatism and created the Media Matters for America Web site that puts the lie to conservative misinformation and propaganda) wrote in *The Republican Noise Machine,* "In 1998 Heritage spent close to $8 million, or 18 percent of its budget, on media and government relations." David Brock, *The Republican Noise Machine: Right-Wing Media and How It Corrupts Democracy* (New York: Crown Publishers, 2004), 58. Spending such sums enables them to keep their name before policy makers, and today conservative think tanks appear to have a far greater influence than moderate ones, even long-established organizations like Brookings. I undertook a rather simple, albeit unscientific, test of the relative strength of the major think tanks on Capitol Hill by noting how often they were referred to on the floor of the House and Senate since 1995. Using the Government Accountability Office's search engine for the *Congressional Record,* I found the following:

Year	The Heritage Foundation	The Cato Institute	American Enterprise Institute	The Brookings Institution
1995	137	87	59	15
1996	63	59	35	11
1997	80	48	40	22
1998	54	22	29	11
1999	49	24	21	4
2000	55	24	19	5
2001	53	23	29	5
2002	48	19	14	8
2003	85	17	51	5
2004	56	56	27	4
2005	70	27	27	6

36. Jean Stefancic and Richard Delgado, *No Mercy: How Conservative Think Tanks and Foundations Changed America's Social Agenda* (New York: Temple, 1997). Work product of the conservative think tanks, however, has become notably predictable, and they are not generating great ideas; rather, they "produce studies with one or more preordained conclusions: that liberal solutions will only increase the power and oppressiveness of government and bureaucracy; that they deprive worthy citizens of their liberty, or that they benefit criminals at the expense of victims; and, most often, that more laissez-faire and lower taxes for business is always the best policy." Herbert J. Gans, "Tanking the Right," *The Nation* (January 27, 1997), 28.

37. Notes, telephone conversation with Senator Barry M. Goldwater, March 1995.

38. Barry M. Goldwater with Jack Casserly, *Goldwater* (New York: Doubleday, 1988), 386.

39. Ralph Z. Hallow, "Weyrich fears 'cordial' ties between GOP and the Right," *Washington Times* (June 17, 2005) at http://www.washingtontimes.com/national/20050617-125248-4355r.htm.

40. E. J. Dionne, "Roasting the Rightest of the Right; Conservatives Turn Out for Tough Guy Weyrich," *Washington Post* (April 2, 1991), E-1.

41. Ibid.

42. Jeff Jacoby, "The Christian Right's Double Shocker," *Boston Globe* (April 26, 2001), A-15.

43. For example, when Michael Deaver left the Reagan White House to set up a highly lucrative lobbying operation—with Canada, South Korea, Mexico, and Saudi Arabia among his A-list of clients—Paul Weyrich called for a special prosecutor to investigate charges of conflicts of interest. (Martin Tolchin, "Conservatives Say Deaver Case Hurts Reagan," *New York Times* [May 1,

1986], A-21.) Although he could not back it up with specifics, Weyrich later shot down Bush I's nomination of Senator John Tower to be Secretary of Defense because he opposed Tower's alleged drinking and spending time with women "to whom he was not married." (Suzanne Garment, "The Tower Precedent," *Commentary* [May 1989], 44.) Weyrich was relentless in his attacks against Bill Clinton. (Anonymous, *New York Times* [November 12, 1995], 6-37.) However, Weyrich wrote thoughtful op-eds critical of conservatives and the Reagan White House, following revelations about the Iran/Contra debacle. He explained that "our government was designed not to play great-power politics but to preserve domestic liberty" through "separation of powers, congressional checks on executive authority, the primacy of law over raison d'état—all of these were intentionally built into our system." He continued, "The Founding Fathers knew a nation with such a government could not play the role of a great power. They had no such ambition for us—quite the contrary." Weyrich also raised a problem in 1987 that remains to this day: "If the executive does what it must in the international arena, it violates the domestic rules. If the Congress enforces those rules, as it is supposed to do, it cripples us internationally." Paul M. Weyrich, "A Conservative Lament; After Iran, We Need to Change Our System and Grand Strategy," *Washington Post* (March 8, 1987), B-5.

44. Anonymous, *New York Times* (November 12, 1995), 6-37.

45. Steve Bruce, "Zealot Politics and Democracy: The Case of the New Christian Right," *Political Studies,* vol. 48 (2000), 263–82.

46. Religion scholar Laurence Iannaccone reported that an "enormous multi-year study, sponsored by the American Academy of Arts and Science, and directed by religious historians Martin E. Marty and R. Scott Appleby . . . enlisted over a hundred researchers to describe and analyze dozens of 'fundamentalist-like' movements across five continents and seven religious traditions" to explain fundamentalism. Yet this "Fundamentalism Project," as it is known, came up with "no clear definition of fundamentalism, no objective criterion for deciding which religious movements are 'fundamentalist,' and nothing approaching a *theory* of fundamentalism." Laurence R. Iannaccone, "Toward an Economic Theory of 'Fundamentalism,'" *Journal of Institutional and Theoretical Economics,* vol. 153 (1997), 100. The Fundamentalism Project, to the chagrin of evangelicals, labels them as a fundamentalist religion.

47. Corine Hegland, "Special Report: Values Voters—Evangelical, Not Fundamentalist," *National Journal* (December 3, 2004).

48. Micklethwait and Wooldridge, *The Right Nation,* 83.

49. Special Report, "You Ain't Seen Nothing Yet," *Economist* (June 23, 2005) at http://www.economist.com/world/na/PrintFriendly.cfm?story_id=4102212.

50. Pew Research Center for the People and the Press, "Bush's Gains Broad-Based: Religion and the Presidential Vote (December 6, 2004) at http://people-press.org/commentary/pdf/103.pdf.

51. Special Report, "You Ain't Seen Nothing Yet," *The Economist* (June 23, 2005).

52. Joel Rogers, "Devolve This!," *The Nation* (August 30–September 6, 2004), 20.

53. Mark Noll explained evangelicalism as the "belief that lives need to be changed"; the "belief that all spiritual truth" is found in the Bible; dedication to active lives in service of God, or to "evangelism" (spreading the good news) and "mission" (taking the gospel to other societies); and conviction that Christ's death on the cross provided reconciliation between a holy god and sinful human beings. See Ethics & Public Policy Center, "Center Conversations: Understanding American Evangelicals, A Conversation with Mark Noll and Jay Tolson" (June 2004) at http://www.eppc.org/publications/pubID.2115/pub_detail.asp.

54. Ethics & Public Policy Center, "Center Conversations," 18.

55. Ibid.

56. Christian Smith, *Christian America? What Evangelicals Really Want* (Berkeley: University of California Press, 2000), 3.

57. Smith polled over twenty-five hundred church-going Protestants in a 1996 telephone survey that he reproduces in the book. He acknowledged the weakness of this type of polling, and the results are now dated. Nonetheless, the surveys have some rather alarming findings. For example, a survey focusing on the South revealed that 87 percent of self-identified evangelicals believed that the United States was founded "as a Christian nation"; 92 percent saw "a serious breakdown of American society"; 68 percent believed "morals should be based on an absolute, unchanging standard"; 69 percent disagreed with the notion that religion is a private matter "to be kept out of public debates over social and political issues"; 55 percent believed "Christian morality should be the law of the land even though not all Americans are Christians"; 68 percent believed the "federal government should promote traditional values in our society"; and 77 percent believed "the mass media is hostile to [evangelical] moral and spiritual values." (Ibid., 200.) In a survey of religious identity and influence, only 35 percent of the evangelicals *disagreed* with the statement "Everyone should have the right to live by their own morality, even when it is not Christian morality." This, of course, suggested that as many as 65 percent of evangelicals wanted to tell others, regardless of their beliefs, how to lead their lives. (Ibid., 201.) This poll also showed that 90 percent of the evangelicals believed "Public school instruction should include Christian views of science and history," i.e., intelligent design and creationism. (Ibid. 204.) A more encouraging result was in the Religious Right Survey (a nationwide poll of over a thousand conducted by Gallup in 1996) that re-

vealed that only 4 percent of all polled, including evangelicals, admired David Duke, who was then running for the U.S. Senate in Louisiana.

Smith and his collaborators also interviewed evangelicals face-to-face from select locations, but it was a very small sample that had not been selected randomly; in addition, these kinds of interviews are not always as candid as anonymous responses. In short, this is not a scientifically representative selection of all evangelicals, but rather a largely anecdotal collection of information gathered from evangelicals willing to talk with sociologists. As another social scientist, familiar with this work, explained, "The sampling procedure is critical, since Smith says his interviews tell us what evangelicals really think and want. That is a big claim and it means he has to have a representative sample. The evidence strongly suggests he does not. This team apparently did two studies using face-to-face interviews. One involved 130 church-going Protestants in six different locations around the U.S., and the second involved 187 evangelicals and others in 23 states. Neither of these is a national sample. If you look at the map in the book, you can see that most of the interviewees (in the second, larger study) came from places near large universities. You can even guess the academic affiliation of many of the sociologists involved by looking at the map. One consequence is that the Deep South, which has the largest concentration of evangelicals in the country, is pretty underrepresented. One might well find that evangelicals who live in university communities have higher educational attainments, etc., than other evangelicals. A second issue is how the researchers found the particular evangelicals in their locale to interview. We aren't told, but in the Acknowledgments Smith thanks the pastors who 'in many cases' granted the researchers access to the interviewees. So it is quite plausible that the investigators contacted the pastors of conservative Protestant churches in their area, and the pastors selected—at least to some extent—the evangelicals to be interviewed. That makes it potentially a very biased and misleading sample."

58. Cal Thomas and Ed Dobson, *Blinded by Might: Can the Religious Right Save America?* (Grand Rapids, MI: Zondervan Publishing House, 1999), 191.
59. Ibid., 52, 58, 59.
60. Ibid., 54.
61. Ibid., 55, 56.
62. Jimmy Carter, *Our Endangered Values: America's Moral Crisis* (New York: Simon & Schuster, 2005), 2–3.
63. Ibid., 34–35.
64. Ibid., 100–101.
65. Ibid., 88.
66. Paul Jalsevac, "Bush Appoints a Pro-Lifer to the UN," *The Interim* (July 2004) at http://www.theinterim.com/2004/july/17bushappoints.html.

67. John C. Danforth, "Onward, Moderate Christian Soldiers," *New York Times* (June 17, 2005), A-27.
68. Bob Altemeyer, *The Authoritarian Specter* (Cambridge, MA: Harvard University Press, 1996), 147.
69. Robert Boston, *The Most Dangerous Man in America? Pat Robertson and the Rise of the Christian Coalition* (Amherst, NY: Prometheus Books, 1996), 25.
70. Americans United for Separation of Church and State, "Religious Leader Approves of Sending 'Squads' to 'Take Out' Foreign Leaders" at http://www.au.org/site/News2?JServSessionIdr005=1uj2ym0jp3.app5b&abbr=pr&page=NewsArticle&id=6179&news_iv_ctrl=1477.
71. Boston, *The Most Dangerous Man in America?*, 164.
72. Ibid., 164, 165.
73. Ibid., 39.
74. Americans United for Separation of Church and State, "TV Preacher Pat Robertson Suggests God Removed Israeli Leader Sharon Because of Land Policies" (January 5, 2006) at http://www.au.org/site/News2?JServSessionIdr006=94g6kp2dr2.app13a&abbr=pr&page=NewsArticle&id=7782&security=1002&news_iv_ctrl=1241.
75. David Van Biema, "What Was Robertson Thinking? With a $50 million partnership hanging in the balance, Robertson tries to make amends for his insensitive comments toward Israel," *Time* (January 13, 2006) at http://www.time.com/time/nation/printout/0,8816,1149156,00.html.
76. Boston, *The Most Dangerous Man in America?*, 39.
77. Joe Queenan, "Bookshelf: New World Order Nut," *Wall Street Journal* (December 31, 1991), A-5.
78. Pat Robertson, *Courting Disaster: How the Supreme Court Is Usurping the Power of Congress and the People* (Nashville: Integrity Publishers, 2004), 236–37.
79. Adam Nagourney, Richard W. Stevenson, and Neil A. Lewis, "Glum Democrats Can't See Halting Bush on Courts," *New York Times* (January 15, 2006), A-1.
80. Robertson, *Courting Disaster*, 258.
81. Charles Colson and Nancy Pearcey, "Who holds these truths?," *Christianity Today* (October 6, 1997), 144.
82. For example, Mark Noll mentions Colson's works when exploring the question "Is an Evangelical Intellectual Renaissance Underway," in Mark A. Noll, *The Scandal of the Evangelical Mind* (Grand Rapids, MI: William B. Eerdmans Publishing, 1994), 223.
83. *Marbury v. Madison*, 5 U.S. 147 (1803).
84. See David E. Engdahl, "John Marshall's 'Jeffersonian' Concept of Judicial Review," *Duke Law Journal* (November 1992), 279, 284–89.

85. Ibid. Professor Engdahl's examination of often neglected data is the basis for the summary I have provided of pre-*Marbury* practices regarding judicial review.

86. See Michael Stokes Paulsen, "The Most Dangerous Branch: Executive Power to Say What the Law Is," *Georgetown Law Journal* (December 1994), 217, 259 n.159. Professor Paulsen argued that presidents do have the power to interpret the law.

87. Lincoln historian Philip S. Paludan wrote, "Although clear evidence is lacking, it would not be surprising if Lincoln had put him up to it, for the president continued to believe that border-state challenges to slavery would deal a heavy blow to the rebellion." Phillip Shaw Paludan, *The Presidency of Abraham Lincoln* at http://www.mrlincolnandfreedom.org/content_inside.asp?ID=56&subjectID=3.

Chapter 4: Troubling Politics and Policies

1. Raymond Hernandez, "At King Event, Mrs. Clinton Denounces G.O.P. Leadership," *New York Times* (January 18, 2006), A-1.

2. David Maraniss and Michael Weisskopf, *Tell Newt to Shut Up!* (New York: Touchstone, 1996), 5.

3. David Osborne, "Newt Gingrich: Shining King of the Post-Reagan Right," *Mother Jones* (November 1, 1984) at http://www.motherjones.com/news/feature/1984/11/osborne.html.

4. Donald T. Critchlow, "When Republicans Become Revolutionaries." In Julian E. Zelizer, ed., *The American Congress* (New York: Houghton Mifflin, 2004), 717.

5. Osborne, "Newt Gingrich: Shining King of the Post-Reagan Right."

6. Critchlow, "When Republicans Become Revolutionaries."

7. Dan T. Carter, *From George Wallace to Newt Gingrich: Race in the Conservative Counterrevolution, 1963–1994* (Baton Rouge: Louisiana State University Press, 1996), 119.

8. Ibid.

9. Ibid.

10. Evan Thomas, Holly Bailey, and Michael Isikoff, "The Exterminator: Expelled, Born Again. Tom DeLay's Rise—and the Risks That Could End It," *Newsweek* (October 17, 2005), 28.

11. See "Texas Congressional Redistricting, Gerrymandering, Minority Vote Dilution, Equal Protection, First Amendment, Voting Rights Act," *FindLaw* at http://supreme.lp.findlaw.com/supreme_court/docket/2005/March.html.

12. John Ydstie, "Profile: The K Street Project and Tom DeLay," *Weekend Edition,* National Public Radio (January 14, 2006) transcript.

13. Lou Dubose and Jan Reid, *The Hammer: Tom DeLay: God, Money, and the Rise of the Republican Congress* (New York: Public Affairs, 2004), 64–65.

14. John Samples, "Same as the Old Boss? Congressional Reforms under the Republicans." In *The Republican Revolution 10 Years Later: Smaller Government or Business as Usual?* (Washington, DC: Cato Institute, 2005), 23. Neither Samples nor the Cato Institute, which published this book, addresses Gingrich's campaign to denigrate Congress. In fact, Gingrich is one of the book's contributors. But the numbers speak for themselves, and Gingrich's attacks on both members of Congress and the House of Representatives itself was certainly not a stealth campaign.

15. See Republicans' 1994 "Contract with America" at http://www.house.gov/house/Contract/CONTRACT.html.

16. Dubose and Reid, *The Hammer,* 87.

17. Ibid., 88.

18. Arthur M. Schlesinger, Jr., *The Cycles of American History* (New York: Houghton Mifflin, Mariner Book edition, 1986), vii.

19. Lee H. Hamilton, *How Congress Works and Why You Should Care* (Bloomington: Indiana University Press, 2004), 47.

20. John Samples, "Same as the Old Boss?," 23–24.

21. For example, William M. Welch, "We Exposed Our Souls in Late-Night Gingrich Debate," *USA Today* (January 8, 1997), A-1, refers to Gingrich's "autocratic and centralized rule of the House majority"; John McQuaid, "Remodeling of House Expected: Livingston to Exercise Restraint as Well as Power," the New Orleans *Times-Picayune* (November 11, 1998), A-1, stated, "Historians say Gingrich has been the most powerful speaker since Joseph Cannon, R-Ill., whose autocratic rule early this century eventually led to an open revolt against him and a reining in of his power"; and Congresswoman Barbara Lee (D-CA) characterized the Gingrich/DeLay refusal to allow a vote for censure of President Clinton rather than for impeachment as "one-party autocracy, which we condemn abroad and which history has proven can lead to authoritarian rule," *Washington Post* (December 20, 1998), A-42.

22. Robert Kuttner, "America as a One-Party State: Today's hard right seeks total dominion. It's packing the courts and rigging the rules. The target is not the Democrats but democracy itself," *The American Prospect* (February 2004) at http://www.prospect.org/print/V15/2/kuttner-r.html.

23. Stephen Moore, "Worse Than Drunken Sailors," *National Review* Online (May 17, 2002) at http://www.nationalreview.com/moore/moore051702.asp. (NRO noted: "Stephen Moore is president of the Club for Growth. This article originally appeared in the *Wall Street Journal* on May 13, 2002.")

24. Norman Ornstein and Thomas Mann, "If You Give a Congressman a Cookie," *New York Times* (January 19, 2006) at http://www.nytimes.com/2006/01/19/opinion/19ornstein.html?_r=1.

25. Kuttner, "America as a One-Party State" at http://www.prospect.org/print/
V15/2/kuttner-r.html. See also, Joseph G. Cannon, as told to L. White
Busbey, *Uncle Joe Cannon: The Story of a Pioneer American* (New York:
Henry Holt, 1927), 243–69. This was an "as-told-to" autobiography pub-
lished after Cannon's death. Cannon made the following observation:

> It is true we engage in fierce combat, we are often intense partisans,
> sometimes we are unfair, not infrequently unjust, brutal at times, and
> yet I venture to say that, taken as a whole, the House is sound at heart;
> nowhere else will you find such a ready appreciation of merit and char-
> acter, in few gatherings of equal size is there so little jealousy and envy.
> The House must be considerate of the feelings of its Members; there is
> a certain courtesy that has to be observed; a man may be voted a bore
> or shunned as a pest, and yet he must be accorded the rights to which
> he is entitled by virtue of being a representative of the people. On the
> other hand, a man may be universally popular, a good fellow, amusing
> and yet with these engaging qualities never get far. The men who have
> led the House, whose names have become a splendid tradition to their
> successors, have gained prominence not through luck or by mere acci-
> dent. They have had ability, at least in some degree; but more than that,
> they have had character.

26. Staff report, *Economist,* "Pyongyang on the Potomac? The Congressional
Elections" (September 18, 2004) at http://www.economist.com/world/na/
displaystory.cfm?story_id=3203239&tranMode=LA.

27. Lou Dubose, "The Man with the Plan," *Texas Monthly* (August 2004), 1.

28. See *Eddie Jackson et al. v. Rick Perry et al.,* brief for Appellants, in Supreme
Court of the United States at http://www.jenner.com/files/tbl_s69News
DocumentOrder/FileUpload500/517/Brief_for_Appellants_in_Jackson_v_
Perry.pdf.

29. Spencer Overton, "Stealing Liberty: How Politicians Manipulate the Electorate," *The Crisis* (January/February 2005), 15. *The Crisis* is an official
publication of the NAACP.

30. Dan Eggen, "Justice Staff Saw Texas Districting as Illegal; Voting Rights
Finding on Map Pushed by DeLay Was Overruled," *Washington Post* (December 2, 2005), A-1.

31. Juliet Eilperin, "House GOP Practices Art of One-Vote Victories," *Washington Post* (October 14, 2003), A-1.

32. Dubose and Reid, *The Hammer,* 6.

33. See Robert K. Murray, *The Harding Era: Warren G. Harding and His Administration* (Minneapolis: University of Minnesota Press, 1969), 432–33.
There is no evidence that President Harding had any involvement with the
influence peddling and illegal sale of government property undertaken at
the "little green house on K Street."

34. Jaun Williams, "The K Street Project and Jack Abramoff," *Morning Edition,* National Public Radio (January 11, 2006) transcript.

35. Jonathan E. Kaplan, "Boehner Can Rely on K Street Cabinet," *The Hill* (October 6, 2005) at http://www.hillnews.com/thehill/export/TheHill/ News/Frontpage/100605/Boehner.html.

36. William Norman Grigg, "Trouble with DeLay," *New American* (October 31, 2005), 21.

37. John B. Judis, "Razing McCain," *The American Prospect* (March 13, 2000), 15.

38. Dubose and Reid, *The Hammer,* 164–66.

39. Sam Rosenfeld, "Then Came the Hammer," *The American Prospect* (December 2004), 51.

40. Jonathan Alter, "Tom DeLay's House of Shame," *Newsweek* (October 10, 2005) at http://www.msnbc.msn.com/id/9557669/site/newsweek/.

41. Story reported by the American Progress Action Fund (January 20, 2006) at http://www.americanprogressaction.org/site/apps/nl/content2.asp?c=klL WJcP7H&b=1331575&ct=1799805.

42. Anonymous, "Corrupted by Lunch: What Speaker Hastert Thinks of His Colleagues," *Wall Street Journal* (January 19, 2006), A-14.

43. Janet Hook, "GOP Seeks Lasting Majority: The Party Dreams of Political Dominion," *Los Angeles Times* (July 21, 2003), A-1.

44. Paul Krugman, "Toward One-Party Rule," *New York Times* (June 27, 2003), A-27.

45. Scott Stewart, "The College Republicans—A Brief History," College Republican National Committee at http://www.crnc.org/images/CRNChistory.pdf (reports on Abramoff's role in the CRNC); People for the American Way, "Right Wing Watch: Americans for Tax Reform" at http://www.pfaw.org/ pfaw/general/default.aspx?oid=9326.

46. Franklin Foer, "Swimming with Sharks: Republicans Learn Their Dirty Tricks by Practicing on One Another," *New Republic* (October 3, 2005), 20.

47. College Republican National Committee, "The National Chairmen of the College Republican National Committee" at http://www.crnc.org/images/ CRNC_Chairmen.pdf.

48. Foer, "Swimming with Sharks," 20–22.

49. Joseph B. Treaster, "College Republicans Open a Drive Against Student Activist Groups," *New York Times* (March 13, 1983), A-28

50. Howard Kurtz and Charles R. Babcock, "Two 'Nonpolitical' Foundations Push Grenada Rallies," *Washington Post* (October 4, 1984), A-1.

51. Michael Hirschorn, "Little Men on Campus (Republican Party College Activities)," *New Republic* (August 5, 1985), 14.

52. Sidney Blumenthal, "Staff Shakeup Hits Conservative Group: 7 Fired at Lehrman's Citizens for America," *Washington Post* (July 27, 1985), A-10.

53. Abramoff's résumé from his days at Greenberg Traurig at http://web.

archive.org/web/20030612020908/http://gtlaw.com/bios/govadmin/
abramoffj.htm.

54. Bell is quoted in Andrew Ferguson, "The Lobbyist's Progress: Jack
Abramoff and the End of the Republican Revolution," *Weekly Standard*
(December 20, 2004).

55. Michael Janofsky, "Senate Opens Hearings on Lobbyists for Tribes," *New
York Times* (September 30, 2004), A-15.

56. Material in this section is based on personal knowledge, which I confirmed
when writing a column on the subject for *FindLaw* at the time the issue of
changing the Senate's rules first arose. See John W. Dean, "The Ongoing
Controversy over Judicial Nominees: What Will It Mean if the GOP 'Goes
Nuclear' on the Filibuster Rules?" *FindLaw*—Writ (May 23, 2003) at
http://writ.news.findlaw.com/dean/20030523.html.

57. See Gang of 14, "Memorandum of Understanding on Judicial Nomination"
at http://en.wikipedia.org/wiki/Gang_of_fourteen.

58. Charles Martin, *Healing America: The Life of Senate Majority Leader
William H. Frist, M.D.* (Nashville: W Publishing Group, 2004), 82. I have
both quoted from and paraphrased this story.

59. William H. Frist, *Transplant: A Heart Surgeon's Account of the Life-and-Death
Dramas of New Medicine* (New York: Atlantic Monthly Press, 1989), 122.

60. Ibid., 123.

61. Ibid., 124.

62. Ibid., 130.

63. The General Laws of Massachusetts, Chapter 272: Section 77 at http://
www.mass.gov/legis/laws/mgl/272-77.htm. The relevant part of the statute
reads: "Chapter 272: Section 77. Whoever . . . mutilates or kills an animal . . . or procures an animal to be . . . mutilated or killed . . . shall be
punished by imprisonment in the state prison for not more than 5 years or
imprisoned in the house of correction for not more than 2 1/2 years or by a
fine of not more than $2,500, or both such fine and imprisonment."

64. David Beiler, "Surgical Precision: How Senate Power Jim Sasser Was
Stomped by a Political Novice in Tennessee," *Campaigns and Elections*
(April 1995).

65. Jeffrey H. Birnbaum, "Letters Show First Notified of Stocks in 'Bind' Trust:
Documents Contradict Comments on Holdings," *Washington Post* (October 24, 2005), A-1.

66. "SEC Ratchets up Probe of Frist's HCA Stock Sale, People Say," Bloomberg.
com (September 27, 2005) at http://www.bloomberg.com/apps/news?pid=
10000103&sid=awvqzH_6IT1o&refer=us.

67. Jeffrey H. Birnbaum and R. Jeffrey Smith, "SEC, Justice Investigate Frist's
Sale of Stock," *Washington Post* (September 24, 2005), A-1.

68. Martin, *Healing America,* 85–86.

69. James Taranto, "The Weekend Interview with Dick Cheney," *Wall Street Journal* (January 28–29, 2006), A-8.

70. See http://www.washingtonmonthly.com/features/2001/0301.marshall.html.

71. Anne Gearan, "Ex-Powell Aide Criticizes Bush on Iraq," Associated Press (November 29, 2005) at http://www.commondreams.org/headlines05/1129-07.htm.

72. David Luban, "Torture, American Style," *Washington Post* (November 27, 2005), B-1.

73. David Luban, "Liberalism, Torture and the Ticking Bomb," *Virginia Law Review* (October 2005) at http://www.virginialawreview.org/content/pdfs/91/1425.pdf.

74. Charlie Savage, "Bush could bypass new torture ban: Waiver right is reserved," *Boston Globe* (January 4, 2006) at http://www.boston.com/news/nation/washington/articles/2006/01/04/bush_could_bypass_new_ torture_ban/.

75. Daniel Klaidman, Stuart Taylor, Jr., and Evan Thomas, "Palace Revolt: They were loyal conservatives, and Bush appointees. They fought a quiet battle to rein in the president's power in the war on terror. And they paid a price for it," *Newsweek* (February 6, 2006), 35–40.

76. Ibid.

77. Ibid.

78. Ibid.

79. Helen Dewar and Dana Milbank, "Cheney Dismisses Critic with Obscenity: Clash with Leahy About Halliburton," *Washington Post* (June 25, 2004), A-4.

80. Barbara Ann Kipfer, ed., *Roget's 21st Century Thesaurus: In Dictionary Form* (New York: Delta, 1999).

81. See, e.g., *The American Heritage Dictionary* (New York: Houghton Mifflin, 1982) or *Webster's College Dictionary* (New York: Random House, 1991).

82. Al Gore, "Transcript: Former Vice President Gore's Speech on Constitutional Issues," CQ Transcripts, *Washington Post* (January 17, 2006) at http://www.washingtonpost.com/wp-dyn/content/article/2006/01/16/AR2006011600779_ pf.html.

83. Joshua Micah Marshall, Talking Points Memo (January 17, 2006) at http://www.talkingpointsmemo.com/archives/007455.php.

84. Joseph J. Collins, "War and Destiny: How the Bush Revolution in Foreign and Military Affairs Redefined American Power," *Joint Forces Quarterly* (First Quarter 2006), 93.

85. Jeffrey Goldberg, "Breaking Ranks: What turned Brent Scowcroft against the Bush Administration?" *New Yorker* (October 31, 2005) at http://www.newyorker.com/fact/content/articles/051031fa_fact2.

86. Steve Mavros, "Letters to the Editor: Cheney and the Politics of Terror," *New York Times* (September 9, 2004), A-32. Also, commentators have, from

time to time, addressed the fearmongering of Bush and Cheney. For example, Bob Herbert, "Get It Together, Democrats," *New York Times* (October 17, 2005), A-19. ("Ever since Sept. 11 President Bush and the G.O.P. have been pushing the nation's fear buttons for all they're worth," Herbert wrote); and Joshua Kurlantzick, "The Rise & Fall of Imperial Democracies," *Washington Monthly* (January/February 2006), 33. ("President George W. Bush tapped a powerful vein of nationalism and fear after 9/11 to expand his authority, intimidate opponents, reward corporations allied with his party, and punish dissent within the government. He then used his enhanced powers to invade and occupy Iraq and to capture and imprison thousands of individuals suspected, rightly or wrongly, of being terrorists," Kurlantzick noted in passing in his essay).

87. Taranto, "The Weekend Interview with Dick Cheney," A-8.

88. Karl Rove, "The GOP Remains the Party of Ideas," January 20, 2006, address to the Republican National Committee at http://www.realclearpolitics .com/Commentary/com-1_21_06_Rove.html.

89. Luke Mitchell, "At Issue in the 2004 Election: A Run on Terror," *Harper's* (March 2004), 79.

90. Jim Harper, "Secrecy fetish hurts war on terror; Assessing the risk is made more difficult," *Orange Country Register* (February 15, 2006).

91. John W. Dean, *Worse Than Watergate: The Secret Presidency of George W. Bush* (New York: Warner Books, 2005), 194. Citing Oren Gross, "Chaos and Rules: Should Responses to Violent Crisis Always Be Constitutional?" *Yale Law Journal*, vol. 112 (March 2003), 1011, 1030–31.

92. Dan Eggen, "U.S. Is Given Failing Grades by 9/11 Panel: Bipartisan Group Faults Counterterrorism Progress," *Washington Post* (December 6, 2005), A-1.

93. Anonymous, "Mortality Fears as Measure of Politics?" *Los Angeles Times* (July 25, 2004), A-23.

94. Associated Press, "More Americans fear terrorists are winning," MSNBC.com (April 22, 2004) at http://msnbc.msn.com/id/4805575.

95. CNN, "U.S. President/National/Exit Poll," CNN.com at http://www.cnn.com/ ELECTION/2004/pages/results/states/US/P/00/epolls.0.html.

96. Martha Crenshaw, "Counterterrorism in Retrospect," *Foreign Affairs* (July/ August 2005) at http://www.foreignaffairs.org/20050701fareviewessay84414/ martha-crenshaw/counterterrorism-in-retrospect.html.

97. Al Gore, "The Politics of Fear," *Social Research,* vol. 71:4(Winter 2004), 20.

98. Robert O. Paxton, *The Anatomy of Fascism* (New York: Knopf, 2004).

99. Bob Altemeyer, *Right Wing Authoritarianism* (Winnipeg: University of Manitoba Press, 1981), 4.

100. Al Kamen, "Scooter Finds Fellowship at the Hudson Institute," *Washington Post* (January 6, 2006), A-17.

INDEX